Thousands of Creative Kitchen Ideas

Thousands of Creative Kitchen Ideas

Virginia T. Habeeb

Funk & Wagnalls New York

Illustrations by Muriel Cuttrell.

Published simultaneously in Canada by Fitzhenry & Whiteside Limited, Toronto.

Designed by Abigail Moseley

Manufactured in the United States of America

Library of Congress Cataloging in Publication Data

Habeeb, Virginia T

Thousands of creative kitchen ideas.

Includes index.

1. Kitchens. I. Title.

TX653.H23 643'.3 75-23318

ISBN 0-308-10227-4

10 9 8 7 6 5 4 3 2 1

To Betty Mae, with love

Acknowledgments

The author wishes to express her thanks to the following people and associations (including their staff and member organizations) for their help and cooperation in supplying information and illustrations: Mary Osborne, Osborne Associates; American Gas Association; American Home Lighting Institute; *American Home* Magazine; American Institute of Kitchen Dealers; Association of Home Appliance Manufacturers; Edison Electric Institute; Gas Appliance Manufacturers Association, Inc.; Home Ventilating Institute, Major Appliance Consumer Action Panel; *Modern Bride* Magazine; National Association of Plumbing, Heating and Cooling Contractors; National Home Improvement Council, United States Department of Agriculture, and the Window Shade Manufacturers Association. And to Dr. Rose Steidl, Cornell University; William H. Kapple, A.I.A., University of Illinois, H. Peers Brewer, Manufacturers Hanover Trust Company; Ben C. Flowers; Robert Houseman, and Doris Piper Lamberson.

Gratitude in large part is also due those many homemakers across the country who have opened their homes, hearts, and kitchens to me in the search for better kitchens and the many home economists, utility companies, and their technical experts who took time to answer my questionnaire.

Special thanks goes to my editor, Ellen Feldman, whose recent experience in kitchen remodeling made her an instant authority on what *to* and what *not to* do in a kitchen and to Abigail Moseley for designing this book.

And to my illustrator, Muriel Cuttrell, who for years sketched a floor plan for every kitchen I planned, developed, and photographed. Her talent is obvious.

Contents

Preface

The sun rose half an hour ago. And someone in the house was not far behind it. She had already taken out the bird, started the stuffing, and put a pot of coffee on to welcome the next one up. Probably she is now humming a little because cooking to her is a labor of love, and Thanksgiving is the biggest love feast of the year.

It need not be Thanksgiving. It can be any holiday you like, an informal party for no reason at all, or a formal dinner in celebration of an important event. But whichever the feast and whatever the reason, you can be sure of one thing: It begins in the kitchen.

You can call cooking a science, if you like, but that's like calling love a chemical reaction or a biological urge. It doesn't say it all. A kitchen isn't a laboratory for methodical dispensing of life-giving foods in measured amounts three times a day. Rather it is the heart of the house—the place where a woman can send out great, warm, good-smelling waves of love to her family, her neighbors, her world. A woman's kitchen is an artist's palette, a musician's studio, a writer's workshop—except that the door is never locked. The kitchen is where it all begins; from sunlit breakfasts to elegant candlelit dinner parties, from Sunday roasts to everyday spaghetti and meatballs, from lunch boxes packed with love to gala family picnics planned with care, from after-school cookies to midnight snacks. It makes no difference what style a kitchen is—Early American or Futuristic Modern, Provincial charm or streamlined chrome-and-steel efficiency—as long as it is a center of warmth and care and reflects the personalities and the predilections of those who work there. Your kitchen is a reflection of your personality.

And like your personality it should have a framework of common sense and an aura of loveliness.

Kitchens, like people, have different shapes. There are U-shapes and L-shapes, one-wall and two-wall designs. But the most important shape of all is the You-shape—the one kitchen that perfectly fits your way of life. Whether you are a free spirit or a model of organization, a traditionalist or a modernist with an eye on the bright world of tomorrow, there is a right kitchen for you.

If you think that right kitchen, that dream kitchen perfectly suited to your needs, is somewhere in the far-off future, you are wrong. It is here now. So stop dreaming and start acting. Your kitchen is just around the corner. In fact, it is right here in the pages of this book. Not only have we assembled for you all the possibilities but we have put them within reach of your pocketbook as well.

That is not nearly as impossible as it sounds. For every kitchen problem there are several solutions, for every kitchen need there are many answers. And that is precisely what this picture book of perfect kitchens is for—to show you the vast variety of kitchen possibilities and help you choose among them wisely and well. The result will be a kitchen that saves time and labor and pays off in endless dividends of sheer enjoyment. The result will be *your* dream kitchen on *your* budget.

Introduction

There are no laws, no hard-and-fast rules of kitchen design. But there are some basic precepts which you ought to keep in mind while planning your kitchen.

On people and kitchens in general: Just as there is no such thing as an average person, so there is no such thing as an average kitchen. Beyond certain basic principles of safety and common sense a kitchen should be designed for the person who will use it most frequently. Certainly a kitchen ought to be pleasing as well as inviting to the rest of the family, but never lose sight of the needs and preferences of the individual who will be in the kitchen most often. Design according to the way in which that person prefers to work and always keep in mind the basic axiom that "form follows function." There is nothing attractive, no matter how beautifully appointed, about a kitchen which does not work.

On creative thinking: A kitchen can always be improved. Whether you have $5 or $5,000 to spend there is something you can do to make your kitchen work better and look lovelier. And remember, the degree of improvement is not always directly related to the amount of money spent. Sometimes, with careful thought and planning, a small expenditure can remedy a large kitchen problem. It is not how much money you spend, it is how wisely and imaginatively you spend it.

Now let's look at the possibilities!

Early medieval drawing of a peasant kitchen shows open hearth for cooking and an early version of a brick baking oven. Note open flame and the hole in the roof to permit smoke to escape. *Courtesy Rutt-Williams*

CHAPTER 1

From Spits to Super Kitchens

Man's First Kitchen

When man first discovered fire he found warmth and a way to make his food more varied and palatable. His first method of cooking was actually a "rotisserie" made from two Y-shaped twigs, supporting a "spit" on which was pierced a piece of meat. As the meat cooked, he turned it slowly by hand over the flames until it was tooth-tender and succulently crisped. Along with the berries, nuts, and seeds of the wilds, this was man's first food, cooked in his first kitchen!

To appreciate today's modern conveniences we should go back to the shallow, in-the-ground fire hole of prehistoric man. Kitchen lore is not only fascinating but it also makes us appreciate the importance of striving to improve our environment and make life easier and more exciting.

In prehistoric times the outdoor fire hole was encircled by field stones and the hearth was devised to keep the fire from extinguishing when it rained. When man moved indoors he brought his fire with him to cook his food and keep him warm. Then came the second step forward in kitchens—a hole cut out of the roof over the hearth to let out the smoke. This was man's first attempt at an indoor ventilating system.

In the Middle Ages the hearth became part of a wall in the form of a fireplace with a "raised hearth." It had a huge smoke hood built over it and the fireplace was connected to a chimney for smoke removal.

The "luxury kitchen" of the thirteenth and fourteenth century was found in castle or convent. Note separation of functions, left to right: storage center, cooking center, cleaning center. The built-in equipment includes plateboards and spit rack on hood.
Courtesy Rutt-Williams

In the average Early American home, the kitchen was part of the general living area concentrated in one room, and the fireplace was the center of activity. As in preceding centuries, cooking was still done on the floor. Trammels were used to suspend pots over the fire, and kettles were hung near the fire to maintain a supply of hot water. Chair next to the fireplace was usually quite low to make cooking easier. *Courtesy Rutt-Williams*

The Kitchen as a Separate Room

It was not until the hearth was moved from the center of the room to a wall arrangement that the kitchen became a separate room. The first "planned" kitchens were found in monasteries around A.D. 1000. In fact these monasteries boasted not one kitchen but several. There was one for baking bread, one for cooking meats, and one for preparing poultices and medicines which were made from plants and herbs. Compared to the peasant kitchens of the time, which consisted of a fireplace, a table, some crude benches, and some boards for utensils, these monastery kitchens were elaborately equipped.

A major reason for separating the hearth from the rest of the home was cooking odor. In recollections of grandmother's kitchen we like to recall a host of pleasant fragrances—roasting turkey, baking bread, a pumpkin pie fresh from the oven—wafting their way from the kitchen. Not so with the early kitchens. There was no refrigeration and trash removal was, at its best, unsatisfactory. Thus came the division of cooking from cleaning. The outbuildings of a colonial estate, for example, included both a kitchen immediately behind the main house and a scullery, separate and some distance away.

There was no concept of kitchen planning as we know it today. Survival was man's first concern and improvisation his only method. Storage and preservation of food were essential to survival so everyone in the family helped with those tasks as well as the cooking and production of necessary equipment, from pots and kettles to baskets and brooms.

All of these tasks went on in a single room which our early settlers in America called a "keeping room." It was the place where the family lived and did all their chores. They lived there because the hearth was there and that was their primary source of heat.

The kitchen was an all-purpose room—a place for cooking, bathing, washing, and ironing. Cooking supplies were stored in a cool room or pantry just off the keeping room or kitchen. As recently as a hundred years ago families were still toting water, stoking the stove, and literally keeping the home fires burning.

The Machine Age in America

Things began to change radically only after the Civil War, when manufacturing plants sprung up all around the country and the machine age began in America. The cast-iron "stove" brought about the most far-reaching changes. It made cooking at once easier and more sophisticated, but its heat, generated first by wood then by coal, was intense in summer, and its ashes required regular removal. By the late 1880s the oil range was advertised for "ideal summer cooking," and at about the same time the gas range appeared on the scene. It did not take long for this magnificent piece of equipment with its many burners, several ovens, a hot closet, and a warming shelf to become woman's best friend. Then in 1910 came the first successful electric range. It looked for all the world like its cast iron ancestor.

The technological revolution of the post–Civil War years affected nearly every item of kitchen equipment. What had earlier been fashioned by the homeowner or by a local or itinerant craftsman was now

McDougall Kitchen Cabinets

reduce kitchen work by half. Each cabinet has the full working surface of an ordinary kitchen table, with an added drop leaf, if desired. No drawers or doors obstruct the table top. The space above and below the table is fully utilized.

The McDougall Idea consists of doing everything possible to lighten the burdens of the housewife, to make life easier for her, to save her innumerable steps and unnecessary work.

To prove to you the value of a McDougall Kitchen Cabinet, we will place any one of them on

30 Days Trial In Your Own Home

Every housewife can afford to place a McDougall Kitchen Cabinet where her kitchen table now stands, under our liberal offer.

You need not take our word for the saving of time and food supplies which the McDougall Kitchen Cabinet will effect. Just put it to the actual test, and judge of its merits for yourself.

Ask Your Dealer to Show You the McDougall Kitchen Cabinets

They are mouse-proof and dust-proof; have bins for flour, meal, sugar and salt; cans for pepper and spices; drawers for table linens, cutlery, and the many little articles needed in kitchen work; most styles have closets for china and glassware.

Illustrated Catalogue Free, showing the various styles of McDougall Kitchen Cabinets ranging in price from $15.75 to $54.00. When writing for the catalogue, please give your local dealer's name and address, and state whether he sells McDougall Kitchen Cabinets, or not.

Look for the name-plate, "McDougall, Indianapolis." It is your guaranty of quality.

Would you like a McDougall Kitchen Cabinet in your home? Then write for our 30 Day Trial Offer, and do it **now.**

G. P. McDougall & Son, 520 Terminal Bldg., Indianapolis, Ind.

''Hoosier cabinet'' popular around the turn of the century had a place for everything: bins for flour, meal, sugar, salt; cans for pepper and spices, drawers for linens and cutlery; closets for china and glassware. Multipurpose unit that became standard kitchen equipment was said to ''reduce kitchen work by half.'' Price range quoted in ad is $15.75 to $54.00. *Courtesy Rutt-Williams*

mass-produced. The dry sink, hutches, and pie safes that were the first kitchen cabinets, hand-crafted from whatever woods were native to an area, were superseded by the "Hoosier" or "Dutch cabinet," depending upon who manufactured it. This freestanding unit was the first significant step in the evolution of today's modern kitchen with its built-in cabinets and continuous counter work surfaces. A Hoosier cabinet boasted a built-in flour bin complete with sifter, built-in sugar bin, spice rack, cutting board, cookbook rack, and a porcelain-enameled or marble work surface. Its advertising was direct: "The new way—a Hoosier Cabinet Makes a Model Kitchen."

Introduced in the late 1800s at a price of $10 to $16, it dominated the American kitchen for the next thirty to forty years. I remember the one in my mother's kitchen on which I leaned heavily in completing all my 4-H cooking projects one by one, from breads to great desserts. This new-fashioned cupboard was made of oak and maple, stained or painted white, and its doors were adorned with white ironstone knobs. Alongside the Hoosier cabinet for convenience were open shelves on which everything else was stored; everything, that is, that didn't fit in the Hoosier cabinet.

"Installed-on-the-job" storage cabinets gradually replaced the open shelves and base cabinets were used to enclose the sink and to provide additional covered storage. Continuous counters appeared as wooden boards covered with linoleum or ceramic tile, then later came steel surfaces with wide, deeply grooved drainboards. The big table in the center of the kitchen where people ate and worked was soon to be covered with "oilcloth," the first washable, wipeable fabric, easy to keep clean. Oilcloth was the first easy-care fabric!

When Kitchen Planning Began

The kitchens of the early 1900s were certainly vast improvements from cooking on an open hearth and toting water in and waste out, but as we devised more convenience we also created more inconvenience. The sink was on one wall, the range on another, the Hoosier cabinet or cupboard on yet another with the big table still in the middle of the floor. There was a good deal of walking, stooping, and bending to prepare a family meal.

As women began to realize that with technology came complexity, professionals began to study woman's work in the home. Eventually time and motion experts, studying women's habits in the kitchen as they moved from sink to range to cabinet to table, found ways to create more efficiency. They decentralized work into meaningful centers or areas, raised and lowered counters according to people's heights, organized storage, and directed work flow according to right- or left-hand tendencies.

About this time came the cabinet sink which gave rise to the concept of built-ins. White-enameled metal cabinets and cabinet sinks could be fitted together in arrangements according to a plan suitable to the size of the kitchen. From this concept gradually evolved today's kitchen and its influence on storage, not only in the kitchen but all over the house. It has made cabinets into furniture, spawned innumerable built-in convenience features, and helped to expand home remodeling into a $17 billion-a-year business!

The Growth of Kitchen Appliances

Of course, appliances too have had a lot to do with that somewhat staggering statistic. Refrigerators, for example, were perhaps the first "status symbol" of modern times. The Roman emperor Nero, whose servants brought him ice and snow from the Italian Alps, had no more comfort or convenience than the first American to own an icebox, which, of course, was just that—a handsomely designed cabinet, divided into several compartments, all chilled by one area which housed a block of ice bought from the ice man. It was, of course, eventually replaced by its even more convenient counterpart, the electric refrigerator which cooled, chilled, and made ice mechanically.

Many of the appliances we have come to take for granted came into use in the late 1930s and early 1940s. A garbage disposer, patented in 1928, did not get underway for nearly a decade. The dishwasher was made and patented in 1914, but it did not come into general use until the late 1930s. The wall oven, though inspired by an electric baking oven in 1936, was not widely merchandised until 1947. It wisely capitalized on two important work habits of the homemaker—that she does 75 percent of all cooking on the surface of the range and that she has to stoop or bend to use an oven that is placed under a range, practically on the floor. Why not separate the oven from the cooking surface, raise it to a more convenient height, and use the space underneath for storage?

The newest appliance on the home scene, the trash compactor, has been used in industry for a long time. It was, however, 1968 before the first household unit to reduce trash to a fourth its original volume was produced and tested by a major manufacturer.

You know the rest of the story. One need only read the current ads to realize all the major breakthroughs in kitchen convenience we have at our fingertips. And the future holds even greater possibilities. Man will continue to have new ideas for the kitchen of the future. (Read about some of them in Chapter 20.) Ideas, in fact, are what this book is all about—simple planning ideas to make your work easier and keep the kitchen a warm, pleasant, and practical place to live and work.

CHAPTER 2

And What of Today's Kitchens?

Family life-styles have changed drastically during the past several decades and so have kitchens, the heart of family living. We have seen that the earliest planned kitchens were "laboratories" or workrooms devised by the experts for efficient meal preparation and quick cleanup. These kitchens were usually single rooms with three walls of cabinets and a fourth wall that supported a sink in the middle with a stove and refrigerator on either side. It was a kitchen designed for a different way of life. Men went out to work; women stayed at home to take care of their families.

Today all that has changed. Women frequently work outside the home. Sixty percent of all working women are married and over five and a half million heads of households are female. There are more single-member households than ever before—career men and women—and more households headed by a divorced or widowed parent. And with the breakdown of the extended family unit and increased life expectancy many older individuals are adapting their own resources for housekeeping. These changes in the composition of families and the American way of life have made new demands upon the kitchen and have elevated it to a new role in the home.

These days people shop less frequently and buy in larger quantities. Thus storage space is more important than ever. In many families the wife and mother holds a full- or part-time position outside the home. In these instances sufficient storage space for convenience foods as well as canned goods and staples is crucial. Specialized equipment which facilitates quick-and-easy meal preparation is especially helpful to these families, as well as to those who live alone, and to senior citizens who may no longer be up to elaborate meal preparation. In all of these cases every appliance that saves time and effort, every kitchen feature that makes cooking and cleaning up easier, is a godsend.

There is, however, another side to the coin. Just as many women are moving out of the home and into the working force, many others are heading back to the kitchen. In the past few years there has been an increased interest in home freezing and canning a wider variety of foods. In many kitchens, therefore, arrangements must be made for the storage of large equipment and supplies as well as the preserved and frozen food. There is a new interest in homemade, unadulterated foods of all sorts. Women are baking their own bread, even making their own ice cream and yogurt (with the aid of sophisticated new equipment which, of course, means more storage space once again).

The majority of homemakers spend approximately 50 percent of their at-home working hours in the kitchen and regard it as the pivot around which their home life revolves. Thus kitchens are becoming not only more convenient and efficient but also more attractive as well. They are more colorful, lighter, brighter, and generally better looking. They bring the outdoors in and take the indoors out. The kitchen is often the warmest, most charming, and versatile room in the house. Most people judge the quality of the entire house by the kitchen, an important factor to keep in mind if you are thinking of resale values.

It is no longer enough to merely hang a cabinet wherever there is an open space on the wall, and today no one wants a kitchen that is hidden away in the back of the house. More than ever the modern kitchen is the center and the very soul of the house. It is the room where family and friends gather for gabfests and coffee klatches. It is a multipurpose room that may serve many functions, including laundry, planning, sewing, hobbies, and child watching. It is at different times of the day a restaurant, a soda fountain, a hot dog stand, a cocktail lounge, a workshop, a sewing room, a laundry, a playroom, an office, and, of course, a coffee shop.

Just as more Americans than ever before are eating as well as preparing their meals in the kitchen—the formal dining room is in the decline—so they are beginning to eat or at least snack all over the house. Kitchen satellites are springing up in dens, family rooms, recreation rooms, on patios and porches, and even in bedrooms.

The possibilities for improvement are endless. Now is the time to consider your choices and plan the perfect kitchen for you.

CHAPTER 3

Now That You Want a New Kitchen

We have taken a brief look at some of the things that are happening to kitchens today. Now let's think about what you want to happen to your kitchen. It is entirely possible to end up with a new kitchen that has all the trimmings, a beauty of a kitchen as attractive as it is efficient, and still not have the kitchen that is right for you.

The first step is to take stock of your present kitchen. Before you go any further it might be fun to rate it. In the checklist* below the number after each "point" indicates how poor or how good you find the various elements in your kitchen. Circle the number indicating your degree of satisfaction, e.g. 1 very poor vs. 6 very good, or any degree in between. Then tally up the total of circled numbers and check results below.

Poor 1 2 3 4 5 6 Good

A. *Storage Space:* Is there enough? Is it easily accessible? Are there hard-to-reach corners? Do you need a stepladder or stool to reach shelves? Good storage where you want it is of prime importance for step-saving work flow. 1 2 3 4 5 6

B. *Workspace:* Is there enough counter space, landing space, and convenient surfaces for food preparation? Twenty-four inches on each side of the sink bowl are needed. A minimum of 15 to 18 inches of landing space adjacent to the door handle of the refrigerator, 18 inches safety area next to the stove top. An experienced kitchen specialist

*Scorecard courtesy American Institute of Kitchen Dealers.

knows these basic rules and will design your kitchen to make your work easier and safer. 1 2 3 4 5 6

C. *Up-to-Date Appliances:* Innovations in appliances will save you time and eliminate many unpleasant chores. These include dishwashers that wash without prerinsing—even pots and pans. Frost-free refrigerators, self-cleaning ovens, cook tops without exposed burners or units, waist-high wall ovens, garbage disposers. 1 2 3 4 5 6

D. *Ventilation:* Will keep your kitchen cooler and looking crisp and fresh longer. It prevents grease deposits on cabinets, walls, and windows, removes heat and moisture. Makes upkeep a breeze for you. 1 2 3 4 5 6

E. *Lighting:* Most kitchens have only one-sixth of the amount of lighting recommended by illumination engineers. Do you have adequate light where you work? At the sink, at the stove? And how is the general lighting of the room? Good lighting makes your work less tiresome. 1 2 3 4 5 6

If your total is:

- 4–10 You are working daily under a severe handicap. Your kitchen is obviously grossly inadequate.
- 11–15 Your kitchen has many serious shortcomings that could be improved.
- 16–20 Although not as serious, you still would benefit greatly from a remodeling job.
- 21–25 Your problems are rather specific—consult a kitchen specialist. The solution may be less difficult than you think.
- 26–30 You are the exception.

Unless your kitchen "scores" 26 or higher you may miss many advantages of an up-to-date modern kitchen. You may be working under conditions that require miles of unnecessary walking, tiresome bending and reaching or under conditions that waste a lot of your precious time.

Now that you have scored your own kitchen, decide which are your problem areas. Actually this is not as simple as it sounds. Too often we learn to live with problems. They become second nature to us and we fail to recognize the toll they take in time and energy. A refrigerator located in the wrong place or one that opens away from the counter means you could be walking miles out of your way each year. Noisy appliances that you have trained yourself not to hear may be the cause of unexplained fatigue and irritation. Storage space too high, too low, or too cramped may be forcing you to bend, stoop, stretch, and constantly shift things from one place to another—a strain on the nerves as well as a "pain in the neck."

Wanting a new kitchen just for the sake of a new kitchen is not enough. The kitchen you end up with must be workable as well as new; it must suit your needs as well as give your spirits a lift. In order to plan that dream kitchen, which will do both, think before you act. Consider the following reasons for wanting a new kitchen. They are the most common, though yours may be different. Perhaps:

•You want to take advantage of the latest convenience features in new equipment and appliances.

•Your kitchen is so poorly planned that you live in constant confusion.

•The space is too small for your changing life-style or growing family.

•The space is too large since the family has scattered.

•Your storage space is inadequate or poorly planned. Have you enough "organized" space for frequently used items, less frequently used items, seldom used ones, staples if you shop infrequently, and for kitchen and dining linens?

•The kitchen is poorly lit.

•It is inadequately ventilated and odor- and grease-prone.

•It doesn't have enough counter space and you are crowded as you work.

•Work surfaces are too high or low for your height.

•You don't have the equipment or appliances you really need—too many features you don't use and not enough of those you would if you had them.

•There is not enough space for other activities such as eating, laundry, sewing, child watching, and hobbies.

•The cabinets are not well designed or installed—wasted corners, stationary shelves, etc.

•It is too humid and hot because the appliances emit too much heat and moisture into an improperly ventilated room.

•You have no place to keep foods warm while other dishes are in the oven.

•An appliance, or several, is located in inconvenient areas.

•A window or door is not in a good location or perhaps you need one or the other.

•It is negatively affecting the sale of your house.

These are just a few reasons, but they are the ones that women complain about from coast to coast. I have been dubbed "the foremost kitchen snooper in the world," for I have done just that in my travels cross-country. I have interviewed homemakers, photographed their kitchens, and discussed their likes and dislikes. I have learned from experience that many homemakers are living in outmoded kitchens, poorly planned, and inadequately designed simply because they have "gotten used to things as they are." And often these are families who can afford to make changes.

On the other hand, many women who know what they want cannot afford the expense of major kitchen remodeling. Yet there are ways to achieve more convenience and improve your kitchen environment without spending hundreds of dollars. It's all in the strategy and planning.

The kitchen is probably the most important room of your house. Why should it be a room which is inadequately planned and perhaps dull and lifeless? And why should you be forced to spend half of your time at home in such a room? Why go on living and working in inconvenience, when you can do something about it? A poorly planned kitchen is a serious obstacle to efficiency and working pleasure. A new kitchen is stimulating. It will improve your surroundings and with it your disposition. It will facilitate your methods of doing things to such an extent that you will actually enjoy your work more. Why? Because you will save steps and time, effort and energy.

If you are a work-away-from-home wife, a work-at-home wife, or both, you will be glad you took the time, and whatever money you decide to spend, to improve your efficiency, cut your work time, and brighten your surroundings.

Here's how!

CHAPTER 4

Where to Begin

Now that you have analyzed all the things wrong with your own kitchen, listed the myriad minor and sometimes major problems, and decided what you do *not* want in a new kitchen, let's consider exactly what you do want.

Kitchens are for people. This one is for you. Begin by analyzing your needs. The result will be not only a better kitchen but one that suits your personality and work habits. But let us add a word of caution at this point. Beware of personalizing your kitchen to the point where it suits *only* you. Other family members and possibly outside help will use it at times, and the kitchen is an important, perhaps the most important, factor in selling a house.

The Important Questions

Begin an analysis of your kitchen needs by answering the following questions. An honest consideration of each of them will help you understand what you really want in a new kitchen, not what you think you ought to want. It will also help you when the time comes to talk to architects, designers, and dealers more intelligently.

1. *What kind of cooking do you enjoy most?* Do you collect recipes and cookbooks and try all the latest dishes? Are you an elaborate cook with gourmet tendencies? If so, you are probably an avid collector of a wide variety of tools, utensils, pots, pans, herbs, spices, and other specialties. Or are you a shortcut cook, always on the lookout for fast and easy ways to get the job done?

2. *How many people will be in the kitchen at one time?* How many family members have you? Does your husband cook? Do you enjoy having guests help with preparations? If so, you will want to increase your counter and work space and duplicate certain utensils. If you have a male chef in the house you will probably find it helpful, if you have the space, to design a separate center for him to perform his specialty whether it be making the salad or broiling the steak.

3. *How do you like to work?* If you enjoy talking while you are cooking, plan a kitchen that allows room for others to assemble close enough to the work center for you to chat, yet far enough away not to interfere with what you are doing. If you prefer to cook alone, then design a compact work area away from the flow of traffic and gathering places, such as eating areas or family rooms.

4. *Will the kitchen be used for dining?* Do you plan to have most of the family meals there? Will you ever entertain in the kitchen?

5. *What about children?* Do you have preschool youngsters you have to keep an active eye on while in the kitchen? Will you need to plan a play area for them somewhere within eye view but at foot's distance?

6. *How do you entertain?* Do you have people over often or infrequently? Do you like large parties or smaller, more intimate ones? Do you prefer buffet dining or sit-down dinners? Your storage needs will vary depending upon the way you entertain. If you give "big bashes" you will need storage space for large platters, bowls, extra dishes, and glasses. If you entertain informally where everyone ends up in the kitchen, you will appreciate a larger dining area in the kitchen or a nearby family room. In some cases, you might want to consider duplicating appliances. Believe it or not, two dishwashers are none too many for those stacks of dirty dishes after a big party. Even a small under-counter compact refrigerator is a big help in providing additional cold storage space for prepared party foods.

7. *How much space do you actually have to work with?* Though two dishwashers or a special work center for the male chef of the house is often an attractive idea, not every kitchen can accommodate such luxuries. It is important to keep the basic measurement of the room in mind to help determine the possibilities as well as limitations and the shape or design that will work best for you.

8. *What other activities will you want your kitchen to accommodate?* If you are considering the installation of a laundry in the kitchen

area, you might want to consider separating it from the cooking center since cooking and laundry activities are not compatible (see page 31). How about your hobby? Is it painting, sewing, gardening, writing? If your space is large enough, devote some of it to your favorite pastimes. A kitchen can be a pleasant place for such fringe activities. For you green-thumbers, a lean-to greenhouse is ideal for growing small plants and herbs. A planning desk makes a lot of sense if you are a work-away-from-home wife or an active community volunteer. You might want a filing drawer for organization of papers, menus, recipes, or homework. Having the tools of your hobby at hand in the kitchen enables you to devote to it spare moments that might otherwise be wasted.

9. *What is your personality?* Bold and daring? Quiet and retiring? Depending on your personal taste, you may love those new, vibrantly graphic wall coverings or prefer a softer background of colorful spring flowers.

Plan on Paper First

The best kitchen is the one you have planned in writing even before the first rough sketch is set to paper.

Write down all the things you plan to do in your new kitchen—cooking, freezing, baking, canning and preserving vegetables from your garden, meal planning, laundry, sewing, flower arranging, entertaining, etc. Now arrange these tasks by priority, placing the most important ones or the ones to which you will devote the most time at the top and the least important last.

Next, list in order of importance the things you cannot do without and the things you definitely do not want in your kitchen. Don't limit yourself. Go all out. This will be the springboard for planning your shopping lists as you go out to look around. You can always cut down later as you trim costs here and there.

Think seriously about how you work in your kitchen. Do a mini time and motion study on your working habits. Jot down how long it takes you to prepare a meal or one recipe, perhaps a macaroni and cheese casserole. Clock the time it takes you to get out the ingredients, prepare them for the casserole, preheat the oven, get out the casserole, fill it, carry it to the oven, bake it, and bring it to the table. Have someone in the family watch you do this and make notes. As you do this several times with different tasks, you will begin to see ways in which you can save time. Pay particular attention to how much you have to bend, reach, and stoop. Then think about how you can facilitate your work and save time and energy. Incorporate these tips in your new kitchen scheme. Remember to list everything, even if it sounds elementary to you. You will be glad in the long run that you took the time to study your work habits now.

Start Collecting Ideas

You have probably been doing this for sometime anyway, but now is the time to concentrate on making up your mind exactly what it is you want. Collect your ideas from everywhere. Magazine pictures, picture books, and kitchen cabinet brochures are excellent sources as are advertisements of kitchens, appliance, wall covering, and flooring manufacturers. Keep in mind that you may not be able to duplicate these ideas exactly due to the differences in space, dimensions, structural layout, and cost, but there is nothing to keep you from adapting the ideas to your specifications.

CHAPTER 5

What Is a Well-Planned Kitchen?

If your kitchen is to be a success, it must be more than merely new and attractive. It must be convenient, functional, and efficient as well. If your new kitchen:

•makes your work easier

•saves steps, time, and energy

•eliminates unnecessary stooping, bending, and reaching

•reduces clutter

•has ample storage—a place for everything and everything in its own place—with some space left for the things you may acquire in the future

•is a pleasant place to be

•serves the family and all its needs—eating, gathering, entertaining, etc.

•makes your work satisfying

•makes you feel good

it is well planned.

To make your kitchen all these things and more, you must follow certain basic principles. It is these essential rules of planning that will guarantee the best possible kitchen. What we are concerned with here are the basic guidelines to designing a functional kitchen. Beyond that, whatever form it takes depends on your personal desires. After you have applied these simple rules, your choices become subjective, and you can adapt whatever ideas and thoughts please you most.

The "perfect kitchen" doesn't just fall together. It requires creative thought and careful planning to make it work. You can apply the basic principles, but if you want a home office or an eating area or perhaps a little greenhouse for growing herbs, you may have to eliminate some part of an otherwise well-planned work area to achieve it. That takes ingenuity and perseverance.

The key to achieving the ultimate design that suits you, your family's life-style, and the architectural design of your house is to give the kitchen some personality beyond the basic plan, but avoid making it so unusual that it could affect the resale value of your home. Your cup of tea may not be the same as that of a prospective buyer. Of course, if selling your home is not a factor, then by all means do whatever you want with your kitchen.

Let's Begin the Planning

When you think of your kitchen in the final stages, it is all right to think in terms of a coordinated room, but during the planning stages it is better to think in terms of parts or *work centers* and what function each will serve. Basically, a kitchen has two types of centers—those that are musts and those that are supplementary. Each major center should contain adequate counter and work space, sufficient storage accommodations, the appliance that does most of the work. Where you put these centers and how large they will be depends on the size of the room, your own needs, and the relationship of one area to the other. First, plan your work centers, then arrange them together in a workable design. What we must consider first, then, are the work centers, and secondly, how they fit into the shape of your kitchen plan.

Work areas include the *sink or cleanup center* which provides water and drainage for food preparation and cleanup; the *range or cooking center* which provides heat for cooking; the *refrigerator center* which provides cold for the storage of perishable foods, and the *mixing center* for storage of cooking staples and facilities for assembling and mixing food. Sometimes the refrigeration and mixing centers or the range and mixing centers are combined. The most functional plan places the sink in the center, flanked by the range and refrigeration areas. This is called triangle planning which we will discuss in greater detail on page 38.

In each center adequate counter and storage space are essential. In discussing the various centers I will list the minimum and maximum counter space recommended for each area. If you plan to combine centers choose the maximum width plus some additional counter space. We will discuss this in more detail when we consider putting all the centers together on pages 38–40.

Various time and motion studies have revealed two important points about storage.

1. Work can be simplified by storing supplies, equipment, and utensils where you will use them first—and most often.

2. Storage should be planned specifically for the items to be stored. Everything has a plàce and should fit into it easily. We will talk more about storage in Chapter 12.

The Sink Center

In addition to the sink, this center could include a dishwasher, waste disposer, and trash compactor. It is the most used center in the kitchen and therefore speeds up work when located between the range and refrigerator centers. Preparations in both these areas involve some auxiliary work at or near the sink. This center is used for cleaning foods before refrigerating or cooking, preparing nonrefrigerated foods, dishwashing, and cleanup. Anything—foods, pots, and pans—requiring water in the first step of preparation is more functional when stored near the sink. Most people store dishwashing supplies here. Because of the hazardous substances and chemicals used in cleaning supplied I would recommend that they be stored near the sink area, but out of reach of small children. Reserve a closet either directly above or above and to the side of the sink and dishwashing area for this purpose.

There should be a minimum of 24 inches (36, if possible) of counter space on each side of the sink. If you are right-handed and in the habit of working from right to left, provide a minimum of 36 inches on the right of the sink for dirty items, food awaiting preparation, or utensils and a minimum of 18 (24 inches if possible) to 30 inches on the left for items that have been scrubbed, peeled, washed, or rinsed. If you are left-handed and work from left to right, place the larger amount of work surface on the left. Do take into account here too how the majority of

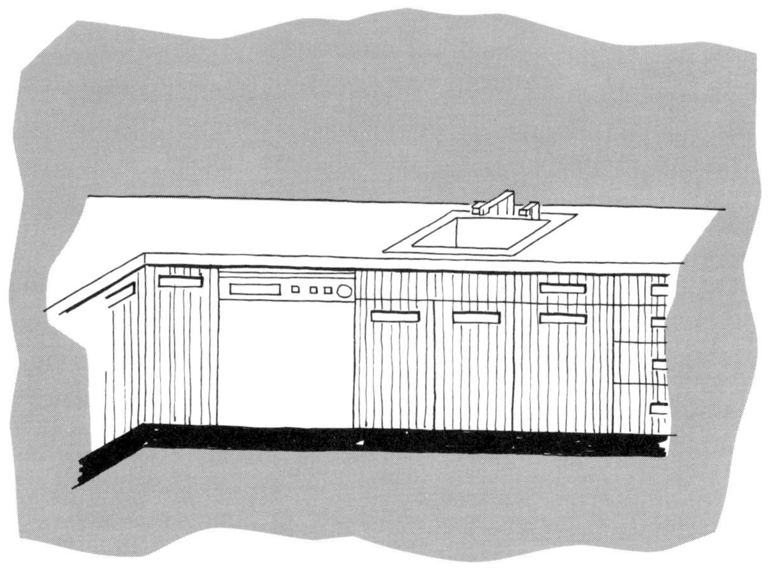

people who use the kitchen will work. Allow more counter space if you usually cook for more than four people or if you are not in the habit of organizing items before you wash them. In the case of hand dishwashing, if you stack them on either side of the sink after they have been dried and before they are stored, allow for additional room there. If a dishwasher is not in the budget at the moment, plan ahead by installing a 24-inch base cabinet which can later be replaced with an automatic dishwasher.

The sink is, of course, the most important item in the sink center. It may have a double or single bowl each of which comes in a variety of sizes and depths. Which you choose will depend on available space and whether you have a dishwasher or plan for one in the future. If you do have a dishwasher, a single bowl sink is usually adequate, if the bowl is large enough to wash pots and pans which will not fit in the dishwasher. If you do not have a dishwasher, it is a good idea to have a double-bowl sink—one for washing, the other for rinsing. Of course, the ideal situation is one in which you have a sink with three bowls—two for washing and rinsing and a third section with a waste disposer for peeling and draining vegetables.

You may be thinking of a corner sink. Generally there are two kinds available—a standard sink inserted into a diagonal base cabinet and a right-angle sink made especially for corner installations. Consider the fact that a diagonal sink does require generous wall area and the right-angle installation may create an inconvenient working arrangement for you. If, however, installing a sink in another location creates a serious sacrifice of convenience in some other situation, by all means install the sink in the corner.

Be sure to plan for drawer space for dish towels and other linen as well as aprons. Don't forget a towel rack for drying soiled and wet towels and a waste container. In discussing each center I have listed certain items which you will want to store in that area. Some utensils are listed in more than one center. Do not hesitate to duplicate certain basic items; it saves time and energy. If duplication is not feasible, choose whichever center suits your particular work habits. Storage space should be provided at or near the sink center for the following items.

EQUIPMENT AND SUPPLIES

aprons
can opener
colander
cutlery (paring knives)
coffee pot
detergents, cleansers, and cleaning supplies
dish towels
funnel
garbage cans and bags
juicer
measuring cups
measuring spoons
paper towels
pot holders
pot and plate scrapers
pot scrubbers
plastic and paper bags
sponges
strainers
tableware—china, glasses, flatware (unless you prefer to keep them in the cooking and serving area)
teapot
vegetable brush
wastebasket

FOODS

canned and dehydrated soups
coffee
cocoa
dried beans, fruits, peas, and lentils
onions
potatoes
unrefrigerated fruits

Range or Cooking Center (also serving area)

This is the area for cooking, serving, and, of course, more storage. Plan to include counter space on both sides of the range, ideally 24 inches on each side. More space should be considered if you are in the habit of placing food directly on dinner plates rather than on serving dishes and platters. A right-handed person may want more work surface toward the right of the range for easier grasp of forks, spoons, or spatulas. The opposite is true for left-handed people. On one side of the range you should plan for at least 24 inches of heatproof surface, such as stainless steel, glass ceramic, or ceramic tile. Somewhere between the range and mixing or refrigeration center it is also wise to include a wood chopping block or counter insert for cutting, chopping, dicing, slicing, and mincing jobs.

Your range selection may determine just how you plan the work surface around it. A complete freestanding, drop-in or slide-in range is self-contained with ovens below or above the cooking surface. If you prefer a separate built-in cooking surface and oven, remember that they will reduce counter space by at least 42 to 48 inches, and therefore will require more space. A separate built-in oven should not block the flow of work from one counter to another. If you do install the oven in

This range or cooking center is self-contained. Freestanding drop-in range, with matching hood, has cooking surface with oven below. Note the minimum 36 inches of counter space to left of range and right of sink. Wall covering is washable and is color-coordinated to match heat-resistant, laminated plastic counter top, range, dishwasher, and window treatment. Wood utensil rack is handy to left of range. Hood provides down lighting at cooking area and range has a built-in convenience outlet, handy for portable hand mixer. *Courtesy Hotpoint*

another area away from the cooking or range center, allow at least 24 inches on one side of it for working and transferring food in and out of the oven. I will talk more about which appliances suit your needs best in Chapter 13.

Don't forget to consider the ventilating system over the range and oven—an exhaust fan and hood for the removal of odors, moisture, smoke, and heat. Some of these systems are built into range or oven; others are separate units. For more about ventilation, see page 127.

If you do use built-in appliances, ideally, the working height for the cooking surface is 32 to 34 inches, although 36 inches, the standard counter height, is most often used. A built-in oven should be placed so the inside of the door, when opened, is 5 to 7 inches below the elbow. See the chart on page 218 to determine *your* best height.

Never place the range next to the refrigerator as both need work space adjoining and the heat from the range can affect the operation of the refrigerator when the door of the latter is frequently opened.

Safety is an important consideration in the placement of a range. It should not be placed at the end of a counter area, if you can avoid it. Locating it under a window is not advisable either and is actually prohibited by city codes in some areas. A corner installation is also not one of the best arrangements as there will not be enough work space on either side for jobs that require "elbow" room.

Store the following items at or near the cooking center:

EQUIPMENT

can opener
casseroles
cooking tools—forks, spoons, etc.
Dutch oven and cover
double boiler (top–bottom should be stored near sink)
deep-fat fryer
deep-fat thermometer
egg poacher
griddle
hand mixer
kettles, steamers
ladles
meat thermometer
measuring cups and spoons
pot holders
poultry shears
pressure cooker
roaster
saucepans and covers
small cooking appliances (to utilize ventilating area—see page 127)
skillets and covers
spatulas
stirring spoons
slotted spoons
serving bowls
tea kettle
tongs
turners
wood spoons
wire cooling racks

FOOD

cereals
condiments
canned goods
flour
instant coffee, tea, chocolate
bouillon
jellies
oil
pasta—spaghetti, noodles
rice
seasonings—salt, pepper, spice, herbs
sauce mixes

Near the range there should be a serving area with sufficient counter space to work and storage space for necessary serving items. Decide whether you prefer to keep china, glassware, and flatware in this area where it is easily accessible while you are serving the food or in the sink center where it can be stored quickly and easily after washing and

This "cooking niche," recessed into a stucco wall, provides the traditional styling of an old-fashioned fireplace in a modern setting. Oak batten doors with block wrought iron L and H hinges reflect the colonial theme. Drop-in range with matching ventilating hood is conveniently located under existing chimney. Air conditioner, top left, also is conveniently installed on the outside wall. *Courtesy Hotpoint*

drying. Be sure to allow sufficient storage space for the following items as well: hot pads, napkins, serving platters and bowls, tablecloths and mats, table condiments, toaster, trays.

The Refrigerator Center

Refrigerator doors may be hinged at the right or left, depending upon the needs of the individuals who will be working in the kitchen and the

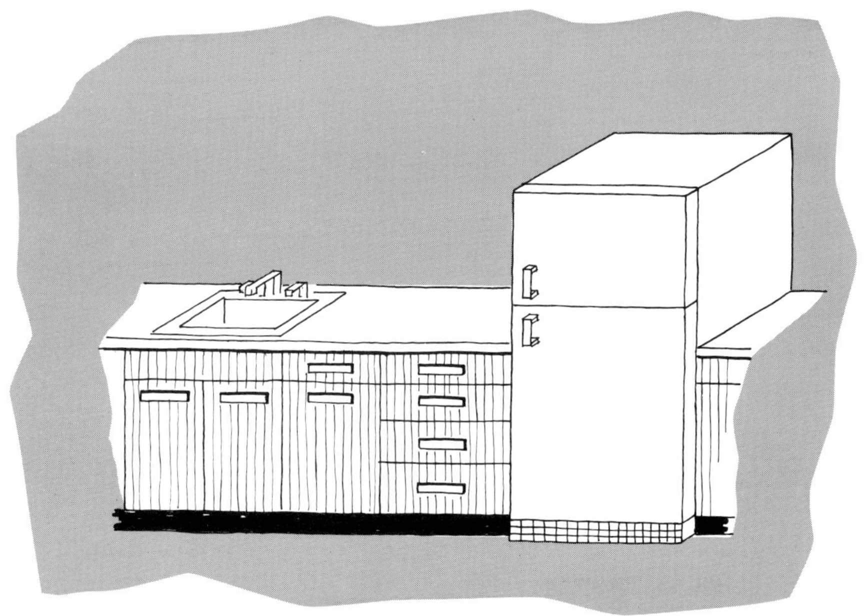

location of the refrigerator. Some refrigerator–freezers are "side-by-side" models with doors opening from the center. Always place the refrigerator so that the door swings *away* from the adjacent counter or if it is a "side-by-side," place it so that the work surface is adjacent to the hinge side of the freezer door. Then you can work toward the work surface from the fresh food compartment by reaching across the closed freezer door rather than by working around the opened door of the refrigerator section. Provide a minimum of 18 inches of counter space next to the latch side where the door swings open. If you combine the refrigerator with some other center, then allow 36 to 42 inches of counter space.

Store the following items at or near the refrigerator area:

EQUIPMENT AND SUPPLIES

aluminum foil
bottle openers
dessert servers
freezer containers
freezer tape
glasses
ice bucket
ice cream scoop
refrigerator containers
paper towels
plastic wraps and bags
waxed paper

FOOD

ice cream cones, decorations, and sauces
sodas
beverages to be chilled

The Mixing and Food Preparation Center

This center may be combined with the refrigeration center, the most popular combination, or with the range area, if it is more suitable to the space available. The amount and types of food preparation you are accustomed to will determine how much space you devote to the mixing center and whether this area is a major one for you. Most kitchens need a fairly good-sized mixing center. You will need at least 36 to 42 inches of counter space for this center and will find it easier to work there if a lower height is used. From 30 to 32 inches rather than the standard 36-inch counter height is generally most comfortable for mixing, rolling pastry, and other tasks.

Depending on your own needs and cooking habits consider installing in this area other conveniences such as a wood chopping surface and special counter inserts of marble or glass ceramic for pastry and candy making. Plan on storage for small appliances needed in food preparation such as a standard mixer, hand mixer, blender, and can opener.

Store the following items at or near the mixing center:

EQUIPMENT

baking pans—cake, pie, muffin, etc.
biscuit and cookie cutters
bread box
can and bottle openers
cookie sheets
chopper
casseroles
cutlery
corers
custard cups
cookbooks
cookie jars
canisters
cake box
cutting boards
flour sifter
food grinder
grater
molds and ramekins
measuring cups
measuring spoons
mixing bowls
pastry cloths
rolling pins
scoops
scissors and shears
sandwich supplies—bags, wraps
skewers
spatulas
wooden spoons

FOODS

- baking powder
- breads, cakes, and cookies
- bread crumbs
- cornstarch
- condiments
- chocolate and cocoa
- cream of tartar
- dried fruits and vegetables
- herbs
- jellies and jams
- flavorings
- flour
- packaged mixes—cakes, cookies, breads, and sauces
- salad oil
- soda
- snacks
- spreads not requiring refrigeration
- shortening
- spices
- sugar
- vinegar

Additional Centers

Now that we have considered the essential work centers, let's look at some of the supplementary areas you may want in your kitchen providing you have sufficient space. Remember, an additional center is no convenience if it cramps the necessary work areas.

The eating area

This is the most common supplementary kitchen center. As our life-styles become more casual, people spend more time in the kitchen and even entertain there more frequently. If this is the way you and your family live, consider setting aside a part of the kitchen or an adjoining room such as a family room or an enclosed porch or patio for casual dining and entertaining. We will discuss the various possibilities for eating areas in Chapter 6, but keep some essential measurements in mind while you are deciding where you would prefer your eating area.

A person seated extends about 20 inches from the table and needs 32 inches to rise from the table. If you want to walk behind a seated person, allow 24 inches of table or counter space per person. If your table is in a traffic passageway, allow 36 inches of clearance around the table.

As for eating counters, the depth depends upon its use. If you serve only breakfast or lunch there, a minimum depth of 15 inches may be adequate. If you serve dinner there, a minimum of 24 inches is a must.

Laundry center

If you want a laundry area in your kitchen, keep it near the plumbing and separate it from the cooking area with an island or peninsula. If the latter is not possible, at least locate it on another wall. For more about laundries see Chapter 19.

Planning or desk center

If you do any sort of paper or telephone work in your kitchen, a desk center will be a great convenience. Allow for a lowered counter (30 inches) with space under it for your knees, drawer storage (file type is excellent), and shelves for books. If you have allowed 30 inches for your counter height, a standard table chair is adequate, but if the counter is higher, you will need a stool with a back support. Other conveniences or necessities, depending upon the type and amount of work you

Lowered counter to right of dishwasher converts to handy planning desk for convenient sit-down chores, an excellent use of space near doorway. Open shelves above provide niche for cookbooks and decorative objects. Louvered windows and doors add tailored touch. *Courtesy Maytag*

Compact kitchen, located at one end of a family dining area, decentralizes cooking center with built-in oven installed separately from cook top and barbecue area. Note extralarge mixing and food preparation center to left of refrigerator (which, incidentally, opens the wrong way!). Island in center of kitchen provides ample wall, base cabinet, and pantry storage as well as planning desk on family room side. Simulated brick wall coordinates with vinyl flooring. *Courtesy Wood-Mode*

do in this area, include a bulletin board, proper lighting, a calendar, slots for papers and recipes, a telephone, and perhaps an intercom and radio.

Storage center

In addition to the storage areas which are an integral part of each center, you may want to build a separate storage area for small appliances, entertaining equipment, or any other special objects which you keep in the kitchen. We will discuss the possibilities for a separate storage center in Chapter 12, but remember that you can often double the use of your small appliances and other items and cut your work in half if you store things within easy reach.

Other centers

As we said before, if you have another chef in the family, or perhaps several of them, you may want to plan a separate center for barbecuing, an extra range area, or whatever the specialty demands.

You may also want to plan a center for plant and herb growing, sewing, or whatever your favorite hobby is. If you have the space in your kitchen, don't be afraid to bring your hobbies into it. For a variety of special centers see the "Young Idea Kitchen" on page 65. Then use your imagination and go on from there!

This spacious kitchen includes a number of specially designed units. The center island of cabinetry, planned with storage units that open at ends of the island, provides an abundance of working space by way of a chopping block counter top. The center island sink is also an extra convenience feature—so handy for preparing vegetables, mixing drinks, or filling vases from its gooseneck faucet. Cabinetry (back center) accommodates a surface cooking unit and barbecue grill located under a beautifully tiled wall in dark contrast to the surrounding frame of white brick. Not visible in the picture is a specially designed base cabinet for dishes, built at a low level for the convenience of young children. An old ceiling fan and flowered paper for walls and ceiling add to the gay decor. *Courtesy Wood-Mode*

The Basic Shapes in Kitchens

Now that you have thought about your new kitchen in terms of individual centers, you are now ready to consider the total plan. In choosing the shape your kitchen will take, consider the space available, the design of the room, any additional centers you have in mind, and whether or not the room is to function simply as a kitchen or to be a part of a larger room such as a family room, an indoor-outdoor kitchen or any other possible combination.

A wall of antique brick dominates this impressive kitchen where the Early American theme is carried out in the cabinetry design—oak with V-joint Colonial styling. The arched cooking area in this wall is reminiscent of yesterday's walk-in fireplace. Extra convenience is incorporated in many features of the island with its spacious counter top, second sink for food preparations, ample storage in drawers and cabinets specially designed to accommodate utensils and equipment in a wide range of sizes. Cabinets housing appliances attractively divide this kitchen from the adjacent family room. *Courtesy Wood-Mode*

Here is a kitchen for spirited people. A soda fountain and built-in barbecue, set into a center peninsula, divides actual kitchen work area from family room. Continuous counter space doubles as service bar, work area. Traditional feeling is amplified through cabinet styling, ceiling beams, wood counters, wallpaper, and accessories. *Courtesy Interpace*

A blend of materials brings a special charm to this combination beverage-barbecue center—natural brick, ceramic tile, copper, wood, glass, and brushed stainless steel. Heavy-duty hood and fan amply remove smoke, cooking odors, and fumes from gas barbecue. Note decorative use of tasteful functional accessories. *Courtesy Thermador Trade-Wind*

The shape of things to come

The three basic work centers—sink, range, and refrigerator—are interrelated and should be arranged so work flows easily from one to the other. In a continuous arrangement, one counter may serve two centers, and as we said previously, it is possible to combine work centers. If you do plan a dual-purpose center, the width of the counter should be the largest width suggested plus an additional 12 to 15 inches.

There are four basic shapes of kitchens with many variations and combinations between.

The U-Shape Plan is probably the most popular and the most functional kitchen shape. Each work center is located on one wall with the sink in the center. In a large room you can build an island or peninsula of cabinets and counter space to separate work centers and cut traffic to a minimum. Corner cabinets make use of "dead space" although some corner storage will be difficult to reach. This shape is advantageous in that it helps to eliminate "through traffic," provides continuous work or counter space, and offers the shortest walking distance between appliances. It is usually the most expensive arrangement. Keep in mind that the back or middle wall should be at least 96 inches (8 feet) to allow a minimum of 48 inches (4 feet) clearance between the two flanking walls.

The L-Shape Plan is practical and more economical for two adjacent walls. It frees space along the other two walls for optional centers such as dining, planning desk, or laundry. It does provide continuous counter space as it turns the corner, but walking distances between appliances and work centers are greater than in a U-shape plan.

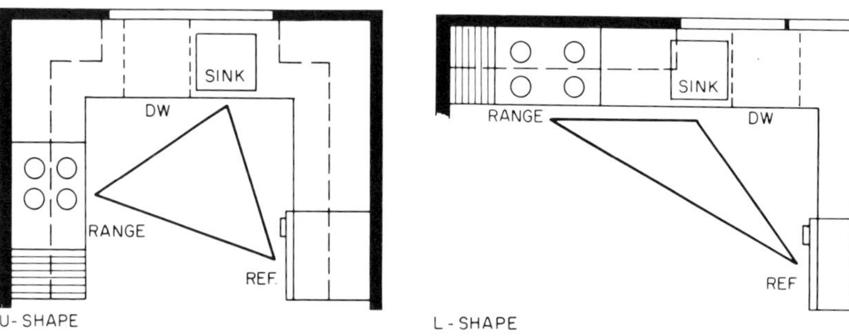

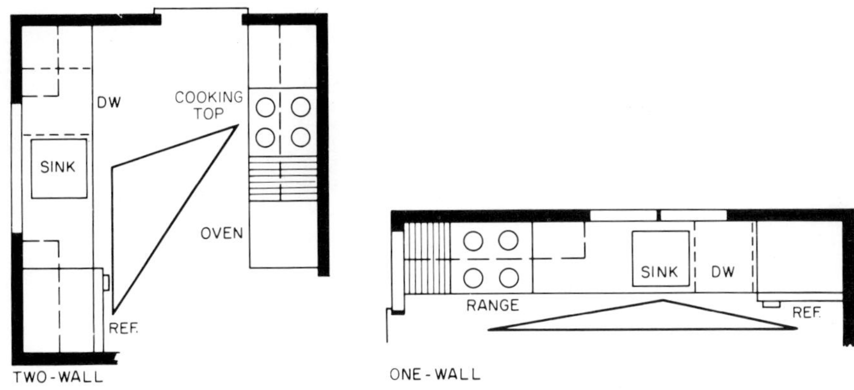

The Two-Wall or Corridor Plan is economical because there are no corners to turn. This plan necessitates a minimum of 48 to 54 inches floor space between the two counters. Actually the floor area should be a minimum of 8 feet and no more than 10 feet wide to provide adequate but not excessive floor space between counters. This plan is most efficient if one end is closed to cross traffic since if the corridor provides a thoroughfare for through traffic it can interfere with your work.

The One-Wall kitchen is perfect for limited space in a narrow room. It is especially popular in small homes and apartments. The main disadvantage, of course, is that it does not provide adequate counter and storage space.

Making variations through islands and peninsulas

If your kitchen area is large and spread out, an island or peninsula can draw areas closer together, while dividing the kitchen from laundry or eating area. A peninsula at a right angle from the wall adds counter and storage space. Sink and range units may be installed here, and wall cabinets opening from both sides suspended from the ceiling.

You can install an island or peninsula if you have at least 4 feet between opposite work areas or an even 3 feet if only a passageway is involved. If you do decide on an island or peninsula, be sure that it does not create an obstacle for traffic or other functions, and remember to provide enough counter and storage space or it may prove to be precisely that obstacle you want to avoid. Stay away from islands and peninsulas if your room is not large since they are very visible and tend to make a kitchen look even smaller than it is.

Center island in clover leaf design adapts to L-shaped kitchen layout and provides space for eating, cooking, barbecuing. Sink center takes advantage of garden view, indoor-outdoor access, and provides sunlight, as well as water for herb garden and plants.
Courtesy Interpace

The Step-Saving Triangle

In your planning consider that the most practical arrangement is one in which the three major work centers are placed so they form the points of a triangle. This arrangement lets you take a minimum of steps to walk from one point to another. Try to have not more than 22 feet around the three sides of the triangle. In addition to the minimum and maximum allowances we have stipulated for the work centers there should be:

- •4 to 7 feet between the sink and refrigerator
- •4 to 6 feet between the sink and range
- •4 to 9 feet between the range and refrigerator

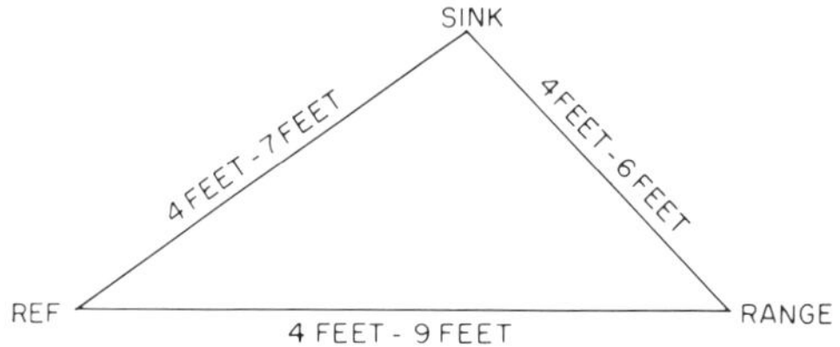

Satellite Kitchens

While you are deciding what shape your kitchen will take and which centers you will include, why not consider some satellite kitchens in other parts of the house. There is nothing new about the idea. You have probably been barbecuing on the patio and cooking in the fireplace for years. There are, however, some very fresh approaches to this tradition of cooking where you eat and live. In fact, satellite kitchens are becoming ever more popular and sophisticated in today's homes. They will supplement, not take the place of, the main kitchen.

Portable cooking appliances and furniturelike refrigerators, freezers, and ranges make it easy to place minikitchens anywhere in the house. Here are some examples of this fast-growing trend. Most of them are available right now; others are just around the corner.

•Set up an automatic coffee maker in the bedroom for that first cup of coffee in the morning. And don't forget the automatic timer to start the coffee for you.

•A guest kitchen allows visitors to rise at their leisure and breakfast at any hour with no inconvenience to the hostess. This satellite might be no more than a counter top built into a closet and outfitted with a series of convenience outlets for a toaster, coffee maker, and fry pan. Install a cabinet or two, a ductless hood and vent, and an undercounter built-in refrigerator. Conceal it all with louvered doors, provide ventilation, and there it is—the perfect convenience for your guests.

•Portable appliances on a serving cart make coffee klatches a breeze. Everything moves easily and at once from kitchen to porch to patio.

•A barbecue grill poolside makes cooking outdoors easy.

•A portable oven in the playroom lets the kids cook their own pizza for a snack.

•If the family room is not located near the kitchen, why not install a second minikitchen there for convenience.

•And how about those midnight snacks when you are comfortably settled in the den? A compact refrigerator dressed up in furniture disguise for beverages and sandwich makings will mean you never have to leave the hearth or miss the last scene of another late show.

In the not too distant future bigger—or should we say smaller—kitchen satellites will provide the following conveniences:

Specially designed for custom tastes: moveable cart with wine rack for indoor-outdoor entertaining; eating area to take advantage of outdoors; raised-from-the-floor cabinets for easy cleaning of floors; built-in ovens to serve both indoor-outdoor functions. *Courtesy Armstrong*

•A breakfast nook in your bedroom could be as simple as a refrigerator drawer for chilled juices.

•A combination freezer-electronic range and laser beam garbage disposer in the playroom might enable teen-agers to order their snacks by voice command.

•A portable cook center on the patio which includes a smooth surface cook top, built-in barbecue, and thermoelectric refrigerator may operate on a self-contained fuel cell.

For more about kitchen ideas of the future see Chapter 20, but before we get lost in tomorrow's dream kitchen let's consider the very real kitchen in store for you today.

How to Adapt a Floor Plan

As you leaf through this book you will find many interesting floor plans. Obviously few floor plans can be duplicated in their entirety in another kitchen, but they can be adapted to fit other room dimensions. Here is a basic floor plan that will illustrate our point.

Use this plan as a springboard

•Note appliances and cabinets and counter space beside them. These work centers can then be juggled to fit your own plan.

•Turn the plan around, look at it from every angle.

•Trace plan on thin paper, flip it over, and study from all directions.

•From another tracing, make cutouts of the work centers; put them together to fit your kitchen.

•Consider using appliances in smaller or larger sizes.

•Try putting one work area at an angle, or on a peninsula or island.

The kitchen below with its overall dimensions is broken into work areas. Dining room is close to cooking top and dishwasher for easy serving and fast after-meal cleanup. Laundry area is compact. Cabinets and built-in oven cabinets are grouped.

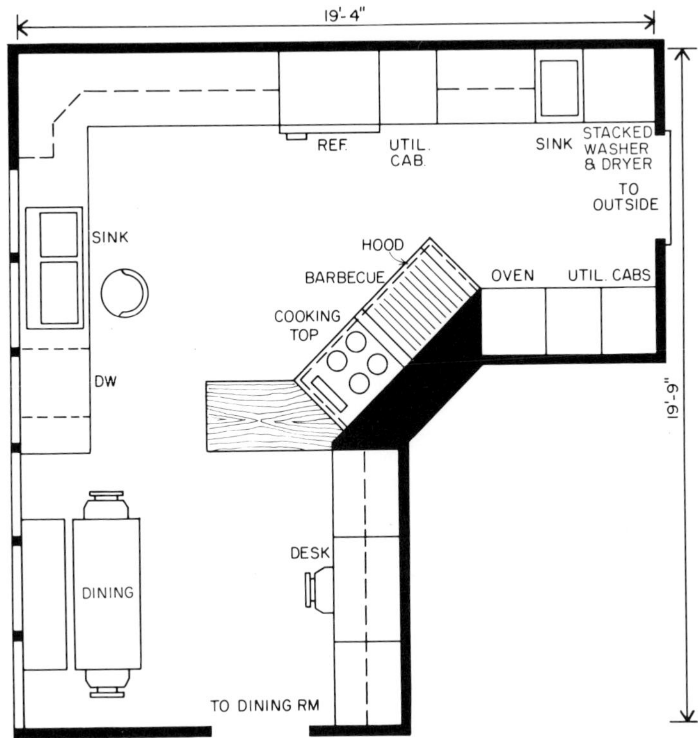

Relate it to a triangle

The relationship of the refrigerator, dishwasher, sink and range is quite similar to the plan above. It is necessary here to use a refrigerator with a left-hand door opening. A single-bowl sink allows more room for counter space. Freestanding range and adjoining cabinets are placed on a peninsula to form an efficient U-shaped work area; wall cabinets are suspended from a soffit over the peninsula. Storage wall in the dining area provides additional space, a convenient desk, and a tall utility cabinet. If you prefer, laundry facilities could replace the desk and some of the base cabinets.

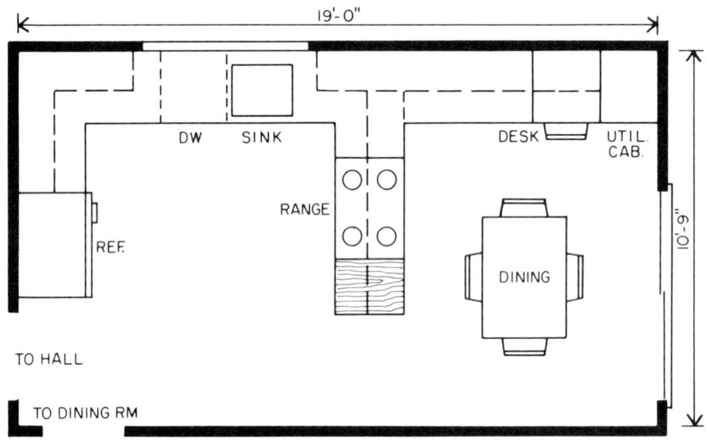

Turn original plan sideways

Note how the major portion of the kitchen on page 41 can be revised to fit into this kitchen plan. The work areas fall into a basic U-shape with the cooking top and barbecue slanting into the main kitchen work area. Putting them on an angle instead of a straight peninsula has the advantage of bringing the cooking area a few steps closer to the refrigerator and sink areas, as well as freeing more space for dining. The wedge-shaped cabinet, resulting from turning the angle, opens into the

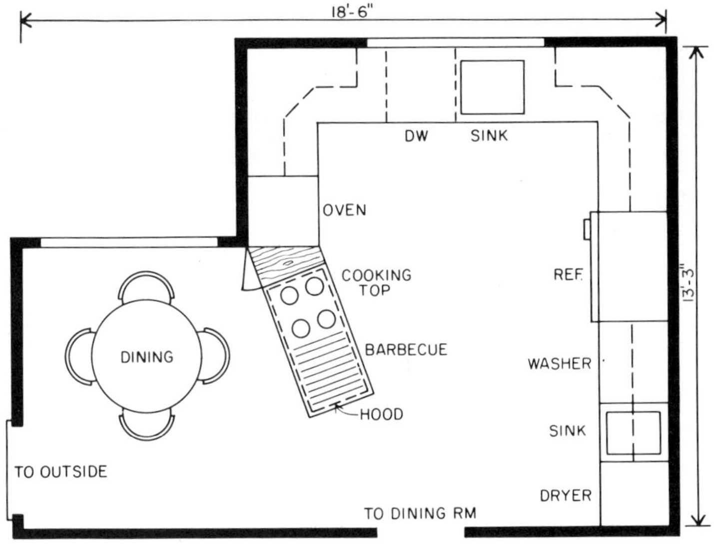

dining area. It can be outfitted with vertical partitions for tray and large platter storage. The laundry area, smaller than the original, has wall-cabinet storage for laundry supplies.

Adapt it to a smaller room

This plan retains the basic elements of the original kitchen (page 41) even though it's much smaller. Cooking peninsula comes straight out from the wall, separates kitchen and family room. Dining bar can be 36 inches counter height or 30 inches table height.

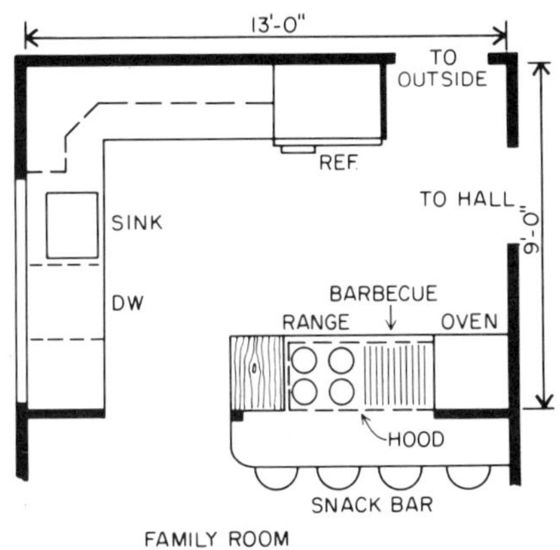

Consider a separate laundry wall

The main kitchen areas (far right) are placed along two walls and on a peninsula—out of the path of traffic from the outside to other rooms. Laundry area has washer and dryer, is completely separated from meal preparation. Since little time is spent at these automatic appliances, traffic is no problem.

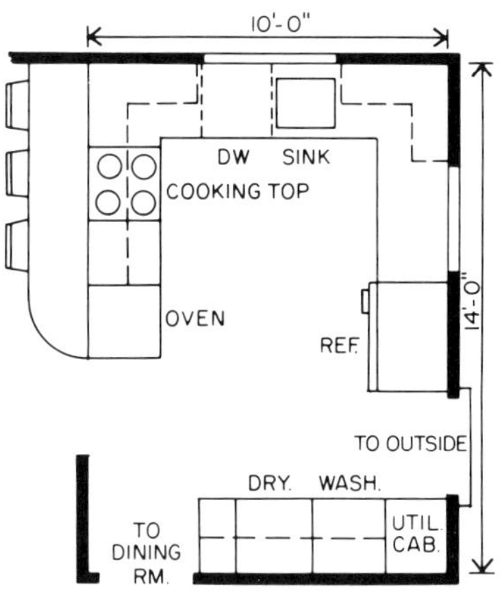

CHAPTER 6

Where Shall We Eat?

Of all the special centers to fill your needs and fit your family's life-style, one is so common to kitchens today that it deserves special consideration. While you are designing your new kitchen, think seriously about planning a special eating area. I have listed in this chapter some suggestions for the dining area that suits your kitchen shape and size best, but you need not stick to these plans. Combine, improvise, or, better yet, if you have the space and do not yet have such a room, consider building a family room that opens onto the kitchen and makes informal dining a convenience as well as a pleasure.

Here is an assortment of eating areas, ranging from minimum to large, adapted to various kitchen shapes. Perhaps one of them will suit your needs.

In a U-Shape kitchen where the space is:

• *Minimum,* build a right-angle extension of the counter, with access below to storage and stools.

• *Small,* build a table-height counter (29–30 inches) along the wall. Taper the sides at traffic and work areas.

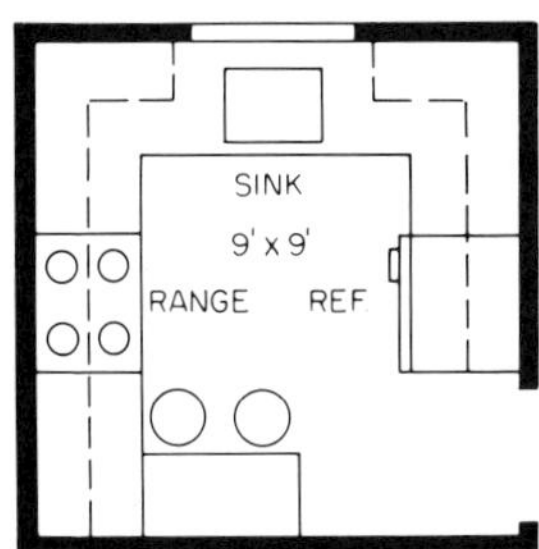

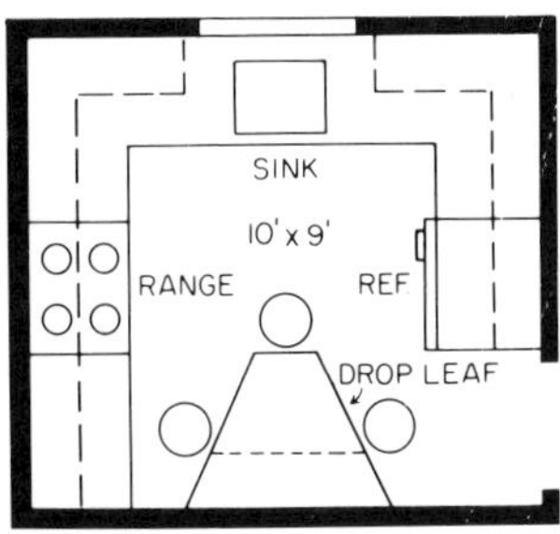

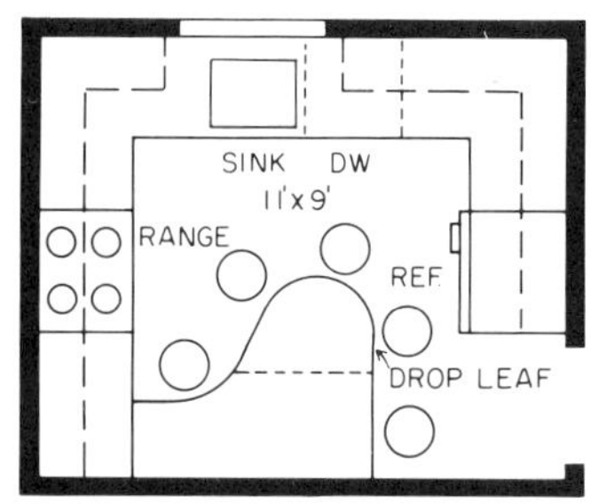

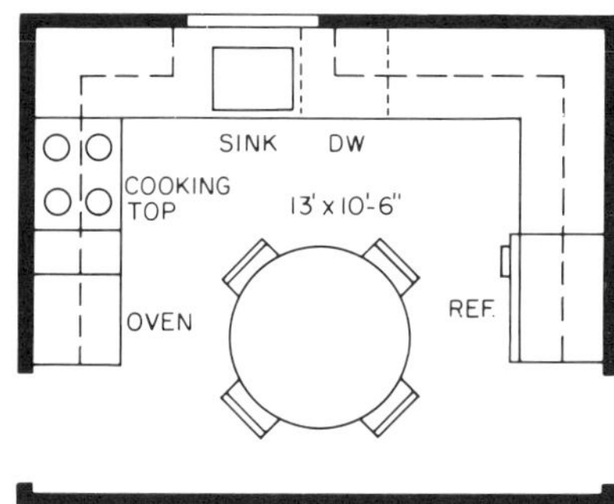

•*Medium,* add a free-form peninsula table to fit space. Casters make the table moveable and a drop leaf extends capacity.

•*Large,* revive the old-fashioned kitchen table in the middle of the room. It will also serve as a spot for various family activities.

In an L-Shape kitchen where the space is:

•*Minimum,* turn a corner into an eating spot with a small rectangular table and gain a work surface as well.

•*Small,* angle a peninsula from corner at 45 degrees (table or counter height) to allow room for several settings.

•*Medium,* place a long table at right angles to the wall allowing room for chairs at both sides. Use a drop leaf if the aisle is narrow.

•*Large,* add a cozy note with a round table as large as space permits. A built-in curved seat will conserve space.

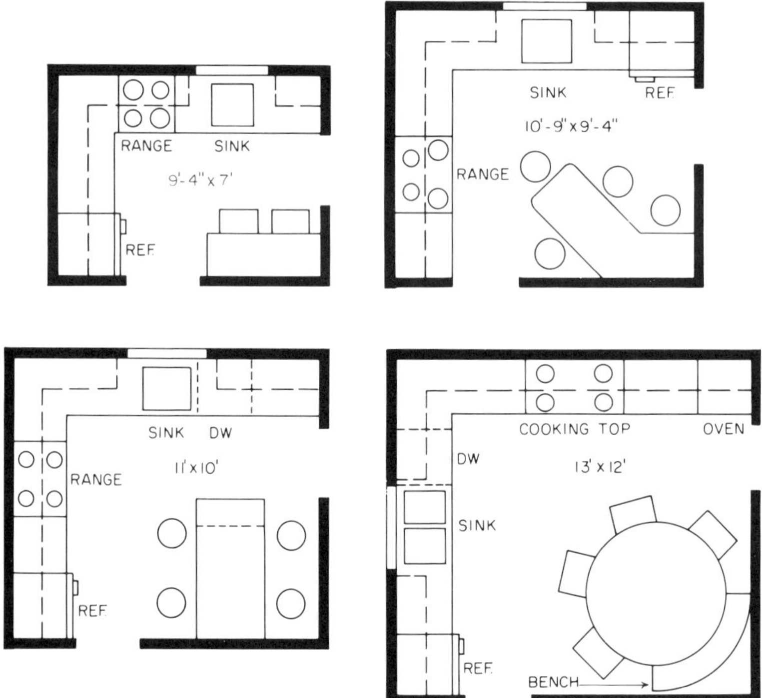

In a *Two-Wall* kitchen where the space is:

• *Minimum,* use every available inch. A hideaway table will pivot into a slot undercounter.

• *Small,* turn a traffic lane into an eating area with a plywood tabletop hinged to wall. The top drops down when not in use.

• *Medium,* hang a long narrow shelf (as deep as possible) on an unused wall and suit the height to either stool or chair.

• *Large,* make a dining area of a long harvest table or use a plywood door on legs. Position the table to allow seating on both sides.

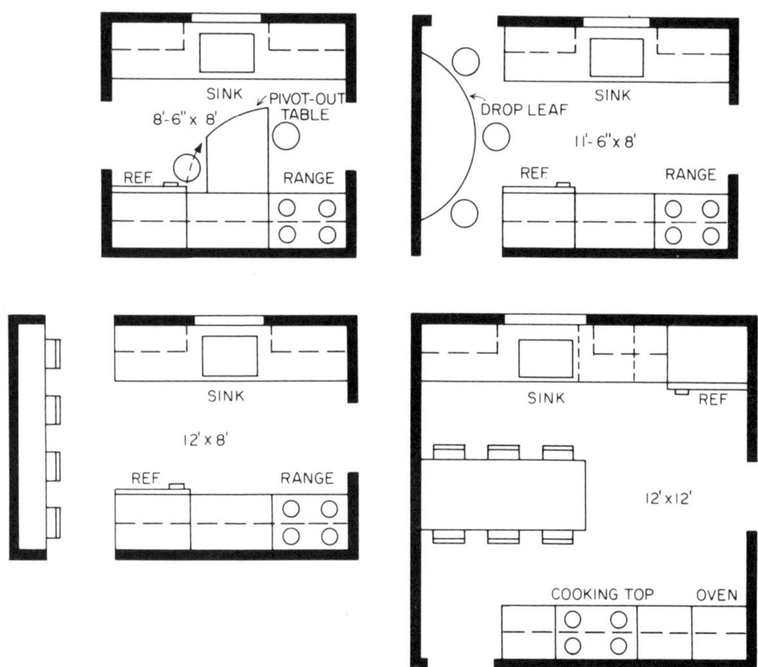

In a *One-Wall* kitchen where the space is:

• *Minimum,* put a narrow shelf under a window at counter height (36 inches) or table level (29–30 inches)

• *Small,* build a 25-inch deep counter area with 13-inch deep cabinets as base. The overhang allows for knees.

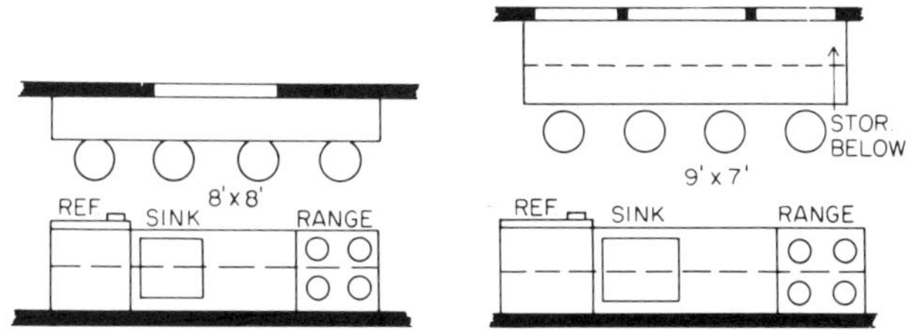

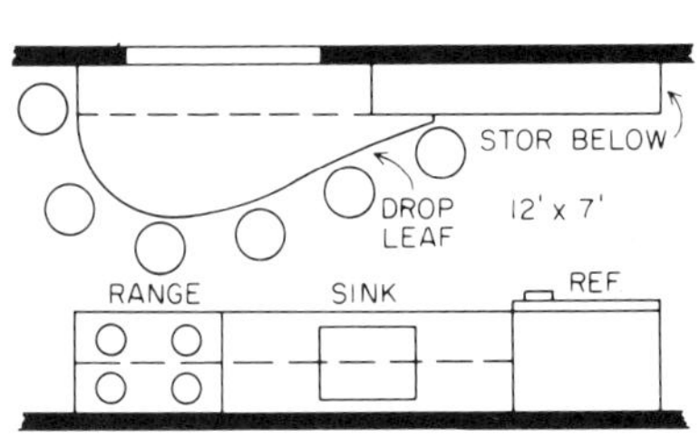

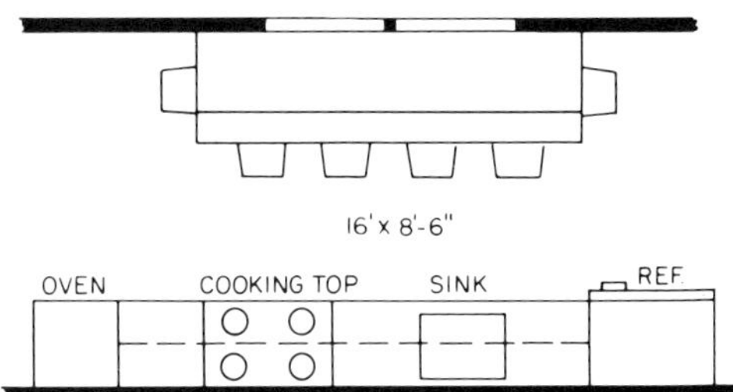

•*Medium,* solve space problem with a free-form counter, hinged to drop flat against wall, or possibly fastened to shallow storage cabinets as above.

•*Large,* consider a harvest table, available in several lengths. It is a perfect solution for hall-like kitchens. Be sure you have planned for space to raise the slim leaf at mealtime.

Cut-Up Kitchens

If you have a cut-up kitchen, here are four ways to add an eating area and gain new convenience.

•*Minimum,* no spare wall space to use? Add on to the end of any counter, perhaps even partially blocking an archway or window. Here we gain an extra work surface in addition to a snack bar.

•*Small,* here's an eating area that doubles as serving space for the cooking center. When you measure for such a peninsula, be sure you have enough space to open the oven door safely.

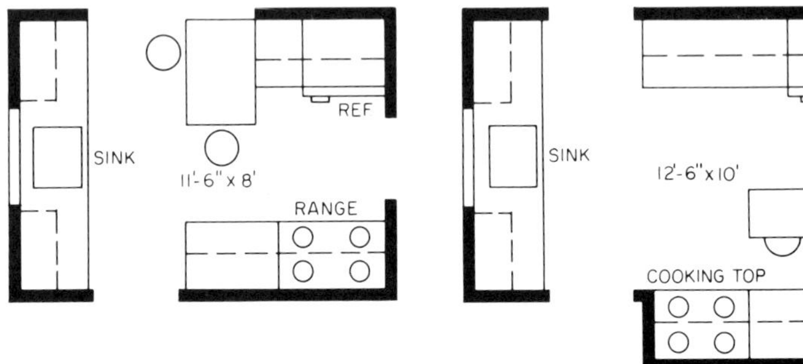

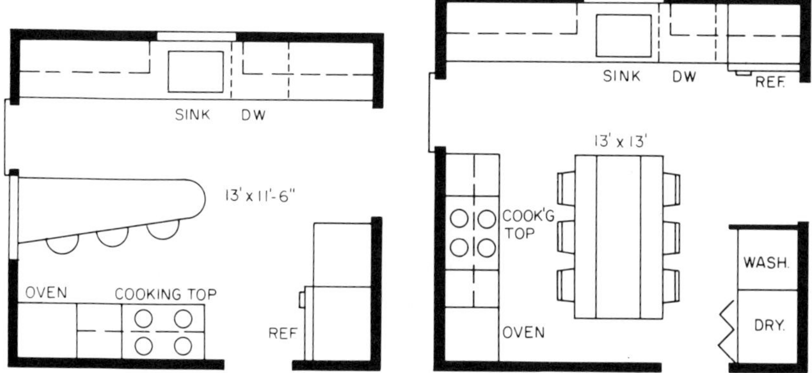

• *Medium,* at first glance, this long counter, built midway between cooking and cleanup centers, seems to be an obstacle. Actually it would save steps in every direction and unify the kitchen.

• *Large,* floor space is the least of your problems, so why not plant a big table right in the middle of the room? It makes a big kitchen seem cozier and gives you room to spread out for cooking.

A delightful eating bar for breakfasts, quick snacks! In a large kitchen is cheerful and efficient; casement windows admit daylight and a sweeping view of lake to meal preparation area as well as to informal dining counter. Cook top and ceramic inset on peninsula, sink, refrigerator-freezer are all within a few steps of each other and of wall oven unseen against long wall. Here as in central living-dining room, the floor is a large-scale ceramic tile whose textured surface and chestnut color complement other materials used, and which is easily mopped clean. *Courtesy American Olean*

Peninsula doubles as eating area, snack bar, and sink center, separating kitchen area from passageway. Light-colored cabinets and sunny yellow counters add spaciousness to a small area. Refrigerator door panels match cabinets. Leaded window in corner wall cabinet adds change of pace in decor—contrasts nicely with brick wall and dark hood.
Courtesy Rutt-Williams

Richly elegant and inviting, this pass-through kitchen makes dining service a cinch. Ceramic tile counter doubles as a snack bar and serving counter. Kitchen is hidden from view behind louvered doors when not in use. *Courtesy Interpace*

Above, left. This "L" kitchen boasts an eating area that doubles as a sit-down work counter. Compact in design, it is big in conveniences—counter-height refrigerator, apartment-sized range with a white ductless hood, and a minisize stainless steel "bar-type" sink. *Courtesy* Modern Bride *Magazine*

Left. Warm, woodsy, and Colonial, this is a kitchen for all occasions. Chopping-block peninsula doubles as an eating area–work surface. Second sink to right serves as a potting area or bar. Washable paisley wall covering, matching window shades, porcelain knobs, painted beams make kitchen distinctive. *Courtesy* Modern Bride *Magazine*

Above, right. A haven on the lower level! This one-wall complete though compact kitchen works overtime. Large eating-work counter does double duty for indoor-outdoor use. Cool shades of green in counters and wall covering and contrasting white cabinets give kitchen a bright feeling. *Courtesy* Modern Bride *Magazine*

Maximum convenience in minimum space! This pull-out table folds into cabinet for complete concealment; pulls out for use when needed. Extra storage space is provided in bottom of cabinet. *Courtesy Wood-Mode*

Have a corner in an attic or dormer? Take your cues from this brightly decorative little kitchen with big ideas. Contrasting white beams show off angled lines of ceiling. Suspended light fixtures offer leveling effect. Raised counter-bar conceals work space, serves as eating area. Wall covering makes the room. *Courtesy* Modern Bride *Magazine*

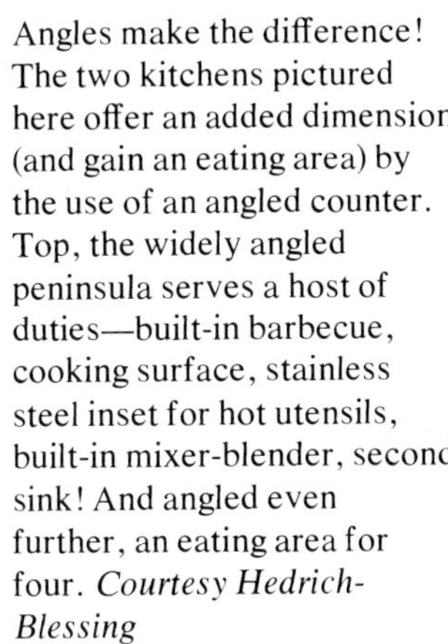

Angles make the difference! The two kitchens pictured here offer an added dimension (and gain an eating area) by the use of an angled counter. Top, the widely angled peninsula serves a host of duties—built-in barbecue, cooking surface, stainless steel inset for hot utensils, built-in mixer-blender, second sink! And angled even further, an eating area for four. *Courtesy Hedrich-Blessing*

Angled counter serves as cleanup area, eating bar! Note free-form ceiling and recessed down lighting; warming shelf under hood. *Courtesy Hedrich-Blessing*

CHAPTER 7

Kitchen Personalities

Beyond the basic principles of good planning your kitchen should reflect your own and your family's life-style and serve the idiosyncrasies of the people who will spend the most time there. First, build some good common sense into your plan; then add the personality notes.

As I have traveled across the country and visited with the many homemakers in whose kitchens I have enjoyed many cups of coffee and warm hours of conversation, I have discovered five basic kitchen types that seem to fit the way most families live. In addition, we have developed several new concepts that you may find particularly adaptable to your own life-style. You can combine any of these concepts with the basic kitchen types or adopt a single plan full scale. The choices are infinite and entirely up to you.

The five basic types include:

1. *The open kitchen.* If you like to entertain informally, wander from kitchen to patio, pool, terrace, or nearby family or living room, if you like to serve directly from the kitchen to any other area, then choose an open plan which adjoins one or more of these areas.

2. *The compact kitchen or the "just-a-kitchen" kitchen.* A small kitchen can be lovely and efficient. If you like everything within arm's reach, if you prefer to work alone without a well-meaning audience, then this is your kitchen! It needn't be a small room. It could be a part of a larger area but enclosed in compact quarters.

3. *The family kitchen.* For you who want family and friends nearby while you work, this kitchen offers area to relax in the form of a family or sitting area. It's also an ideal plan if you want a children's play area so you can keep a watchful eye while you work.

4. *The dining kitchen.* For the family that's on the run yet likes to eat together, the dining kitchen is simply a place to cook with an area large enough for the family and even friends to eat. It can even serve as a place for informal, casual entertaining.

5. *The fun or hobby kitchen.* Are you or your husband a gourmet cook? Do you like to hang all sorts of lovely utensils or display a favorite collection? Would your family like a soda fountain? Do you enjoy sewing, arranging flowers, or growing herbs? Would you like some extra "office space"?

These are the five basic plans. In the portfolio that follows, you will see how they can be adapted to the personalities and life-styles of the people who live and work in them.

Basic Concepts

Pantry-Shelf Kitchen—Fresh New Look in Design

The concept behind a pantry-shelf kitchen is twofold:

It is based on the premise that the kitchen is primarily for cooking, and everything for that function should be at hand.

It recognizes the fact that the most common complaint of homemakers everywhere is the lack of adequate and convenient storage space for the important items.

In the pictures and floor plans below, note how this concept takes shape:

- All wall cabinets have been eliminated, giving the *utility cabinet* a chance to be what it was designed for in the first place—a large pantry storage area within the kitchen itself.
- The basic core of the kitchen is the food preparation center which has a full-height pantry wall for refrigeration and storage including a refrigerator-freezer and 24-inch deep utility cabinets for the storage of linens, food, cleaning supplies, small appliances, and utensils.
- The staggered-height work island has a variety of undercounter storage cabinets.
- Basic plan includes a pull-down serving and eating counter; sliding, on-the-spot midway shelves for storing ingredients and utensils in strategic areas; a planningdesk,and two 13-inch-deep utility cabinets for glassware and dinnerware.
- Twenty-four-inch utility cabinets have easy-to-adjust pull-out shelves.
- Even though the refrigerator-freezer is not adjacent to a counter, a half-turn away is the work surface on the island opposite it.
- With limited counter space ($7^1/_2$ feet in this kitchen) the entire island was topped with hardwood. If you've more space perhaps it would be a good

idea to choose a variety of surfaces, including stainless steel, laminated plastic, or a combination of all three materials.

•Counter heights are 36 inches except in the mixing center. Here it's 30 inches high for easier working.

•The height of the midway storage cabinets over the island helps to hide the unsightliness of food preparation and cleanup in an open-plan kitchen.

•Fold-down snack area is illuminated by lighting installed under the midway units.

•Encompassing the entire island and brightening the work area is the hood of lights. The ventilating fan and exhaust system are directly above the range. Metal duct, supporting the hood and designed for the removal of grease and odors, now becomes decorative and functional.

•Wallpaper has a washable acrylic finish.

All photographs in this section are courtesy American Home *Magazine; Photographer, Lyman Emerson.*

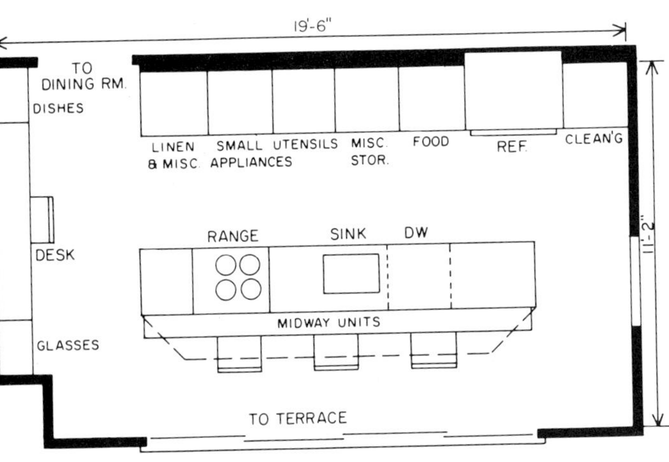

Below, right. Linens, vases, Thermos jugs, paper supplies, and a variety of serving pieces are stored in the utility cabinets near the dining room and terrace —where they are most often used.

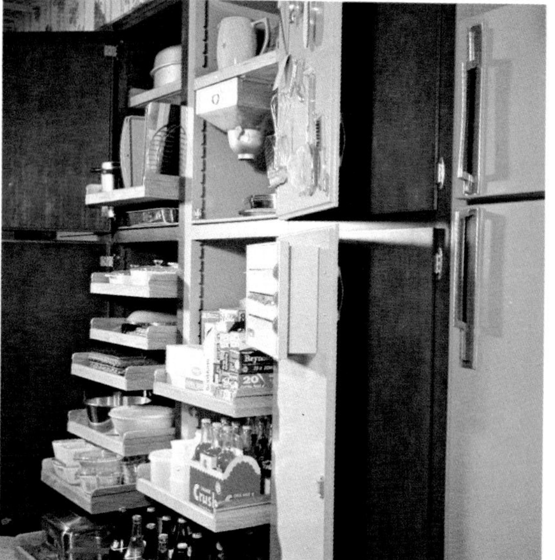

Top. Small electric appliance storage is a problem to many homemakers. On the easy-to-roll-out shelves of this utility cabinet we have more than a dozen appliances. Shelves are adjustable and can be arranged to fit the height of any equipment.

Bottom. Pots and pans, casserole dishes, a large roaster all find space in these closets. For storing baking utensils there is a vertical slotted wire holder. Combination flour container and sifter is attached to one shelf. On the door hang small utensils and a three-way dispenser.

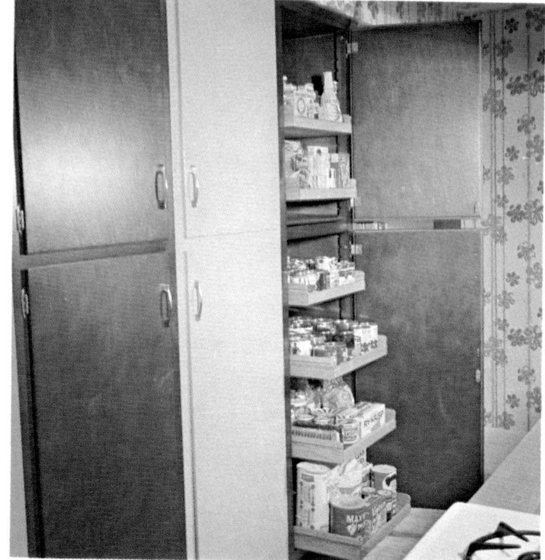

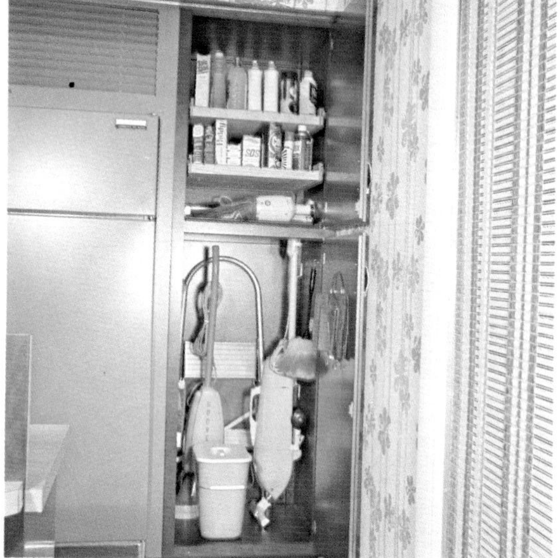

Top. The food storage cabinet contains all necessary food supplies and staples. There is never any reaching or guesswork to find a specific item. Food inventories are easy to keep.

Bottom. Cleaning equipment is stored in the lower half of this closet. The brooms and brushes hang from cup hooks and a wire bag holder is installed on the door. Above are all necessary waxes, detergents, soaps, polishes, plus a handy portable vacuum.

Top. The 30-inch high counter at the end of the island work area is a perfect mixing height. Mixing equipment and nonrefrigerated vegetable storage are below. An electric outlet at the back of the counter allows you to use small appliances on the spot. Midway units hold an extra supply of spices and small utensils.

Bottom. Slide-in compact gas range gives you a large 30-inch oven in a minimum amount of space. Adjoining cutting-board counter is convenient. An extra slide-out cutting board and hidden trash basket are featured in this area.

Top. Snack bar behind island work center can be used for serving buffets or for quick family meals. It folds out of the way when not in use. Midway storage services both sides of island—condiments and serving accessories are easy to reach at mealtime or for use on the other side in food preparation.

Bottom. Desk area is ideal for planning meals, talking on the phone, or writing letters. When necessary, heatproof laminated plastic desk can be used as additional counter space. On each side of desk are adjustable shelved closets for dishes and glasses.

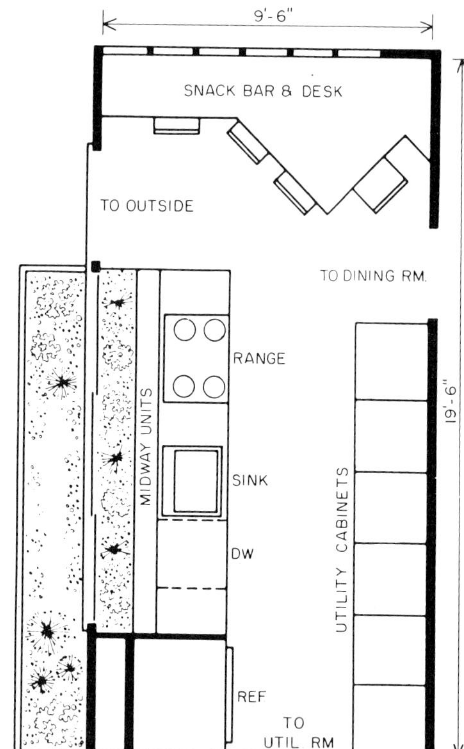

Pantry-Shelf Kitchen Variations

A corridor or two-wall kitchen variation of the basic design moves the refrigerator to the working wall, giving one additional utility cabinet. The desk and snack bar are one, designed a bit more dramatically and offering additional counter work space when needed. For the gardener a large indoor planter, accessible from the outside through sliding glass doors, is behind the midway units.

A scaled-down adaptation utilizes a kitchen-work area only, without eating and planning facilities.

19'-6"
TO DINING RM.
UTILITY CABINETS
REF.
UTIL. CAB.
TO HALL
OVEN
COOKING TOP
SINK
DW
10'
TO OUTSIDE

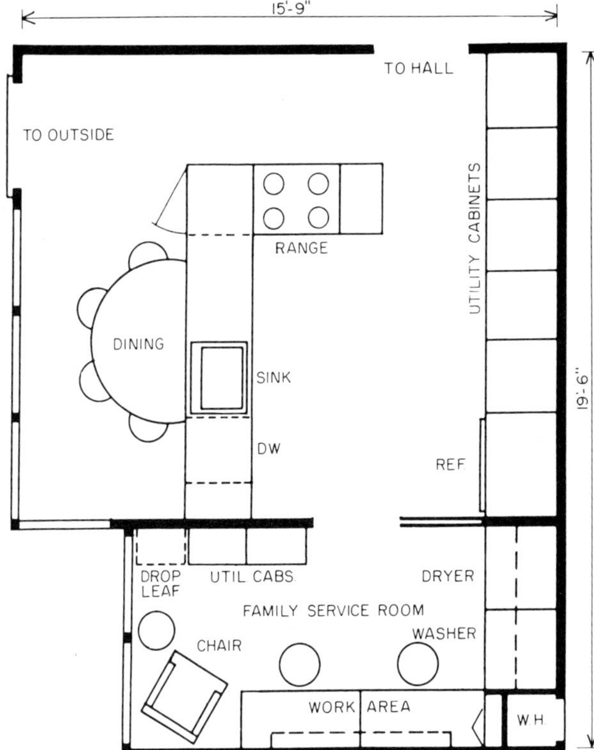

An L-shaped design variation adds a family service room adjacent to the kitchen for laundering, ironing, hobbies, or sitting, plus two more utility cabinets for additional storage. This room lends itself to what we call "planned chaos" where the ironing board can stay up all the time, the gift wrapping on the table, or the material on the sewing machine. Just slide the door closed and hide the working clutter.

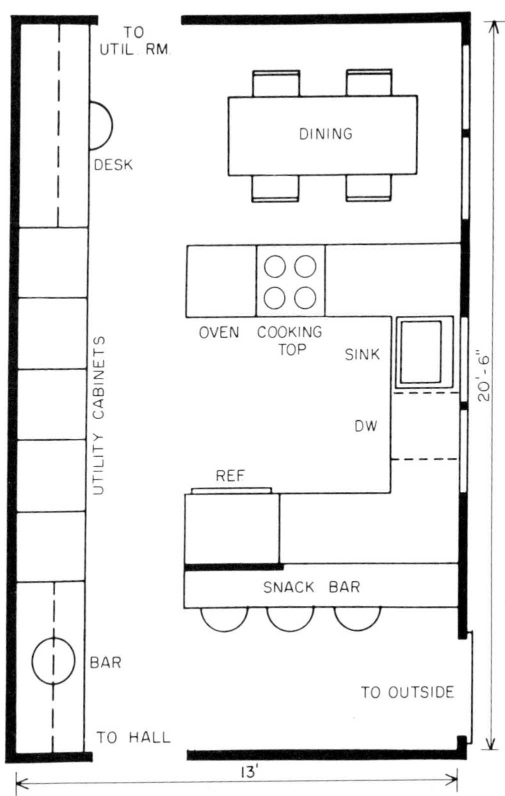

The U-shaped kitchen
variation will appeal to those who enjoy eating family meals in the kitchen. The cooking center features a built-in oven and cook top. The range-area counter top doubles as a serving counter for the dining area. The snack area is ideal for after-school cookies and milk or a quick cup of coffee. The built-in bar conveniently services nearby entertaining areas of the home.

U-shaped work area designed for arms' reach working, yet out of traffic flow.

Functional Kitchen—Hub of the House

This kitchen was designed with two goals in mind: it had to be *functional* (to suit family life-style) and it had to be the center of all family activities. The plan and pictures below show how they achieved their goal:

•Dining area end faces a secluded garden court at the rear.

•The other looks out to a deck, reached through a door in the adjacent dining room.

•U-shaped meal-preparation area has all the necessary appliances including a counter top, eye-level range.

•Roll-out exhaust fan above the range removes grease, smoke, and odors.

•Pass-through serving counter with china cabinets that open from both sides, is convenient to dishwasher on one side, dining room table on the other.

•Opposite the kitchen eating area are some large pantry-type closets for storing food supplies and necessary cleaning equipment.

•Note relationship of indoor cooking to outdoor serving.

All photographs in this section are courtesy American Home *Magazine; Photographer, Lyman Emerson.*

Pass-through serving counter does double duty as a snack bar for quick dining.

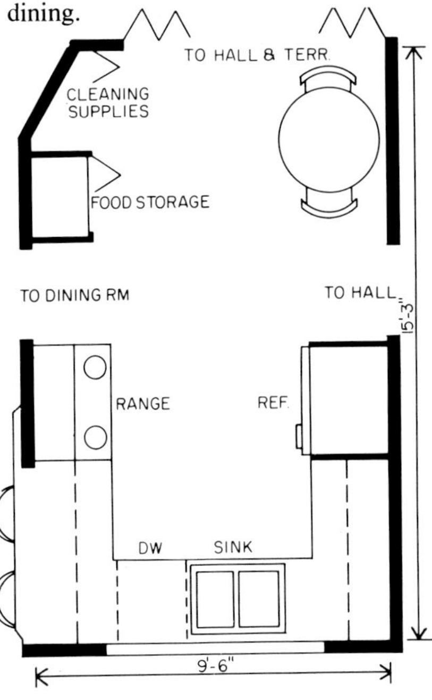

Salt

Removeable counter insert leaves enough room so sewing-machine base fits flush with counter top. With insert in, counter is gift-wrapping area.

It didn't take much to equip a small corner of our snack counter with the necessities for breakfast.

Young Idea Kitchen

Warm, yet functional. A complete description in three little words for this young idea kitchen designed for the woman who loves to cook and who cares about where she cooks. Because she cares, her kitchen goes beyond the ordinary and becomes an extension of her personality. This is a kitchen where everything—the plan, the materials, the decorative accessories—works together to bring out that warmth and convenience.

This is more than a "kitchen proper." It includes an indoor barbecue, a laundry center, a desk, a snack area, a sewing nook, a gift-wrapping area, complete storage facilities, and a cozy corner for relaxation. It's chock-full of ideas meant especially for the woman who's young at heart. She is one who has the courage to brighten her kitchen with lively colors and gay wallpaper, to combine a print with a plaid; she's endowed with the creative spirit to investigate the use of handsome, lacquered butter molds for cabinet hardwares, use

The heart of every kitchen tells the story of the way you cook. Here, practical, hard maple chopping block counters are "decorated" with favorite herbs, spices, cooking staples, while everyday gadgets and utensils hang within easy reach from ventilating hood over the range.

Enclosed shelves above snack counter turn it into a multipurpose activity area. Practical tile walls in the barbecue become a focal point of interest when a decorative tile design is added. Another great idea for the barbecue is a two-burner cook top to supplement gas-fired barbecue unit.

latticework to enclose a restful nook; she has the irrepressible urge to comb antique shops for finds such as a carved cookbook "stand"; and the sensibility to demand up-to-date materials that are easy to take care of.

You don't have to reproduce this kitchen as is, but it could be to your advantage to copy and adapt many of its ideas, fifty of which are listed here.

All photographs in this section are courtesy American Home *Magazine; Photographer, Horst Ahlberg.*

Kitchen Conveniences

1 Pull-out flour sifter.
2 Tile insert in counter next to oven for hot pans.
3 Gadgets and utensils hang from ventilating hood around cook top.
4 Built-in oven to supplement oven in freestanding range.
5 Open shelves beneath wall cabinets for measuring cups and small mixing utensils.
6 Foot-operated sink faucet in salad center.
7 Dual-level, enameled cast iron kitchen sink with detergent and lotion dispenser. Wooden cutting board formed to partially fit over sink.

Family sitting area located at end of kitchen island provides a cozy nook for resting, coffee klatches, or for needlework.

In addition to serving as the cleanup area (with double-bowl sink and cutting board with opening to complement garbage disposer), center island separates that work area from the rest of the room. Dishwasher is raised for easier accessibility. Broken counter heights combine hard maple and glazed ceramic tile counter materials.

8 Raised dishwasher for easier loading and unloading.
9 Gas cook top next to barbecue.
10 Cleaning closet includes all the aids to make housecleaning as quick and easy as possible. (Lightweight vacuum for quick cleaning, standard vacuum for thorough cleaning, floor scrubber-polisher, assorted floor polishes, rug cleaners, etc.)

STORAGE TIPS

11 Cake pans stored in sliding lid rack.
12 Step stool spice rack.
13 Slide-out vegetable bin for assorted cookie, biscuit, and doughnut cutters.
14 Pastry drawer for a variety of rolling pins, pastry cloth, pie crimper, etc.
15 Sliding-shelf units installed in base cabinets.
16 Envelope holder for packaged envelope mixes.
17 Open-shelf storage for sheet wraps such as plastic wrap, aluminum foil, wax paper.
18 Wastebasket pulls out from undercounter on slide-out shelf unit.
19 All shelves lined with durable rubber mat shelf lining.
20 Two-way dish storage from dishwashing to eating area.

Two-way sliding shelves are a great plus feature for storing dinnerware and serving dishes.

Storage space behind dishwasher is compartmented for vases, etc. Raised counter is ideal flower arranging area. Paperware is stored below.

21 Low storage compartmented for paper plates, cups, and napkins.
22 Gift wraps on dowels near sewing center.
23 Compartmented drawer insert for sewing supplies.
24 Snack counter breakfast center.
25 Turntables and stacking units help stretch pantry storage.
26 Perforated hardboard on otherwise unusable wall space in pantry and cleaning closet for hanging often-used utensils.
27 Small baskets hung on perforated hardboard to hold small cans of snack foods, etc.

DECORATING IDEAS

28 Lacquered butter molds used for handles and drawer pulls.
29 Antique bookstand for cookbook.
30 See-through canisters on counter top for colorful staples and decorative food garnishes.
31 Mix/match designs of floral wallpaper and plaid fabric.
32 Bright wallpaper pattern is treated with a soil-resistant finish.
33 Unusual window treatment.
34 Fruit basket attached to hanging scale.
35 Decorative tile over barbecue.

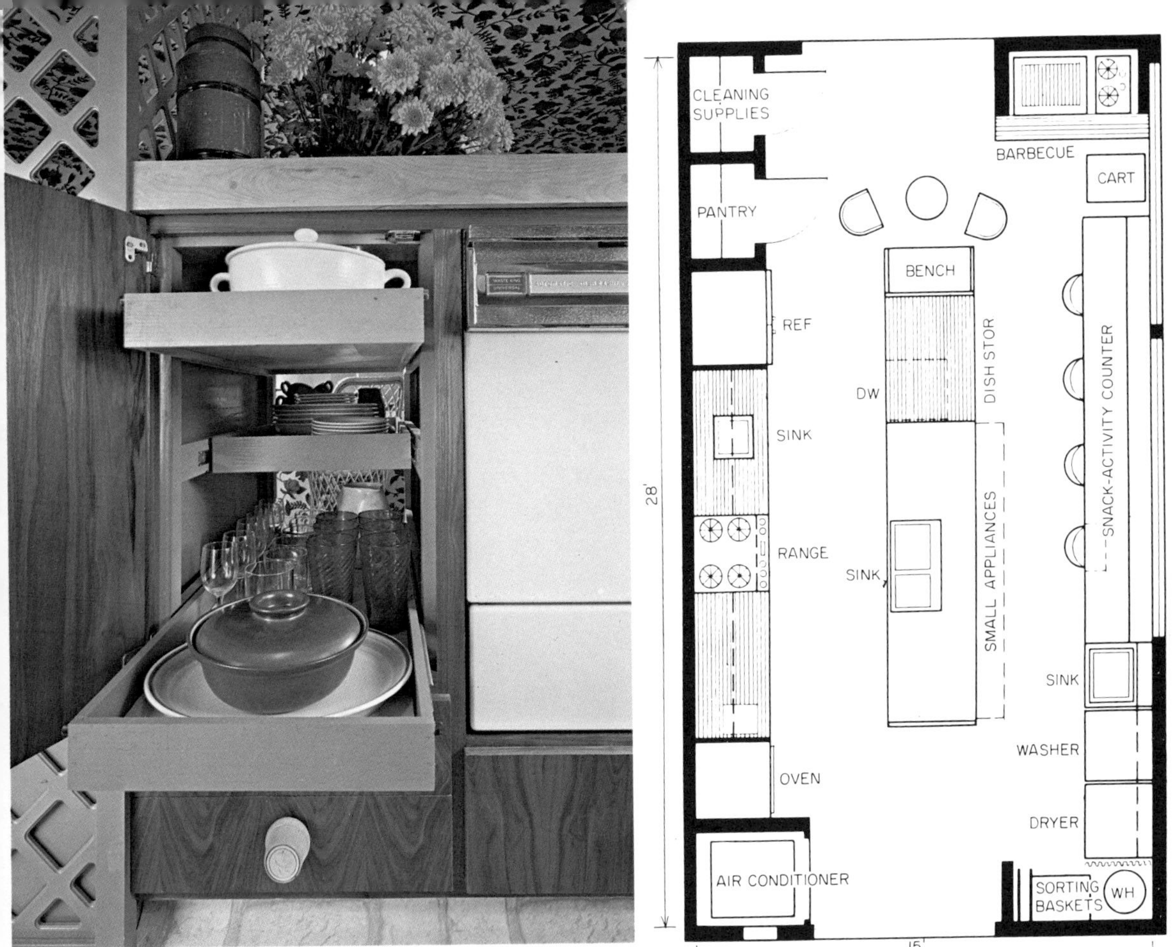

FOR THE LAUNDRY

36 Sorting baskets in laundry.
37 Stain-removal shelf above laundry sink.
38 Bulletin board for hangtags in laundry.
39 Decorative hat rack to hang ironed garments on in laundry.
40 Cut-out in laundry shelf for large detergent boxes.
41 Open shelves above washer and dryer for laundry supplies.
42 Chemistry beakers as decorative yet useful containers for laundry aids (water softener, detergent, powdered bleaches, etc.).

PLANNING IDEAS

43 Sitting area in kitchen.
44 Raised counter for flower arranging.
45 Compartmented storage for flower arranging.
46 Small appliance cooking and storage center.
47 Dual purpose center island.
48 Enclosed shelves above snack counter.
49 Removable counter insert for sewing machine.
50 Built-in toaster.

New Concept—A Two-in-One Kitchen

If you find yourself doing more and more casual cooking, entertaining from one end of the house to the other, then consider having a two-in-one kitchen or perhaps two kitchens. Why not, if you have the space, the inclination, and the money! The idea of decentralizing kitchen equipment to those areas where it will best serve your family's needs is a basic concept and a logical one. The second kitchen, as you will note in the floor plan shown below, adjoins the main kitchen. Yours could easily be located in the family room, basement, recreation room, porch, patio, carport, garage—even in the bedroom wing. A

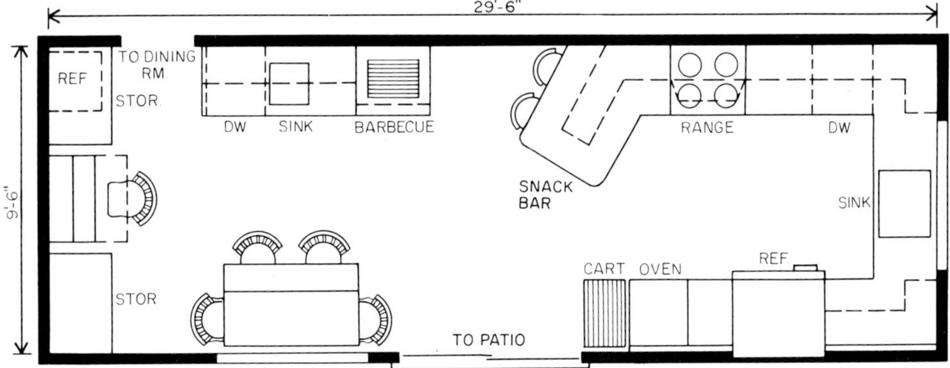

second kitchen should certainly be more compact and budget-conscious than a main kitchen. It could be a little more than a storage wall equipped with a bar-size sink, counter area with outlets for small appliances, or a portable range unit.

This decentralized kitchen, below, with its colonial-designed walnut and oak cabinets and traditional hardware is chock-full of ideas:

•A 4-cubic-foot refrigerator (handy for beverages and snacks) designed into the storage closet of the second kitchen.

•Easy-to-maintain wall behind the gas barbecue is actual brick facing (it can be nailed on!).

•Both kitchen areas have dishwashers—one for pots and pans, the other for dishes from the dining table.

•Cooking is divided: main kitchen has a compact freestanding gas range with extralarge oven plus a built-in oven on the opposite wall. Second kitchen has the "fun" appliance—a gas barbecue unit.

•Refrigeration is divided: main kitchen makes use of standard refrigerator-freezer while second kitchen boasts a small refrigerator for food items used mainly in the dining area.

•Cleanup: Both kitchens have stainless steel sinks and each has a dishwasher—one does the pots and pans, the other the dishes.

•Serving: main kitchen features wide counter; second with its limited counter space relies on the serving cart, directions for which you'll find below.

•Cabinets in blond oak (in main kitchen, not shown) and walnut finish show how two styles and finishes can be used in the same room with harmony.

•Flooring is a twentieth-century version of old wide-planked floors. Rosewood vinyl planks pegged with white vinyl and separated with divider strips make a handsome pattern underfoot.

•Overall lighting comes from illuminated ceiling panels, recessed lights in open soffit areas, and under cabinets.

•Decorating scheme calls on an old favorite—black and white with red and brown accents.

Courtesy American Home *Magazine; Photographer, Ernie Silva.*

Above. The pantry features open shelving—another special request of the owner, a busy professional working mother. With open shelves, impromptu table setting can be quickly assembled, children and household help can find things easily.

This kitchen, in a home converted from an old stable built in the late 1920s, is warm, rustic, and functional. It has all the attributes desired by the owners, along with the practical aspects of a combination living-dining-cooking area . . . serving both indoor-outdoor living and large enough for a big family with lots of friends; also, and most important, it is easy to maintain. The center cooking island, kitchen's focal point, functions both as cooking center and serving buffet for courtyard parties and midnight snacks. Special request of homeowner was a cooking area without a suspended center vent fan and hood–thus a surface cook top with its own built-in ventilating unit. Counter tops are all hardwood maple, rustic in feeling, and functional for sandwich making, chopping, mincing, and dicing. Note also the scanner to left of sink used for special recipes, built-in food center to right of sink, trash compactor to left of dishwasher, roll-out cart to left of the refrigerator for ease in transporting items to courtyard.

Decorative highlights feature "south-of-the-border" feeling–white walls and ceramic tile for floors and wall areas. The wall serves as a storage area for baskets, pots, and pans collected from all over the world. Dining table and chairs, from Mexico, nestle snugly near the fireplace, in constant use during winter months. Message center, next to cushioned fireplace seat contains intercom and telephone. *Courtesy interior designer, Ben C. Flowers; Photographer, George Mayhew; Residence of Mr. and Mrs. B. W. Morris*

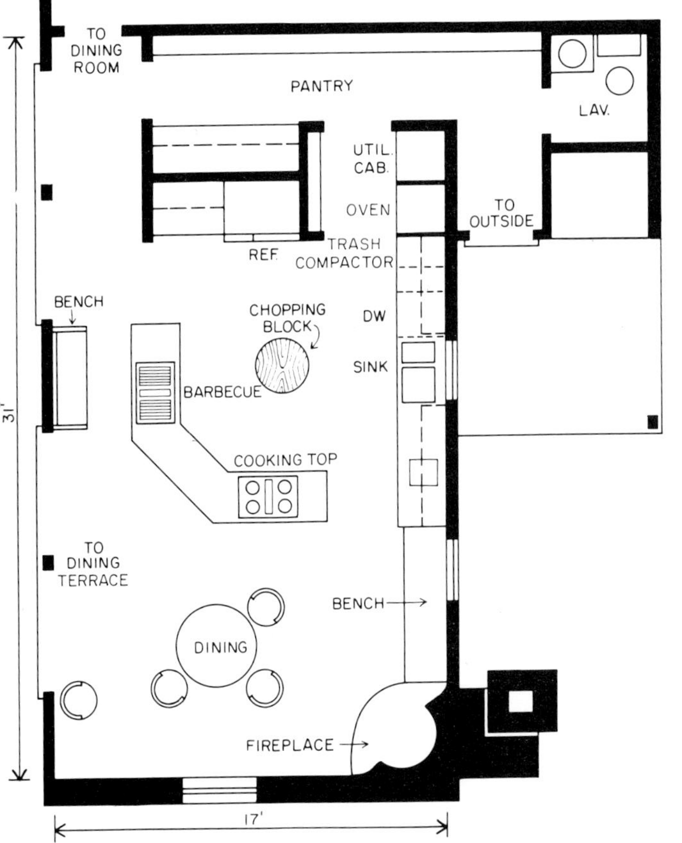

Laundry room is functional with laundry equipment, drip-dry closet, and sorting counter. Note shelves above sorting counter that boast individual baskets for children's clothes—great family organizer!

Here is an easy-care dream kitchen come true—a warm, charmingly traditional design using dark finish V-groove cabinets with antique brass hardware, laminated plastic butcher-block patterned counter top, a beige-colored sink, and no-wax vinyl flooring. Note cooking peninsula that helps to incorporate added work and counter space, and colorful accessories above cabinets. *Courtesy Maytag; Photographer, William N. Hopkins*

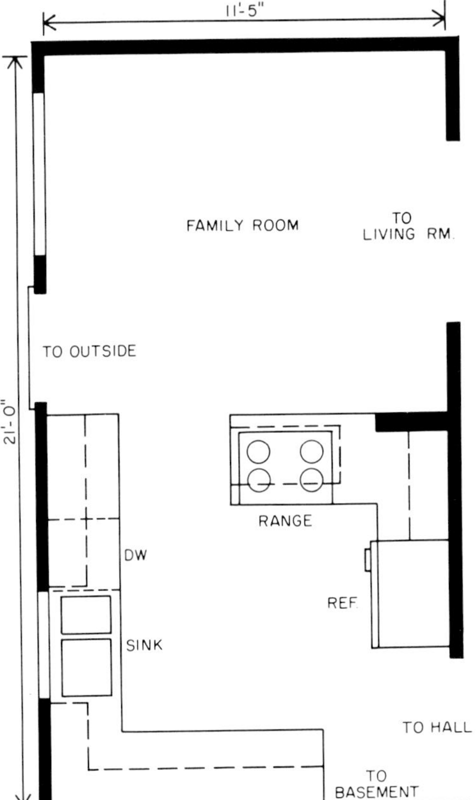

This corner area provides ample space for work between range and refrigerator. Copper-colored appliances offer a striking contrast to red-checked wall covering.

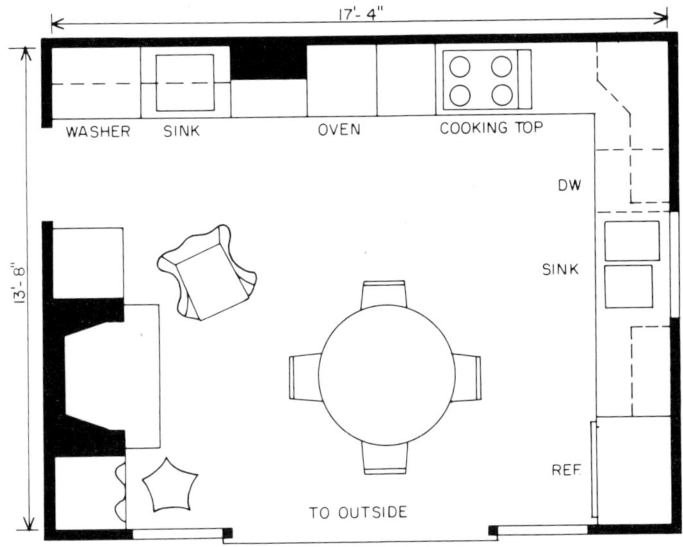

Contemporary Colonial

Practical L-shaped floor plan of this contemporary colonial kitchen provides a superefficient working area, with a cozy living and dining area that is close enough for convenience. The color palette, borrowed from the colonists—barn reds, blues and plaster white—adds immeasurably to the authenticity of design.

To create this kitchen, the designer dipped gently but firmly into the eighteenth century for homeliness, warmth, security, and romance—ingredients somewhat lost in twentieth-century planning of efficient, automatic kitchens. The joy in decorating today is being able to weave a bit of the past with modern mechanization. The feeling of traditional dignity and proud heritage in this kitchen almost belies the existence of automatic appliances arranged in a convenient work pattern. There is a bit of the Queen Anne style in the furniture and fine cabinets, a touch of Vermeer and the Dutch influence in the delft tile laminated plastic wall covering and the floor tiles. But there's more to this kitchen than tradition. Every detail was carefully planned to provide the utmost convenience, efficiency, comfort, and charm. All of a kitchen's pleasant functions were considered and combined in the most appealing arrangement possible. There are areas for cooking, laundry, dining, and sitting by the fire. Note how the cabinets almost rival the style of fine furniture. The finish is dark and smoky, with a patina of old satin. The beveled paneling of the doors and drawers is deeply recessed and antiqued in delicate shadings of the dark stain. The hardware boasts a pewterlike finish.

Dark-stained wooden beams repeat the rich wood tones of the cabinets and dining furniture. The traditional dining table is well placed in relation to cooking and serving center. Stainless steel double sink and laminated plastic counter tops keep their good looks and are easy to maintain. The laundry area in its own quiet corner of the kitchen (behind lounging chair) boasts a combination washer-dryer, shelf for laundry supplies, and cabinets for storage.

Designer, Robert Houseman; Photography, Krantzen Studios.

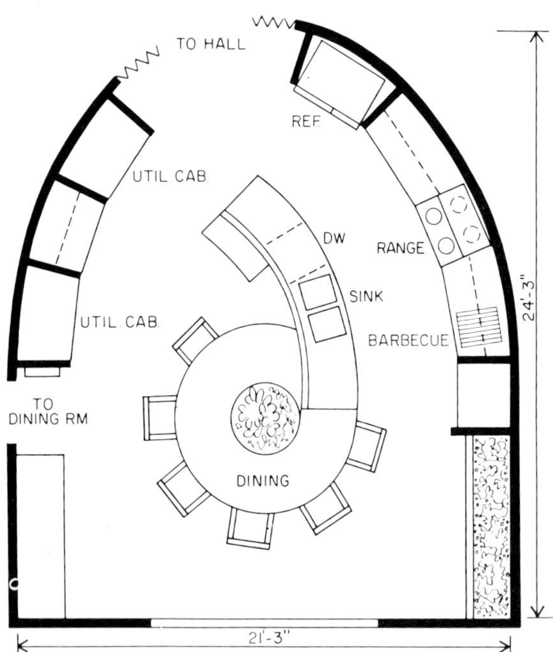

A "tree" for all seasons growing smack in the middle of an open-plan kitchen is the focal point of the fabulous circular ceramic tile dining center, a peninsula off the circular kitchen counter. Greenery throughout with tile, pitched beams, wood ceiling, and pottery clay objects of art gives an atrium "south-of-the-border" feeling. Circular design of kitchen counters, serving area behind the sink center and the dining area provide free expanse of space and easy mobility—a flexible use of a long narrow room. *Courtesy Interpace*

Left. A cheerful kitchen in the round. Space above the cabinets was furred out to allow room for fluorescent lighting around perimeter of the room. Plastic lens that shields the tubes from view also directs the light down onto the work counters where it is most needed. Food preparation area to left of sink with built-in food center, mixer, blender, and cutting board uses deluxe cool white fluorescent lamps. Wallpapered ceiling is focal point. *Courtesy General Electric*

Bottom, left. It almost looks like a kitchen from outer space—but if you look closely, it's only an illusion. Appliances and accessories are today's products—designed into an oval setting, proving you can have a kitchen-in-the-round if you have the space. All white color, super graphic lines all help to create an aura of tomorrow. *Courtesy General Electric*

Bottom, right. Range or cooking center is replete with two built-in ovens, smooth-surface cook top with hood and fan, and a microwave oven for superfast cooking. Lighting fixture carries out futuristic theme. *Courtesy Hotpoint*

Have Kitchen—Will Travel

This kitchen belongs to yours truly—and her husband, Mitch. Because we both have active jobs that carry us well beyond the 9 to 5 routine, there is no opportunity for commuting. So we picked this high rise that towers above the tallest bridge span along the East River in Manhattan. Before we moved in we had several stipulations that the kitchen had to meet. It had to have enough room to help us make the most of everything we planned to do there—cook, entertain, do the laundry, and provide enough counter space to spread out food preparation and cleanup. It had to have a feeling of permanence; a wonderful place to come home to and allow us to add all the personal touches that would make it uniquely ours. We're avid collectors of everything from string to empty glass jars.

Usually when a couple lives in an apartment, it is on a temporary basis and the sad part of it is it usually looks temporary. My theory is to get the most out of your present surroundings . . . live a little . . . design your kitchen to suit your habits and the way you like to live. That's what we did with our kitchen. And when and if we should ever move, most of the things we've grown to love and all the gadgets we've collected can go right along with us.

For example, the wall-mounted maple shelves can be easily dismounted. They are the same length as the butcher-block table—48 inches. The washer-dryer combination was a must and is another investment that could be transferred to another location. The same is true for the butcher's meat rack. We could move to Pasadena tomorrow and never know we'd left home!

Some of the philosophy that went into this kitchen plan includes the following thoughts:

I like things out in the open, where I can reach them. That's the reason for the graduated, wall-mounted maple shelves. They're 6, 8, 10, and 12 inches deep. Why graduated? So I won't bang my head while working at the butcher-block table beneath. The shelves hold measuring utensils, canister filled with staple ingredients, spice casseroles, and fancy pots and pans.

The major work center pivots around the 34-inch high butcher-block table. It's perfect for dining when you use stools and great for working. It's two inches lower than the regular counter top. Here's where I mix, cook, bake, eat, write, and study.

Certain small appliances are a must and I like them on the counter top, organized in working groups where I use them most often. One group includes a toaster, mixer and food grinder, citrus juicer, and food scale. Another includes a blender, coffee mill, and can opener.

The butcher's meat rack serves as a place to hang saucepans and to dry sausages and green herbs. Underneath is the washer-dryer—not the ideal place, but in an apartment it's a logical place to put it. It's surely better than running down to the basement to do the laundry.

The carpeting is foam-cushioned acrylic that is easy to keep clean. Best of all it's soft underfoot and adds warmth to the kitchen. Other easy maintenance features include washable wall covering and matching window shade, as well as easy-to-launder, permanent-press cafe curtains.

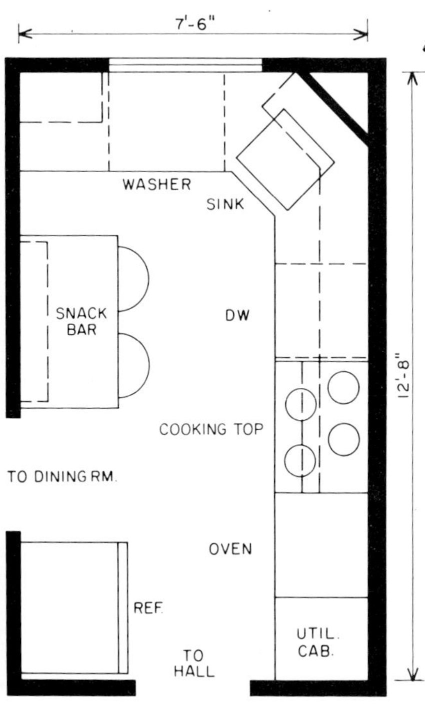

Perforated hardboard above the sink holds all small working tools. It's also where Mitchell makes his favorite cheese. He pours yogurt into a heavy muslin bag and hangs it on an extended hook to let it drip into the sink until all the whey disappears.

Wall and base cabinet hold the things seldom used. Additional supplies and accessories are stored in a large pantry, which was once a coat closet and is located just outside the kitchen.

A corner sink is not the perfect arrangement when two people are using the kitchen at once. But it does utilize space that is normally used for corner cupboards or dead storage and it did free space for the laundry equipment.

Self-cleaning oven (a must in my book) surface cooking top with ventilator and hood, dishwasher, refrigerator that never needs defrosting (another must), are the nucleus of the well-rounded kitchen I had in mind. I cover the cooking top with an asbestos pad when I use the electric skillet, waffle iron, and other appliances since they require ventilation just as any saucepan or skillet does on a range.

Courtesy American Home *Magazine; Photographer, Harry Hartman.*

A Kitchen in the Shaker Theme

This kitchen, designed with the Shaker precepts of regularity, harmony, and order in mind, combines maximum utility and the native charm of this unique American culture. *Courtesy St. Charles; photographs, Bill Hedrich, Hedrich-Blessing*

Above, left. In the preparation and cleanup center, a creamy whiteness of alabaster-textured steel base units contrasts nicely with unadorned pecan wall and utility units. Knobs are pewter finish and pulls are satin chrome. Beams, posts, and wood trim are stained to match the cabinet wood color. Wall cabinets are joined together with valances behind which are light strips for indirect lighting that call attention to decorative objects. A double-bowl stainless steel sink with faucet deck is centered under the window. A linen shade, in lieu of curtains, folds up with draw strings. A dishwasher with textured front to match the cabinet is at left and a special purpose unit with a slide-out cutting board, two wastebaskets, and vegetable storage bins are at right.

Above, right. The cooking center boasts a self-ventilating range with lift-out ceramic glass tops which can be converted to a grill and griddle accessories. The utensil rack of authentic pegs is typical of those used around the walls of Shaker homes. A full high 36-inch wide pantry unit to the left of the range is fitted with swing-out shelves, with half shelves behind them and sliding shelves in the lower section. The upper section has a revolving shelf and tray storage utilizing leftover space. In the foreground is a peninsula with second sink. Hand-hewn corbels pegged to the posts support a dropped canopy-type soffit over the peninsula forming a separation to the dining area.

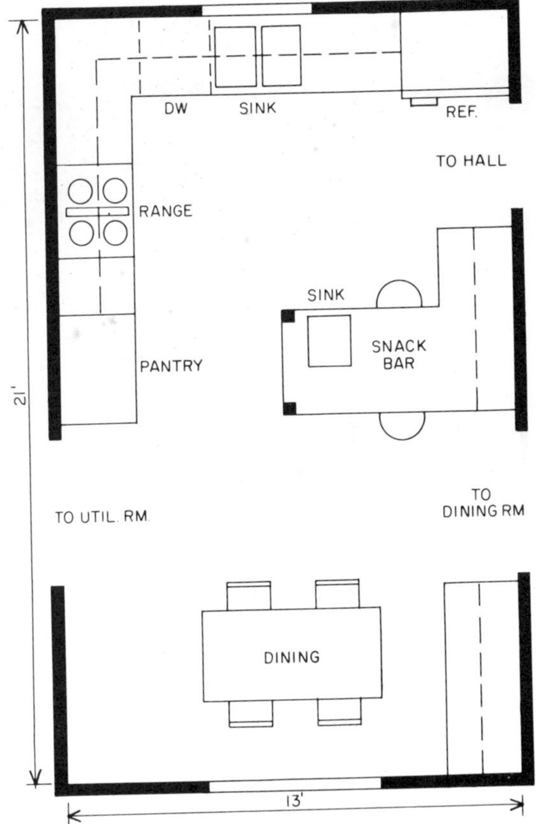

Below, left. The peninsula complete with utility sink and open undercounter space has stools on either side for sit-down work and snacks. Generous storage wall cabinets have open lighted shelves below for handy storage of utilitarian and decorative accessories.

Below, right. In the dining end of the kitchen, cabinetwork is designed to form a hutch effect with a lighted open step shelf and a 30-inch high counter for serving. Spacious upper cabinets allow storage for dishes, glassware, crockery, etc. Cabinets below the counter are fitted with slide-out trays for flat storage of linen and a variety of sliding storage shelves, some of which are lined with Pacific Cloth for silverware.

The simplicity of the hutch design is balanced by a lacquered Parsons-type table. The straight post chairs with swamp rush seats are authentic Shaker antiques.

The peg rail, level with the window top, surrounds the room and is typical of Shaker usage. Note hanging decorative objects.

This corner window apartment kitchen featuring plastic laminate cabinets, is predominantly Contemporary in design with a touch of the Mediterranean. Springtime colors of lettuce, grass green and yellows are set off by surrounding areas of clean white, providing a light, airy and cheerful atmosphere. *Courtesy St. Charles; photographs, Bill Hedrich, Hedrich-Blessing*

Above. L-shaped kitchen utilizes open-shelf niche to right of range for spices, books, and a recessed area for portable television. Note white appliances, counter tops, work area, wall surfaces, ceilings, beams, and other woodwork. A stainless steel corner sink is placed to take advantage of the garden view.

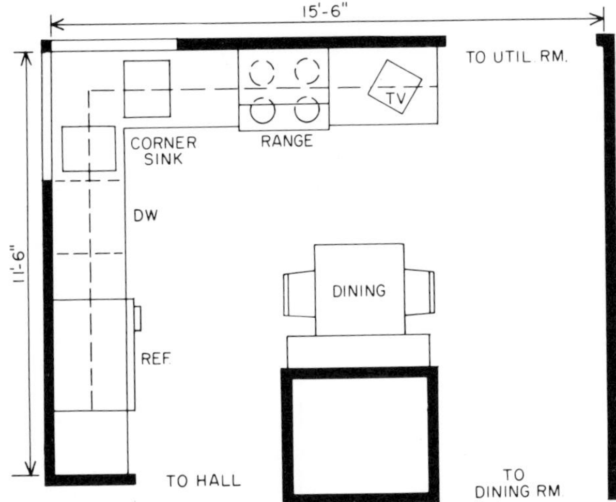

Breakfast table with laminated top is attached to a tiered shelf structure or herbarium. All shelves have special lights designed for growing plants and herbs behind valances. Plexiglass doors create vaporization to promote growth of herbs.

U-Shaped Kitchen

This U-shaped kitchen, classically designed with sink in center flanked by cooking and food preparation areas, can be easily adapted to a variety of decorative themes as you will see in the kitchens below. *Courtesy St. Charles; photographs, Bill Hedrich, Hedrich-Blessing*

Above. Butcher block acts as center island. Recessed cooking center is hooded, lighted, and backed by wipeable Dutch ceramic tiles which are repeated in cornice over windows. Gingham wall covering was selected to give kitchen a country look.

Right. Refrigerator or mixing center to right of sink utilizes midway cabinets for easy-to-reach storage in space that is otherwise wasted. Note how sheet vinyl flooring runs up toe space. Recessed down lighting over sink provides spot illumination and wood ceiling beams complement country look.

It is clearly evident that it is possible to mix and match patterns successfully. Wall covering on ceiling and walls blend uncannily with flooring and window shades. Wall area behind cooking center is stainless steel for easy cleaning.

Cart was designed to serve as moveable island. Excellent as a buffet server or as a center for food preparation. Cutting board inset is also lid for plastic trash container built in below. Drop leaves help to conserve space when not in use. Ball-bearing casters provide easy glideability.

Strictly Contemporary kitchen throughout—including the window treatment. Shades do the job and are decorative in their simplicity. Window shades and drawer panels on wall cabinet to left of dishwasher take their cues and hues from horizontal vinyl flooring strips.

Midway cabinet doors pick up color from flooring. Mixing and preparation area to left of refrigerator also doubles as breakfast and sandwich bar; is near dining table. Wood cutting board with knob is handily built into base cabinet assembly.

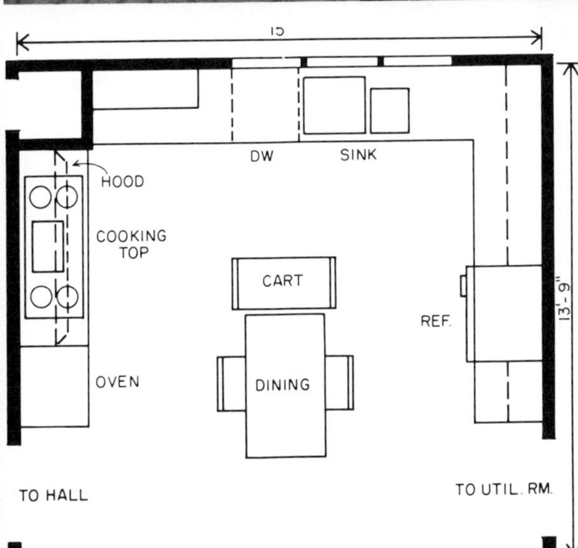

Recessed cooking center with coverall hood is the focal point in this up-to-date kitchen with a yesteryear theme. Since hood and fan cover entire area, counter is ideal for using small cooking appliances. Wall cabinet to left of dishwasher is built flush to counter and resembles hutch; holds dinnerware and flatware used in kitchen. Proximity to dishwasher and dining table makes storage convenient.

A peninsula in the center of things divides the kitchen from the dining area. Laminated butcher block counter, deeper than standard two-inch thickness, offers substantive feeling for heavy duty use. Provincial wood cabinet doors contrast pleasingly with sleekness of metal cabinets.

Beverage center, at end opposite peninsula, is outfitted with stainless steel bar sink and gooseneck faucet. Ice maker could replace base cabinet to right of sink. Area also perfect for counter top microwave oven to left of sink. Under cabinet lighting is practical as well as warm. Shelf above sink great for glassware, condiments, bar accessories. *Courtesy St. Charles, Hedrich-Blessing*

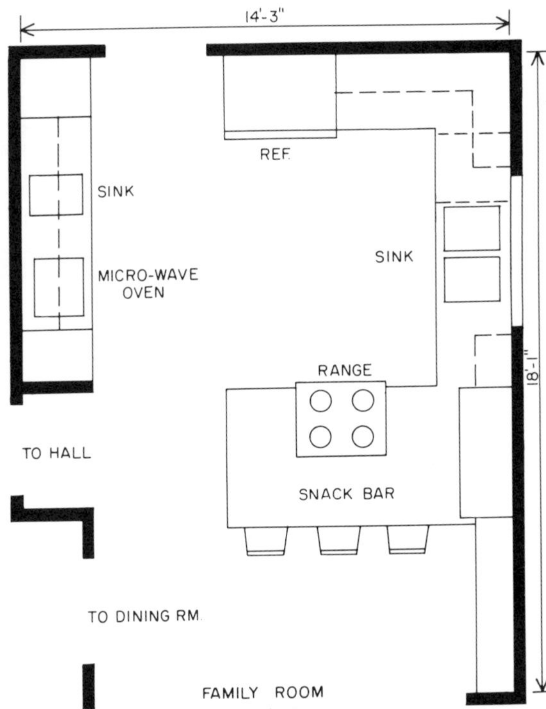

Drop-in range offers continuous flow to toe-in space below. Glass door curio cabinet to left is outfitted with built-in wine rack. Note peninsula height is 32 inches—perfect for ease in working, and in using standard dining chairs.

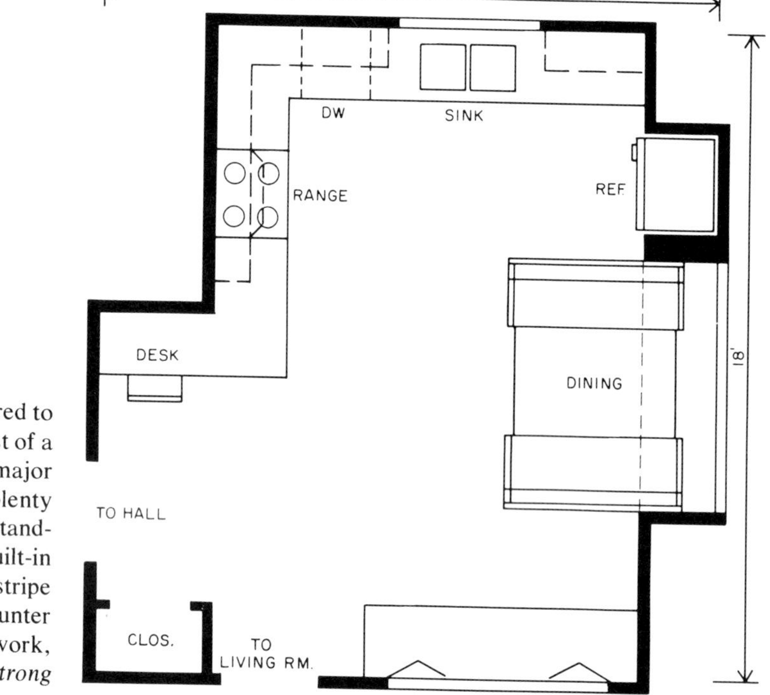

This cushy dining booth upholstered to match window shades makes the most of a pastoral setting. While it takes up a major portion of the floor space, there is still plenty of room for work area to the left. Freestanding refrigerator recessed into wall has built-in look. Tailored window shades pick up stripe pattern in wall covering. Overhang counter at left leaves knee space for sit-down work, snacking, or telephoning. *Courtesy Armstrong*

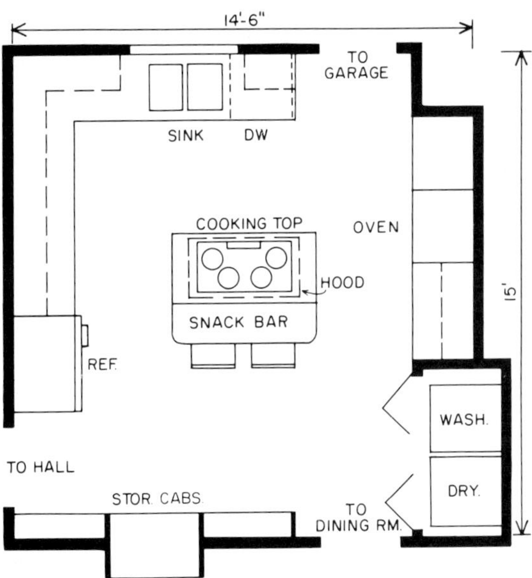

Every inch of this small-scaled kitchen has been engineered for easy-does-it efficiency. Notice the well-defined and uncluttered work centers, easy-to-clean surfaces, generous storage cabinets, proper cooking area ventilation, and bright, cheerful lighting. For the gourmet cook, there's plenty of elbow room to dice, slice, shake, and stir. For everyday cooking here's a gay sunny place to work. Note the snack bar for the children or coffee-sipping neighbors. Conveniently accessible to other rooms and the outdoors, the kitchen also incorporates a laundry area tucked behind folding doors and away from the food preparation area. *Courtesy* American Home *Magazine*

A kitchen for the gourmet cook who loves to entertain! Open shelves instead of wall cabinets, pegboard instead of drawers, tables instead of counters are all practical solutions to the space problem, especially when you want to serve in the kitchen. Note butcher-block table, French cook knives and "add-on" wine rack. Flooring is easy-to-clean, no-wax vinyl.
Courtesy Armstrong

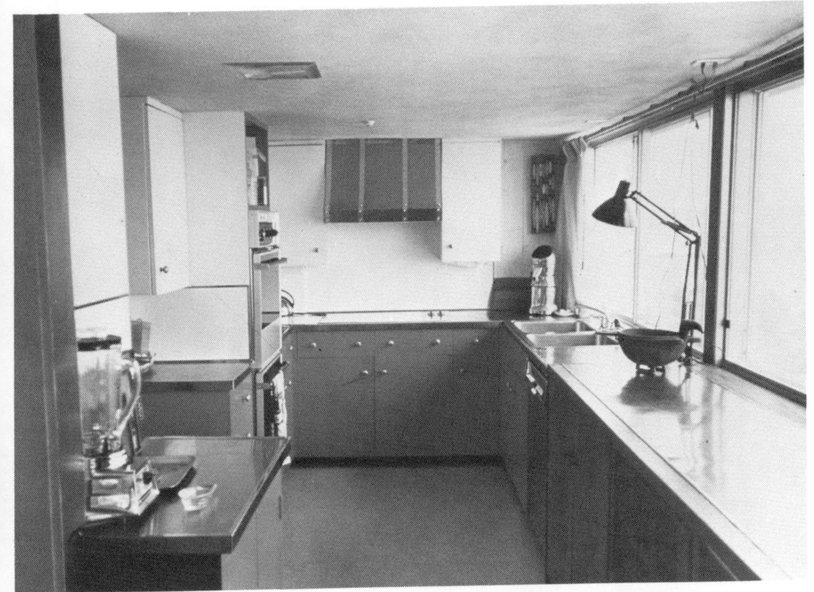

Remodeled kitchen with successful results. U-shape design utilizes wall area to gain added counter space. Double-bowl stainless steel sink overlooks pleasant view outdoors while wide window expanse lets in light. Two-tone cabinets are bright, cheery. Note how brass hardware complements hood. Open shelf above oven provides quick and easy access for breakfast cereals. Counter to left serves work area next to oven. *Designer, Doris Piper Lamberson*

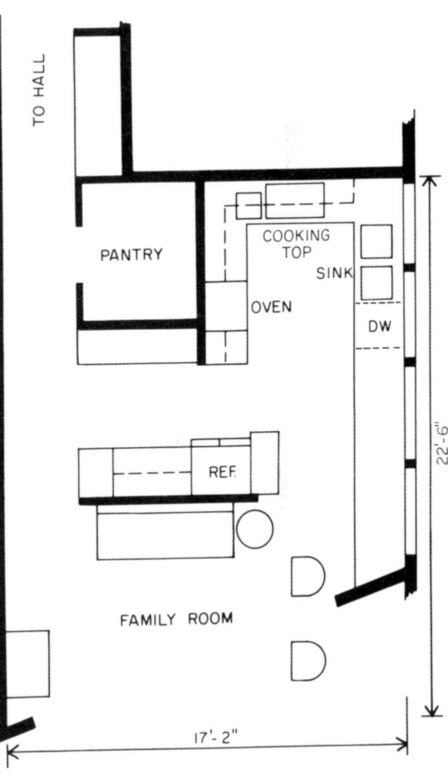

Right. The warm tones of browns, copper and wood make this kitchen cozy and inviting. Wood beams, traditionally styled cabinets, and period furniture set a Colonial theme—a perfect setting for the antique churn, copper utensils, and clock. Laminated butcher block peninsula separates cooking center with pewter hood from sink and cleanup area. *Courtesy Nevamar Kitchens, N-I-N-E, Inc.*

Left. Another version of tomorrow's kitchen today. In black and white the lines are clean and stark. Admittedly drastic, this kitchen does work with ample wall and base cabinet storage, drawer storage, and lower counter to left of cook top for mixing and baking. Note microwave oven angled into wall to right of oven. *Courtesy Hotpoint*

Right. Unique contemporary installation for cooking center is circular off-the-floor counter, open underneath. Range hood, flanked by cabinets, is ductless.
Courtesy Hotpoint

Left. Indoor-outdoor kitchen serves two sitting and dining centers. Woven wood shades provide privacy, pull up for easy access to sliding doors. Sliding window over sink acts as pass-through. Note carpeting in sitting area, vinyl flooring in kitchen, ceramic tile counter.
Courtesy Del Mar Woven Wood

This kitchen opens up entirely to the patio—and then closes up when it rains! Great for large parties you don't want to have indoors. Note large expanse of ceramic tile serving counters, smooth surface cooking top, drop luminous lighting fixture that covers work area. Two different floral designs—one on wall covering, the other on the ceiling—mix and match well. *Courtesy Interpace*

Serving counter on patio just outside sliding window is of same tile as indoor counter—easy to clean, weatherproof. *Courtesy Interpace*

Here is a good example of what I call "just a kitchen kitchen." It does very little more than cook—but it is planned to do that as efficiently as possible. The center island, or cooking center (which has a built-in ventilating system), helps to bring all work centers into close proximity. Built-ins, such as mixer-blender and paper caddy to left of refrigerator, make mixing and food preparation center more convenient. Kitchen carpeting is easy underfoot and easy to clean. Note additional storage behind island to right of eating area.

Almost a chalet, with a pitched beam ceiling, this kitchen was designed for the owner who "always wanted red cabinets." And what's more, she proved it could be done in a small space. It works well with white laminated plastic counters, white appliances, orange shag carpeting, and white hardware. Enameled porch furniture, saucepan rack, and sophisticated window treatment add personal touches. Note handsome objects over cabinets. *Courtesy* Modern Bride *Magazine*

This kitchen is all red—but in tone-on-tone textures. Note refrigerator paneled with wall covering material and dishwasher paneled to match cabinets. Sleek lines of cabinetry, with magnetic latches, are enhanced by indirect lighting above, "task" lighting below. All against a white wall designed to reflect light. *Courtesy Maytag*

Wonderfully efficient two-wall corridor kitchen opens onto the dining room, but hides behind louvered doors when necessary. Luminous ceiling provides a wash of light throughout while undercabinet lighting provides spot illumination. Porcelain enamel sink is color-coordinated with avocado green appliances which blend naturally with warm brown cabinets. *Courtesy* Modern Bride *Magazine*

Indoor-outdoor, L-shaped kitchen is all set for family dining or entertaining. Carpeting blends with the green grass outdoors, is soft underfoot. Dining table in center acts as work counter when not in use. Double-duty light fixture-utensil rack is practical yet decorative. *Courtesy* Modern Bride *Magazine*

Remodeling enlarged and brightened this kitchen. Width is visually extended by roughhewn ceiling beams. Spotlights recessed in ceiling assure proper lighting of work surfaces. Custom-made Tiffany-type hanging lamp creates a warm pool of light for informal dining. Other details combine charm with utility. Wide-tiled windowsills are ideal for houseplants and trays of herbs. Built-in hutch cabinet stores china and provides extra serving counter. Textured Tuscany ceramic tile on floor and counter tops, in keeping with oak cabinetry, is durable, easy to clean. *Courtesy American Olean*

The thoroughly modern kitchen is seen through sliding glass doors leading to an atrium herb garden. The chopping block table serves as a room divider and as a work surface. *Courtesy American Olean*

A "keeping room" in the Provincial tradition blends modern convenience and taste. A combination dining room-kitchen, each area can function separately or as part of the whole. The natural look of the quarry tile floor ties it all together into a warm, harmonious whole.

The seat cushions are a variation of the print used on the wallpapered ceiling, and antique cooking utensils are displayed on a wall near the kitchen. *Courtesy American Olean*

Right. This two-wall kitchen makes use of otherwise wasted space. A 32-inch counter was installed below windows—and a drop down leaf extended in front of the door. Note the 34-inch high sink counter to the left, ideal for food preparation and sitting to cook; also dinnerware storage above dishwasher. Clever window treatment lets in light while providing privacy. *Courtesy Frigidaire*

Left. In this kitchen, midway shelves behind the counter separate dining area from kitchen and obstruct view of kitchen clutter. Sliding doors provide easy access for storage inside. Note Early American styling with batten doors, L and H wrought-iron hinges and recessed cooking niche. Brick wall, tile-design wall covering, and braided rug complement the colonial feeling. Note recessed down lights over peninsula, wooden beams, and plate rail oven wall cabinets. *Courtesy Coppes Napanee, Hedrich-Blessing*

Right. A refurbished kitchen with happy results! The job, primarily a decorating and accessorizing one, included spraying cabinets in shades of blue and green, new wall covering, a Victorian lighting fixture, Victorian-styled side chairs bought in a secondhand store and reupholstered with blue leather fabric. Contemporary-designed dining table, and beaded decorative window curtain —all for under $1,000.00. Note handy pass-through shelf in window, used as a convenient service buffet for indoor-outdoor dining. *Courtesy* American Home *Magazine*

Left. Large kitchens made smaller: Center island serves as pivot around which all work areas center and are brought closer together.

Note two-unit cook top installed in island—excellent for short-order cooking and keeping foods warm. Island storage is functional with bakery bin located under counter to right of snack counter, foreground left. It features a handy pull-out cutting board plus abundant storage space for all kinds of baked goods. Base cabinet at far right of island is a tray storage unit which can convert into a storage area for bulky items by removing laminated surfaced dividers. Corner base and wall cabinets between cooking and sink center turn full-circle and eliminate the hard-to-reach corners. Midway units between wall and base cabinets serve as spice rack, solving problem of where to store small items. Entire kitchen is designed for easy maintenance—cabinets and counters are laminated plastic, behind range is ceramic tile, floor is no-wax vinyl. *Courtesy National Industries, N-I-N-E, Inc.*

Custom-designed kitchen—a study in wood and ceramic tile. Geared to large- and small-scale entertaining, the actual kitchen area is small but very functional. Mixing and cooking areas directly opposite sink center open onto dining area—convenient, accessible for food service and buffet. Base cabinets open in either direction for easy access. Service bar in dining area opens onto patio for indoor-outdoor entertaining. Fireplace opens both ways to sitting-dining room. Steps, foreground, lead to living area. *Courtesy* American Home *Magazine*

Simplicity and low maintenance are the main features of this modern corridor kitchen with broad expanse of laminated counter top, plexiglas cabinet sliding doors, and enameled, easy-to-wipe appliances. Note off-the-floor-cabinets for easy access to carpeting with vacuum cleaner. *Courtesy General Electric*

Warm and charming, this homey kitchen emphasizes its cooking functions. Island is topped with large ventilating hood that serves both cook top and barbecue activities and covers ample counter space for the use of portable cooking appliances. Dining center wall, designed to look like a large hutch, provides storage space and plan desk. Vinyl tile floor, easy underfoot, looks like the real thing, as do the ceiling beams, which are actually lightweight plastic.

U-shaped kitchen serves dining area conveniently. Note how backsplash of cook top shields cooking from view of diners. Dishwasher, paneled to match cabinets, is handy to wall and base cabinets used to store dinnerware. Cabinets open in both directions for easy access. Undercabinet and underhood lighting provide shadow-free convenience. *Courtesy Coppes Napanee; Photographer, Hedrich-Blessing*

Though airy and spacious, this kitchen retains the efficiency of compact work areas with its large center island. It's a great work surface and a family favorite for eating breakfasts and reading the newspaper—you can spread the whole paper out flat instead of reading commuter-fashion, according to the homemaker who planned this kitchen. Lighting is an important factor, since entire island needs so much of it. Honeycombed light fixtures supplement sunny skylight; massive rack holds cooking utensils. Note shallow shelves near cook top installed in the island surface . . . narrow to hold one layer spices and condiments needed quickly for seasoning.

In adjoining pantry closet, height of each of the open shelves was carefully measured to accommodate canned foods, salad bowls, and casseroles. Pantry shelves are shallow so there is no guessing or digging to get things out—a good idea for otherwise unusable wall space.
Courtesy American Home *Magazine*

Two-toned cabinets highlight the decorative scheme, offer a traditional feeling. While the amount of counter space to right of refrigerator and left of range is not really adequate, there is enough expanse of counter space to the right to make up for the advantage gained by designing peninsula-counter-divider separating dining from kitchen activities. Cabinets over peninsula open both ways for easy access. Eagle-design wallpaper, treated for easy cleaning, carries out traditional feeling. *Courtesy Coppes Napanee, Hedrich-Blessing*

This kitchen picks up the same design as the previous one although work areas are made more compact by the addition of a center work island, which incorporates second sink and a built-in food center to accommodate mixer-blender attachments. Note ventilating hood with a warming shelf over surface cooking top. *Courtesy Coppes Napanee, Hedrich-Blessing*

A blending of wood ceiling and wood and tiled floors complement raised panels on cabinet doors and give this kitchen a coordinated look. Buffet counter, with its curved dining-table peninsula, also serves adjoining family room. Plate rail, over wall cabinets, adds decorative note for collection of antique plates. Stainless steel backsplash behind surface cooking top protects wall from grease spatters. Rolled matchstick shades at windows provide privacy, and clean, uncluttered look. *Courtesy Coppes Kitchens, Hedrich-Blessing*

In this remodeled kitchen the eating area adjoins pantry-buffet, providing easy access to foods and dinnerware. Pleasantly decorated, plaid wall covering adds cheerful note. Carpeted floor is nice contrast to vinyl kitchen tile. Eating area opens onto patio. *Courtesy J. Josephson*

CHAPTER 8

Consider Your Choices

Now that we have discussed the different kinds of kitchens and you have decided what you do and do not want in yours, let's think about how you can achieve your ends. How much do you want to spend? If you are on a strict budget, you will want to cut corners without cutting efficiency. You may want to begin with just a few changes such as a new appliance or some additional cabinets in the hope of finishing the job at a later date (I will say more about that later) or you may decide to go all out. The point is that you have several options. Let's look at what they are.

A. *Give your present kitchen a cosmetic face lift.* Perhaps there is nothing seriously wrong with the kitchen you have now. All you really need is a few new conveniences or some pretty new decor. In this case consider adding some new functional accessories, a few colorful pots and pans, a little paint, a new wall covering, perhaps a new floor, or even simply some cabinet accessories in the form of shelf organizers to create order out of chaos. You might choose to install new counter tops, paint your old cabinets, get new lighting, or add some wall shelves. Some or all of these alterations will give you a change for the better.

B. *Plan a basic remodeling* with new cabinets, a new counter top, new appliances, and some of the cosmetic face lifts mentioned above. In this case you will keep structural changes to a bare minimum, such as moving a radiator or changing the location of a door or window, or opt to make no structural changes at all.

C. *Go all out!* This will include whatever structural changes you deem necessary, such as moving a wall, adding or extending a room, or combining several rooms. In this case you will probably want to change all or most of your appliances for the latest models with the features that meet your needs and choose the cabinets that provide you with the custom features you want. This full-scale renovation will give you the option to add multipurpose areas such as a laundry center, dining area, sewing nook, child's play center, or even a full family room, or an indoor-outdoor kitchen.

If you are planning an all-out remodeling, think carefully about structural changes. Some alterations such as closing up a door or making a new one are not as costly as you might think, and even major structural changes may be more economical in the long run. Why build a spanking new kitchen around your old structural problems? A single investment now may pay off in years of increased efficiency and additional pleasure. (For some specific solutions to your structural problems see pages 219–221.)

If you do decide on structural changes, there are a few rules to keep in mind. Before moving a wall, make sure that it is not a load-bearing one vital to the support or operation of the house itself. In the case of doors, I recommend keeping them to a minimum. Try to place them so that traffic will not pass through a vital work area. Similarly, try to locate windows so they do not interrupt continuous wall space so valuable to wall and base cabinets. If you are starting from scratch and can plan as many windows as you want exactly where you want them, keep in mind that, ideally, the window area of your kitchen should equal one-fourth to one-fifth the floor area. If, however, structural changes are out of the question and you must work with what you have, don't despair. The treatment a window receives is as important as the window itself. See page 205 for helpful hints and guidelines.

What about remodeling in phases? This is one way to do it, but you will probably pay more in the long run and will be living in a state of incompletion for longer than you would like. If you opt for step-by-step remodeling, make sure you have an overall plan before beginning. Leave space for any equipment you plan to add in the future and keep in mind your overall plan while making immediate purchases. For example, if you buy a dishwasher, select a convertible one which can be used as a portable now and can be converted to a built-in later. It is usually a good idea to do all your counter tops in the first phase. The same is true of any electrical or plumbing changes you find necessary.

If you do elect to remodel in phases, ask your bank about financing through a unit-by-unit modernization plan. I will say more about financing in the next chapter.

Cutting Costs

Although you may have opted for going all out, there are still ways to cut costs without sacrificing efficiency or beauty. The key word here is waste. For example, if you know exactly what you need in the way of appliance features you can avoid buying the most expensive model with all the top-of-the-line features, some of which you might never use. The secret is careful thought and planning before you act.

Think creatively. Do you really need to move a window just because you've always wanted one over the sink? Perhaps a window would be just as pleasant over a planning desk? Is it possible to place the new sink where the original plumbing connections were in order to avoid plumbing changes as long pipe runs? If you want a laundry in the kitchen, is it possible to install it back to back with the sink and dishwasher in a peninsula or island installation and thus cut down on the amount of new plumbing necessary?

If you are planning a major kitchen renovation, you might consider doing other remodeling such as a bathroom, laundry, heating system, or electrical work at the same time. In this way your contractor can save time and money which will consequently add up in savings to you. There will be less paperwork and fewer transportation expenses; he can make all the estimates on one visit and have all materials shipped at one time. You can also cut down on labor costs in this way. A contractor usually charges for a minimum of a half-day's labor which includes paying the workmen from the time they arrive at the shop until they return. You can see then that combining several remodeling jobs might mean a lower cost for each.

If you do plan to have other repairs and remodeling done at the same time as the kitchen, decide to do it before you start, not when the workmen are well into the job. It may be impossible at that time and it will probably cost you considerably more.

The important thing is to know exactly what your problems are and which changes you want to make. Only then can you decide how much remodeling you need and exactly what sort it will be.

CHAPTER 9

How Much Will a New Kitchen Cost?

In deciding how extensive you want your remodeling to be, one of the major considerations will be cost. I said one of the major considerations rather than *the* major consideration because you can sometimes spend more on minor changes than on a total remodeling. It all depends on the equipment and appliances you choose and how resourcefully you work with the space and structural limitations you have at hand. Remember too that even the smallest investments can mean a major improvement in your kitchen. Perhaps all you really need to whip your kitchen into top working order are a few minor purchases. It doesn't necessarily take a complete set of expensive custom-made cabinets to improve your storage space. You can spend as little as $5 for a plate and cup organizer or as much as $50 for a whole passel of cabinet arrangers which will vastly improve your efficiency. Or you might invest in a swivel stool that will allow you to sit down to do some of your counter top chores. These are all small purchases, but they will pay big dividends in kitchen pleasure.

Or you can spend as much as $10,000—or more—and come up with an entirely new kitchen that boasts all the latest appliances and most expensive materials. The important thing is not what you spend but how you spend it. Know what you want and what you will get for your money.

According to the Association of Kitchen Cabinet Dealers the average cost of a kitchen remodeling is about $4,400. If, however, you have $2,500 or $3,000 to spend, you can get a few cabinets, perhaps a floor, a new counter top, and possibly two or three new appliances with basic convenience features.

Some Typical Costs

Here are several kitchens of varying designs that will give you some idea of costs in relation to shape and materials. None of these estimates include *major* structural changes. All are 100 square feet. These estimated costs applied to the midwestern United States in 1972.* Prices will vary depending on quality, specific appliance features, and geographical location. Add about 15 to 20 percent for costs to these examples at publication date of this book, and perhaps more each year as prices increase.

1. A luxurious *two-wall kitchen* with *top-of-the-line* products:

cabinets and counter tops	$1,796.00
appliances, including sinks, built-in oven, cook top and hood, dishwasher and side-by-side refrigerator	1,653.00
accessories, floor covering, lighting	905.00
labor for installation	850.00
Total	$5,204.00

2. A *two-wall "middle-of-the-line"* kitchen. The cabinets and styling are more modest; the appliances have fewer special features.

cabinets and counter tops	$1,222.00
appliances, including sink, free-standing range and hood, dishwasher, and refrigerator/freezer	1,349.00
accessories, floor covering, and lighting	248.00
labor for installation	695.00
Total	$3,514.00

3. A *two-wall* kitchen in the *economy* class. It meets a tight budget but gives good performance.

cabinets and counter tops	$693.00
appliances, including sink, drop-in range, dishwasher, and one-door refrigerator	$755.00
accessories, floor covering, and lighting	156.00
labor for installation	475.00
Total	$2,079.00

* *Examples courtesy The Tappan Company.*

4. An *L-shape* kitchen in the *luxury* class:

cabinets and counter tops	$2,109.00
appliances, including built-in double oven, smooth-surface cook top, dishwasher, sink, and side-by-side refrigerator	2,081.00
accessories, floor covering, and lighting	316.00
labor for installation	1,128.00
Total	$5,634.00

5. An *L-shape* kitchen in the *medium* quality bracket:

cabinets and counter tops	$2,172.00*
appliances, including sink, range, dishwasher, refrigerator, and hood	1,490.00
accessories, floor covering, and lighting	150.00
labor for installation	592.00
Total	$4,404.00

6. An *L-shape* kitchen in the *economy* class:

cabinets and counter tops	$838.00
appliances, including dishwasher, drop-in range, refrigerator/freezer, sink and faucet	804.00
accessories, floor covering, lighting	177.00*
labor for installation	497.00
Total	$2,316.00

7. A *U-shape* kitchen in the *luxury* class with no budget restrictions:

cabinets and counter tops	$3,012.00
appliances, including sink, two built-in wall ovens, cook top and hood, dishwasher, and refrigerator/freezer	1,907.00
accessories, floor covering, and lighting	792.00
labor for installation	993.00
Total	$6,704.00

8. A *U-shape* kitchen in the *medium* class:

cabinets and counter tops	$1,298.00
appliances including sink drop-in range and hood, refrigerator/freezer, and dishwasher	1,403.00

*In some cases you may elect to spend more on a particular aspect of a remodeling even though your overall budget may be lower.

accessories, floor covering, and lighting	294.00
labor for installation	795.00
Total	$3,790.00

9. A *U-shape* kitchen in the *economy* class:

cabinet and counter tops	$1,106.00
appliances including sink, slide-in-range, dishwasher, and refrigerator/freezer	848.00
accessories, floor covering, and lighting	196.00
labor for installation	525.00
Total	$2,675.00

Cost in Relation to Your Home

A complete kitchen, designed by a professional, could run anywhere from 10 percent to 15 percent of the appraised value of a home. And what is better, it can increase the resale value of your home by about the same amount. On the other hand, if your kitchen needs to be remodeled, you can decrease the resale value by about the same amount.

The cost of a new kitchen is dependent upon many things—what you want, the possibilities or limitations of a given amount of space, any structural changes necessary, and the kind and quality of the materials chosen. For example, the cost of cabinets varies greatly and can account for as much as one-half the total remodeling cost. Then there are such hidden or implicit costs that are less visible, e.g. energy consumed by appliance lighting and other factors. By making yourself aware of these hidden elements you can be guided wisely in your choice of appliances and other items for higher efficiency, lower operating costs.

You will at some point wonder whether or not it is worth the investment you will make. Count on the fact that the investment will be worth it if all other things are equal, e.g. if the value of the house is not affected by economic, environmental or geographical change. The kitchen is usually the first room that a home buyer wants to see, and he will usually choose the house with a newly remodeled kitchen. A good kitchen can be an incentive to a buyer's quick decision so if you are remodeling to sell, remodel where it counts—the kitchen!

The Ins and Outs of Financing

When you build a house, a sizeable investment goes into the kitchen; when most people remodel, bringing the kitchen up to date is the first thing they plan for—and rightly so, for it is the thing many houses need most. The majority of kitchens in this country are at least ten years old because the majority of homes in this country, forty-five million out of seventy million, are that old or older. (A ten-year-old kitchen that has not been remodeled probably needs to be updated for more convenience.) That means a lot of kitchens are in need of remodeling if new features and designs are desired. It also means that a lot of homeowners must find ways to finance that remodeling.

The elements that add up to a new kitchen—new appliances, cabinets, carpentry, paint, flooring, wall covering, lighting, electricity, and plumbing—can run into money, and the cost totes up quickly if you go all out! It is undoubtedly worth it. Ask the homemaker who has a new kitchen and she will tell you that every cent invested has bought a dollar's worth of efficiency and pleasure. Nevertheless, not many people can afford to pay cash for the whole thing at once, nor need they. The practice of financing kitchens through loans, mortgages, and other types of borrowing has become widespread and for the most part practical even in these times of inflation, increased costs, and tight money. If your credit profile is good and/or the bank has appraised and approved your home, you should have no trouble in financing a new kitchen.

Some contractors may wish to arrange your financing for you, but generally you can secure better terms on your own. If a dealer or contractor does your financing, he may then "sell his paper" to the bank for financing, in which case it will cost you more. Estimate what your kitchen improvements will cost, then discuss the methods of financing them with your banker, finance company, dealer, or other lending institution to see which type of borrowing is best for you.

Borrowing money always costs money, of course, and the longer the term of the loan, the higher the total sum you pay out as interest. But long-term loans are a boon to many families because they mean smaller monthly payments. Interest rates, which fluctuate with the economy, may vary in different parts of the country and will depend upon your own credit profile as well as where and how you borrow the money.

There are 4 main avenues of financing:

1. *Refinancing an Existing Mortgage.* Special home improvement

loans cost money—substantially more than a standard house mortgage loan. It might be wise for you to investigate refinancing your present mortgage in which case you will utilize the equity you have already built up in your home. Naturally your chances are better if the unpaid principal that remains is comparatively small.

When you choose to refinance, the bank gives you a new mortgage that covers the outstanding balance plus whatever they are willing to give you for your kitchen remodeling. Your mortgage probably carries a lower interest rate than the refinanced mortgage will, *so be aware that you will be paying more interest on the outstanding balance than you would had you not applied for refinancing.* There also may be the matter of additional closing costs and legal fees. This could significantly increase monthly payments. In any event, work out all the figures with the bank and compare values. You will have to decide if the additional cost is offset by what you save in refinancing.

2. *The Home Improvement Loan.* This is a popular method of financing. It is a fairly easy loan to obtain, the monthly payments are relatively low, and the loan can be financed for terms as long as seven to ten years. Since a kitchen remodeling adds immeasurably to the resale value of a house, the bank normally considers it a safe investment, but how much money the bank will lend is usually dependent on the collateral you offer in support of the loan, your credit standing, and your ability to pay. A bank will usually provide a maximum of $10,000 on a home improvement loan of five to eight years' maturity for an 11 to 13 percent annual rate of interest. As a guideline, the amount of the loan will vary by geographical location and institution.

One note of caution: how much money you actually receive can be influenced by whether the bank uses an "add-on" method or discount method for the interest rate. In the *discount method* the interest is deducted at the time you take the loan from the total amount and you receive a net amount. For example, if you borrow $3,000 under the *discount* method and you *need* $3,000 you will be surprised to find that you receive considerably less than the face amount of the loan. With the *add-on* method the finance charges are added to the face amount of the loan so that you actually receive the desired amount. In comparison, simple interest, used most often when a mortgage is refinanced, is charged only on the declining or remaining balance.

3. *FHA Title I Loan.* You may also want to investigate the federally insured loans such as the FHA Title I Property Improvement Pro-

gram, backed by the Federal Housing Administration. This short-term loan often offers up to $10,000 with a repayment period from one to seven years at an annual percentage interest rate of around 12 percent. A longer term FHA improvement loan may be available at a lower interest rate, but in these times of tight money and higher interest rates it is becoming increasingly more difficult to find anyone willing to make these low-rate loans.

4. *Personal Loans, Cash, and Other Possibilities.* A *personal loan* is another possibility when you need relatively small amounts of money for short periods of time. You can borrow against your savings account passbook or securities directly from the bank or from other institutions, depending upon your credit profile. A savings account passbook loan rate is generally lower than an FHA property improvement loan rate. A personal loan is a fast way to obtain cash, but be prepared to pay a high interest rate for the privilege and keep in mind that your collateral is secured until the loan is paid.

Other methods of obtaining the money for your kitchen remodeling include loans from a *credit union or against your life insurance.*

Or you can *pay cash!* If you do choose to pay cash, there will usually be three or four payments involved in a kitchen remodeling. In the case of four transactions, the payments are usually as follows: an original deposit; a payment upon delivery of the materials; another at some previously specified stage, perhaps halfway through the work; upon completion of the work to your satisfaction. This means you have checked to see that everything agreed upon in the contract has been completed as originally stipulated.

In the case of three payments, the total amount is divided into thirds: one third when you sign the contract; one third when the materials have been delivered; the final payment upon completion. (Note caution in point number four, above.)

The Cost of Borrowing

One last word of caution about financing—keep in mind that the more you borrow and the longer you take to make the payments, the more money you will spend in interest. As I have said before, it costs money to "rent" money! But remember that interest is tax deductible, and that can help to ease the pain.

CHAPTER 10

Who Will Do the Work?

Now that you have an idea of what the costs of your new kitchen will be, it is time to think about who will do the work—and make no mistake, work it is! You have two options. You can do the job yourself or you can have professionals do it for you.

My first inclination is to warn you against do-it-yourself remodeling. It is my idea of a nightmare and many who have lived through it agree. The job is bound to take longer. Even if you can work at it full time, which is unlikely, you will be working alone or at best with some member of your family who is sufficiently qualified. In this case the job is bound to go more slowly than if you have a team of skilled workmen on hand.

In addition to the extra time you will spend and the blood, sweat, and tears you will shed, you ought to have a certain talent for carpentry and a longstanding facility with the screwdriver and claw hammer. And even then be forewarned. Many who have remodeled their own kitchen swear that they would never do it again.

If you are still determined to do it yourself, grit your teeth, roll up your sleeves, and see Chapter 16 for guidelines and directions. Remember too that no matter how skilled you are, you will probably have to rely on outside help for plumbing, wiring, and certain "licensed skills." If, on the other hand, you have taken my warning to heart and have decided to hire professionals, consider your options.

There are many different kinds of professionals. Some will do all the work for you from the first stages of planning to the ordering of supplies and subcontracting of installations; others will merely sell you the materials and appliances and install them.

Though working through a kitchen specialist may seem like an unnecessary expense, it is often more economical in the long run. An expert will be able to interpret your needs quickly. He knows how to order materials and subcontract the work. Most important, he knows how to avoid the costly mistakes you as an amateur might make.

Whichever kind of professional you decide to use, be sure to familiarize yourself with everything available on the market and your own needs and limitations before you consult him. It is even a good idea to take your own measurements and draw up a rough plan before you approach a kitchen specialist. (See Chapter 15.) Eventually he will make his own plan, but your rough sketches and lists will present a clear idea of exactly what you have in mind.

Who Are the Professionals?

Kitchen dealers are specialists in kitchen remodeling. They usually have a showroom with one or more kitchens designed to display their products and capabilities. They are well qualified to take over your kitchen remodeling job from start to finish—planning, specifications, supplying the products and materials, labor and installation, and, quite often, decorating advice. Many kitchen dealers also do bathrooms and similar installations. They usually have a portfolio of completed jobs and will gladly share it with you along with client references.

Leading kitchen dealers are members of the American Institute of Kitchen Dealers. To become members they must provide proof of their performance and financial responsibility, as well as some written declaration of their professional status. Requirements also include a two-year business history, the prominent display of AIKD Standards of Conduct, and a one-year written warranty upon completion of the job. They are listed in the Yellow Pages under the heading AIKD. Most of the best specialists—either the dealer himself or one or more of his employees—are accredited by the AIKD and qualify for the acronym CKD after their names. This means that they are *certified kitchen designers*. To receive this designation they must have passed specific tests and submitted proof of their capabilities along with sample plans, specifications, and client references.

A kitchen dealer may have a complete staff including installation experts as well as designer, or he may subcontract the plumbing, electrical and sheet metal work, carpentry, flooring, wall covering, and other specialized work. Whether he subcontracts the work or does it himself, the dealer is responsible for the completed job.

A good dealer will always put everything in writing and their best advertising is done by word-of-mouth through satisfied customers. Some kitchen dealers, especially those with a CKD designation, charge a professional fee for the original estimate, which includes a visit to your home, a personal interview, preliminary measurements, a plan, and specifications. If you contract them to do the job, this fee is credited to the total cost.

If the dealer does not charge a fee, you are not entitled to keep the original plans and specifications.

When you contract a dealer, the contract price is based upon an estimate of the cost of equipment and labor and an overall percentage for overhead. Generally a total price is quoted and you will get a breakdown of cabinetry, appliances, other materials and equipment, and, of course, labor. Usually each cabinet is not included in the breakdown, but it is a good idea for you to ask for it.

Some leading *cabinet manufacturers* may have local retail outlets which offer kitchen planning services through dealer specialists. Others franchise local kitchen dealers to handle their products.

Many *department stores,* especially the larger ones and chains, have kitchen departments, which are managed by specialists in the kitchen remodeling field. Like a kitchen dealer, these departments will usually have one or more kitchens on display and a separte sales staff of qualified professionals. Always ask for a portfolio of completed jobs and, if you wish, client references.

Building supply or lumber dealers usually sell all material and equipment needed for kitchen and home improvement remodelings. They may not have a design and installation service, but if you are doing the work yourself you will not want this help. Some dealers can arrange for subcontractors to do installations as well as plumbing, electrical, and sheet metal work. If you do arrange your work through these dealers and they are not professionals in the kitchen remodeling field, be sure to have in writing who is ultimately responsible to guarantee the work. Most likely it will turn out to be the individual contracted for each job. Make certain you know exactly what they plan to do, how they will do it, and what the price is before you sign a contract. In any event, get it *all* in writing, before you begin.

Home improvement centers or remodeling contractors do interior and exterior work and will usually do kitchens. The best ones will have showrooms with samples of their work on display. If you are having them do other work, consider letting them do the kitchen as well. Combining all remodeling work, as I have pointed out, is often economical, and major home improvement jobs can be financed over long periods. Some of the best and largest remodeling contractors will be members of the National Remodelers' Association or the National Home Improvement Council.

Cabinetmakers usually make cabinets in the shop or on the site and install them. Some may take on the job of complete remodeling and subcontract the rest of the work, but most confine themselves to cabinetmaking and installation. They may be members of the National Remodelers' Association or the National Home Improvement Council.

Plumbing and electrical contractors may qualify as kitchen specialists, but if they do, they should have separate showrooms and someone on hand to design and supervise the entire remodeling.

Other contractors you will need include those who do heating, sheet metal, flooring, tile, and masonry. At some point in your remodeling, you may need one or all of these skilled tradesmen.

Appliance stores carry only appliances. Occasionally, however, they have a kitchen planning specialist on their staff who can provide a complete design. Most appliance stores do have an optional installation service.

Architects are indeed qualified to plan kitchens, but when they do they are usually concerned with the kitchen in relation to the entire house. Actually, we have found that most architects prefer not to do individual kitchens. Nor does it pay for them to do so. If, however, you are involved in a major redesign of your home, adding a room or two or making major structural changes, you may very well need an architect to supervise the complete job including the kitchen.

Interior designers usually fall into the same category as an architect. If you are redesigning the entire house and have retained an interior designer to do the work, he (or she) may be willing to take on the entire kitchen remodeling as well. Interior designers generally charge a high fee, and while familiar with decorating materials and home furnishings they frequently do not know as much about appliances and other kitchen equipment and will have to subcontract most of the work.

Utility companies may offer kitchen planning services in your area, in addition to providing specialists for consultation on lighting and wiring requirements.

Associations

Some of the trade associations we have mentioned have lists and directories of their members. If you cannot find them in the Yellow Pages write to them at the following addresses to find out who their members are in your area:

The American Institute of Kitchen Dealers (AIKD)
114 Main Street
Hackettstown, New Jersey 07840

The National Home Improvement Council (HIC)
11 East 44th Street
New York, New York 10017

The National Plumbing, Heating and Cooling Contractors
1016 20th Street, N.W.
Washington, D.C. 20036

The National Remodelers Association
50 East 42nd Street
New York, New York 10017

For a complete listing of where to go for information, see Appendix, page 263.

Making the Decision

Now that you know who *can* do the work, who *will* do it? The decision is up to you. Visit the showrooms. It's always better to see things firsthand than to rely on brochures or telephone interviews and letters. Ask questions. Is there a design specialist on hand? Does the firm design and install? Do they assume responsibility for whatever work is subcontracted, such as plumbing, electrical work, and other licensed skills? Are they franchised or authorized dealers for specific manufacturers of appliances, cabinets, or other materials? What kind of services and guarantees do they offer?

Take your plans and ideas with you and make sure that the specialist you choose can take care of all your needs. Find out if he is a member of any trade associations. Ask for references and be sure to check them.

Insist on a firm and definite price when receiving an estimate. Make sure that you have a contract which puts everything in writing and read the contract thoroughly before you sign it. Ask questions *now.* After you have signed the contract it will be too late.

CHAPTER 11

What Makes a Kitchen Run?

It is all very well to dream about how that new kitchen will look after it is finished, but now is the time to do something about its parts, to separate it into components, and to see what makes it tick. There are certain basic elements vital to the very heartbeat of a kitchen. These are the arteries that supply the life-giving nutrients that make it run—the electricity, plumbing, water, heat, ventilation, lighting, and storage.

Early on I mentioned that you will find ways to cut costs here and there. Four areas where I do *not* recommend cutting costs are *wiring, ventilation, lighting,* and *plumbing.*

Wiring, of course, is necessary for the safe and efficient operation of your appliances—those you have now and those you may be planning to add in the future.

Adequate and proper *ventilation* is a must if you are to remove grease, smoke, odors, heat, and moisture that result from cooking and possibly laundry. A good ventilating system in the kitchen will reduce the need for frequent cleaning of walls, curtains, draperies, and furniture throughout the entire house.

As for *lighting,* you need it to see. It is as simple as that. Poor light—harsh, dim, or not enough of it—can result in accidents, eye strain, and fatigue.

Good plumbing, of course, is essential to the proper operation of your water supply, drainage, dishwasher, disposer, and laundry equipment.

Let us consider these and other important elements one by one.

Wiring and Electricity

You need adequate wiring for major and small appliances, lighting, and ventilation. Plan enough convenience outlets and sufficient current where you will need them most. What you do need:

•A separate 240-volt circuit for an electric range or built-in electric oven and cook top, electric dryer, and air conditioner.

•A separate 120-volt circuit for a refrigerator-freezer combination, freezer, dishwasher and disposer (one circuit), washer, and air conditioner.

•Two 120-volt, 20-amp circuits for small appliances, a gas range, automatic ice maker, compact refrigerator, and trash compactor.

•One 120-volt, 15-amp circuit for lights, clock, exhaust fan, and perhaps a radio. It is wise to check with your local utility company about your electrical needs. Most offer analysis and recommendations for home lighting and wiring either free or for a nominal fee.

•One duplex outlet for every four feet of counter space or plug-in wiring strips.

Ventilation

The kitchen is the one room in the house that provides the most indoor pollution. Grease-laden vapors, cooking odors, moisture, and heat are the culprits. These impurities can cause serious housekeeping problems when they are allowed to deposit on walls, surfaces, fabrics, and furniture, and to permeate the air generally.

A good ventilating system with a well-designed hood and fan will supply the fresh air you need in the kitchen. It will stop odors and trap grease and fumes where they originate. You need a ventilating hood and fan anywhere cooking takes place—over the range, barbecue, built-in grill, built-in wok, and even in areas where you use portable cooking appliances most.

There are two types of ventilating hoods and fans—the *ducted* type and the *ductless* variety. Naturally, a ducted style is the best as the fumes, odors, and grease-laden vapors are filtered and exhausted to the outdoors through specially installed metal duct systems. If, on the other

Cooking center with built-in microwave/stay hot/self-cleaning oven combination and cook top griddle grill boasts a brushed stainless ventilating hood with warming shelf. Trash compactor paneled to match cabinets is convenient at range area. Cabinets above and below ovens hold baking pans. Base cabinet under cook top has pull-out shelves for fingertip reach. Wall cabinet over hood houses ventilating mechanism. *Courtesy Thermador*

hand, it is impossible to duct a ventilating system, ductless hoods are designed with satisfactory filtering systems that inhale the air, clean it, and then exhaust it back into the kitchen. They are better than none at all.

Selecting a ventilating hood and fan

You will find hoods in many varieties and in almost any color you want to match a particular appliance or cabinet finish. If you have something very special in mind you can have a hood made to order either by the cabinet manufacturer or a special fabricator. Whether you buy a ready-made system or have one made to order, however, keep one thing in mind. Not all ventilating hoods and fans are equally efficient. Before you buy anything, check the mechanics of the operation. Any system manufactured by the members of the Home Ventilating Institute is rated according to performance and sometimes for noise or "sone" level as well.

Make sure that ventilating hood and fan have enough power to remove all kitchen impurities and to carry them through the length of

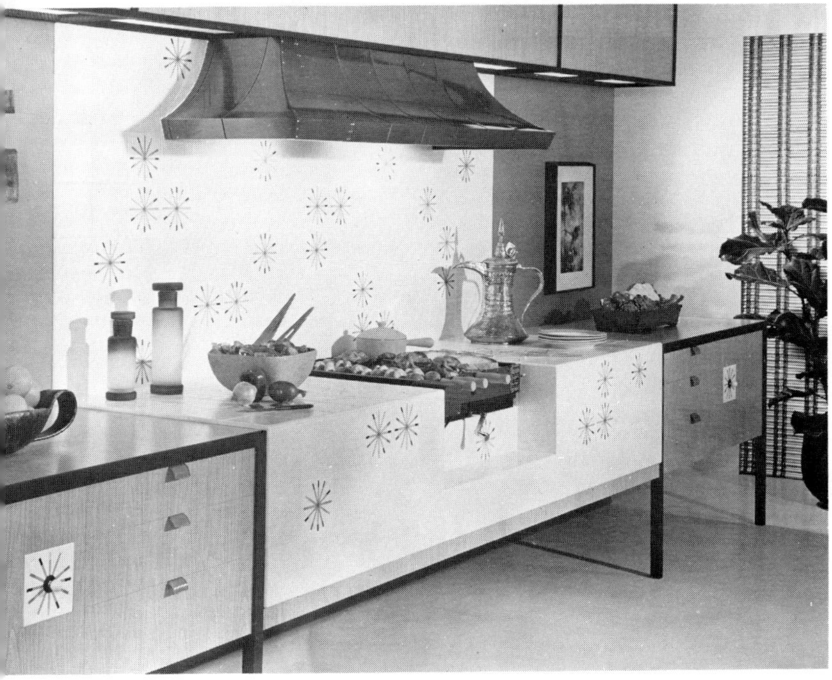

Barbecue center at one end of a large family kitchen doubles as buffet for entertaining. Heavy duty ventilating hood and fan absorbs smoke and cooking fumes. Matchstick tile design picked up on cabinet hardware adds festive note. Off-floor cabinets makes cleaning easy. *Courtesy Thermador; Photographer, George de Gennaro*

the duct and any turns that may be necessary for your installation. The system should contain a good grease filter and fan. The filter should be no less than a half-inch thick and removable for easy cleaning.

A good system (hood, filter, and fan), installed properly, should exhaust up to 85 percent of all cooking fumes and have an air removal capacity of at least three hundred and preferably four hundred cubic feet per minute (CFM). Ventilating fans are rated by the number of cubic feet of air they can move per minute. A change of air every four minutes is recommended for kitchens. In order to determine the CFM rating necessary to achieve this air exchange in your kitchen, multiply the number of square feet of the kitchen floor by two. For example, a kitchen with 150 square feet of floor space would utilize a fan with a 300 CFM rating in order to change the air fifteen times every hour. If your kitchen has a ceiling higher than eight feet, the fan should have a somewhat higher rating. Check the building codes for your area. They may stipulate minimum CFM ratings. Both the Home Ventilating Institute and the Federal Housing Administration require a fan that will deliver a minimum of 40 cubic feet of air per minute per foot of hood length.

Check on the noise level of the fan as well as its efficiency. In some

Can't you just taste luscious pancakes made on this griddle cook top recessed into cooking niche? Vent hood and fan will absorb heat, fumes, and odor while infrared warming shelf keeps sausages hot. *Courtesy Thermador*

cases it is possible to install fans in more remote areas in order to cut down on localized noises.

If you have any questions which your dealer cannot answer about the performance rating of a system, write to the Home Ventilating Institute, 230 North Michigan Avenue, Chicago, Illinois 60601.

The mechanics of operation and installation

When installing a hood and fan over the range, make sure it is deep enough to cover the entire cooking surface. The bottom of the hood should be a minimum of 21 inches above the cooking surface and never more than 30 inches.

It is best to locate the range on an outside wall so that the ventilating hood and fan installed above it will exhaust directly to the outdoors. Be sure that the exhaust does not open onto your own porch or patio or that of a neighbor. If you have to locate the range on an inside wall or in the center of the room in an island or peninsula, the duct can go up and, with one turn, straight out through a soffit over the wall cabinets. Keep in mind that the more turns in the ductwork, the less effective the system. Depending upon the structural design of your house, it may be possible to carry the ductwork straight upward and vent it through the roof. But remember, long duct runs decrease efficiency.

Lighting

There are three types of lighting necessary in every room throughout the home, but especially the kitchen: *general illumination* to provide a low level of light throughout the room, creating a soft and pleasant atmosphere; *task or functional lighting* at work areas for specific tasks; *accent or decorative lighting,* if you desire, to emphasize areas, pictures, or objects of art. I like to think of this as mood lighting.

General illumination

This is provided from large center ceiling fixtures, ceiling panels, or a luminous ceiling. Fluorescent fixtures with low brightness and cool operating temperatures are excellent for general illumination. Deluxe warm white tubes provide a soft, warm atmosphere. If you prefer a "daylight" effect or cooler atmosphere, Deluxe cool white fluorescent lamps may be used.

Consider these guidelines in selecting tubes and bulbs for ceiling fixtures: Per each 50 square feet of room use 150 to 200 watts incandescent or 60 to 80 watts fluorescent.

Task or functional lighting

Special task or local lighting will help you avoid working in your own shadow. In the range area a 36-inch fluorescent lamp is suggested. For incandescent light, use two 60-watt bulbs. Lights on the range and ventilating hoods may provide some or all of the light needed near the range or cooking area.

In the counter areas lights installed under cabinets or mounted on the wall under the cabinets are excellent. When using fluorescent light, 3 feet of counter work area require a 24-inch fixture.

In the sink area, even if there is a window to provide natural light, you will need spot lighting for night work. Use either fluorescent or incandescent fixtures, shielded by a decorative valance or recessed into a soffit installation. Decorative down lighting is also effective.

If there are no windows, you may want to find some other means for providing natural light, such as a skylight or glass brick placed between wall and base cabinets, or consider placing windows high enough to permit cabinets to be located beneath them.

THE WORK AREA

Mount fluorescent channels to the underside of the cabinet, as close to the front as possible. To shield, you can side-mount the channels and use the back of the channel for shielding, or cut shielding from one-quarter-inch plywood to blend with the style of the kitchen. Over the sink and range areas, you can use this same arrangement, or mount a bullet type of fixture on the side of the cabinet and aim it at the task area. Wiring can be run through a small hole drilled in the cabinet.

Another effective solution is to build a luminous shelf. Make a wooden frame with a fluorescent channel mounted to it. Use a diffusing plastic or frosted glass for the top. This lights the work area and supplies a place for storage and display. Be sure the lamp is centered over the work area. This application is also good for meal planning and study areas if a 40-watt fluorescent lamp is used.

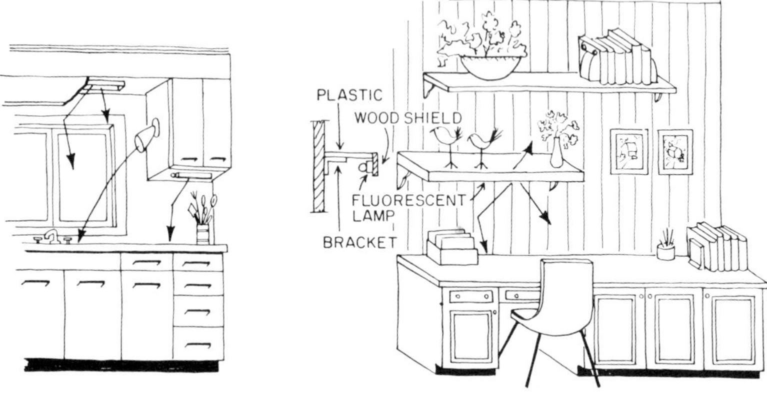

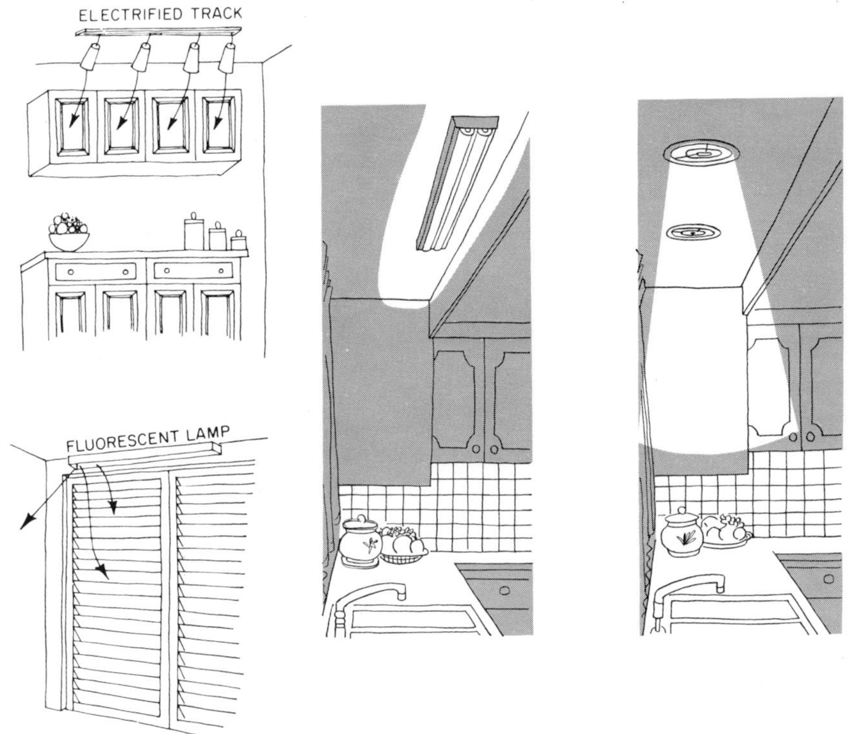

CABINETS

If cabinet fronts are carved or textured, accent by mounting electrified track to the ceiling and aiming the housings on the doors. This also aids in giving additional light to the inside of the cabinets.

CLOSETS

For closets, if the door is louvered, mount a fluorescent lamp at the inside of the door header. Run the wire to an outlet.

Task lighting is especially important in the various work centers. In the sink or range area, when there are wall cabinets on either side of the appliance, use bare bulbs or tubes for cabinets joined by an 8-inch minimum depth faceboard. If you prefer fluorescent lighting, you might use deluxe warm white tubes in a two-lamp fixture mounted close to the faceboard and sized to the available space. Use three tubes in areas where 20-watt fixtures are required.

If you prefer incandescent lighting, try two 75-watt R-30 floodlights or two 75-watt soft white lights spaced 15 inches apart. Mount these on soffit 3 to 4 inches behind the faceboard.

RECESSED FLUORESCENT

SURFACE MOUNTED FLUORESCENT

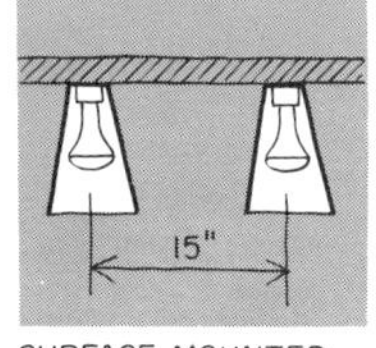

SURFACE MOUNTED INCANDESCENT

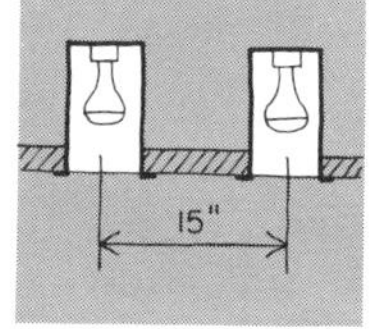

RECESSED INCANDESCENT

If there are no faceboards, you might consider recessed fluorescent lighting. Two 30-watt, 24-inch tubes of deluxe warm white will do the trick. If you desire a "daylight" effect or cooler atmosphere, use deluxe cool white fluorescent lamps. Shielding louvers, frosted glass, or ribbed clear plastic add an attractive decorative note.

Surface mounted fluorescent lighting is another possibility. In this case you can repeat the center ceiling fixture directly above the work area. If two work areas are treated in this way, the need for a ceiling fixture is minimized depending upon the size of the room.

For recessed incandescent lighting you might try two 75-watt R-30 floodlights in louvered "high-hat" fixtures spaced 15 inches apart.

If incandescent surface mounted lighting is more appropriate to your work center, consider two metal housings 15 inches apart using 75-watt R-30 floodlights or soft white 100-watt bulbs, though the floodlights are preferable in this arrangement.

If there are wall cabinets above the sink or range, follow the suggestions given for illuminating the food center on page 131.

Task lighting is made easy if you use the ventilating hood over your cooking center. You can choose a single bulb, 100-watt soft white or, if the socket is in a base-up position, try a 75-watt floodlight. You can also use two 60-watt soft white bulbs.

The food preparation center is another spot for special task lighting. If there are wall cabinets above your work counter, fasten fluorescent channels either to the bottom of the cabinet at the front (the preferable treatment) or directly under the cabinet on the back wall. (Deluxe warm white is preferred, unless cool or "daylight" atmosphere is desired in which case deluxe cool white is a better choice.)

The channel may be painted to match the wall or you can install an opaque shield of metal, wood, or laminated plastic to match the counter top. For a counter of less than 24 inches, use an 18-inch, 15-watt tube; for a 36-inch counter use a 24-inch 20-watt tube, and for a counter of more than 48 inches (but not more than 6 feet), select a 48-inch 40-watt tube. Use the longest tube that will fit, and make sure to cover at least two-thirds of the counter length.

If your work area is a right-angle counter with no cabinets above, try a fluorescent channel mounted lengthwise under center of upper cabinets. Install opaque shielding on both sides of the tube. The lengths necessary here are the same as above.

Other solutions to the right-angle counter without cabinets above are louvered, surface-mounted, semirecessed cylinders, or recessed, louvered "high hats" containing 75-watt R-30 floodlights, spaced 20 inches apart from center to center. If the counter doubles as an informal dining area, a pulley fixture or several pendants are attractive as well as functional.

Illustrations and information courtesy General Electric Lighting Institute, Nela Park, Cleveland, Ohio.

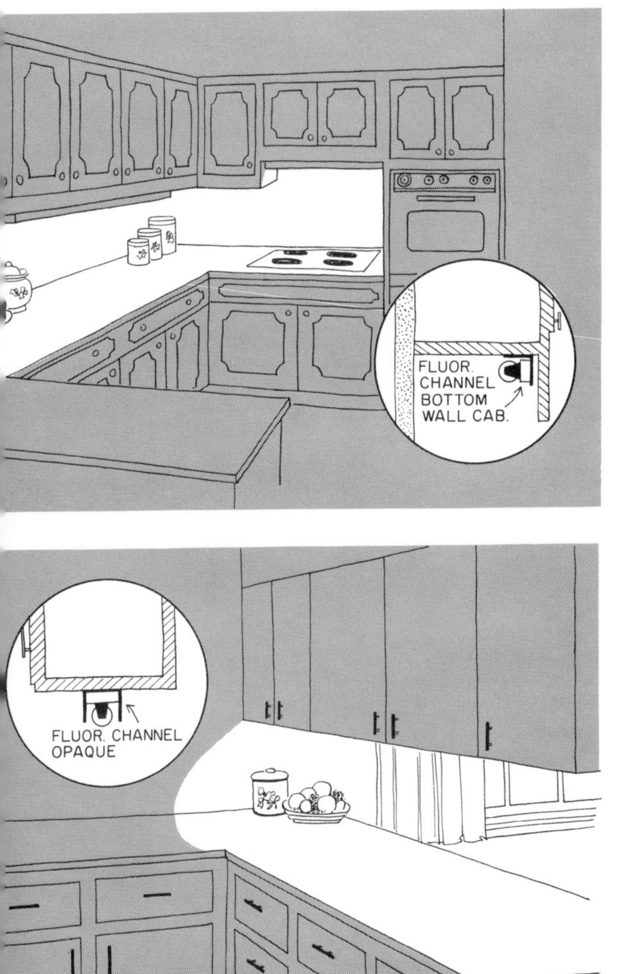

OTHER SOLUTIONS

Lighting from a luminous ceiling floods the kitchen with a daylight effect while lighting recessed over the sink and under each wall cabinet provides continuous illumination over the counter tops. All lighting is deluxe warm white fluorescent. *Courtesy Westinghouse*

Storage, as well as lighting, is the key in this remodeled kitchen. The central divider houses the sink, dishwasher, and disposer as well as being a mixing and serving counter. Storage cabinets above it, containing glasses and dishes, open to both sides. Cabinets along the left wall store portable appliances, canned goods, cereals, and bottles. Condiments and other ingredients for cooking are stored in the area of the platform range and built-in double oven. Cabinets and table top are laminated plastic. Both cabinets and counter tops are easily washed without concern about wearing the finish. *Courtesy Westinghouse*

Undercounter lighting—including a fixture located in the range hood—provides the proper amount of light for work surfaces. General room illumination is provided by recessed incandescent down lights in the ceiling including one unit that illuminates the artwork on the left wall. A small fixture is located at the desk to light that area. *Courtesy Westinghouse*

Remodeled "open kitchen" is lighted as for an intensive work situation by an efficient utilitarian four-lamp 40-watt fluorescent surface-mounted fixture. Perimeter lighting, at all work areas, is in good balance with general lighting. For casual use and entertaining, perimeter lighting alone provides a pleasing atmosphere—effectively and economically eliminating the need for a decorative center fixture. *Courtesy General Electric, Nela Park*

Reflection of available surfaces as well as the need to increase illumination levels and lighting distribution were all considered in relighting this apartment kitchen. Cabinet doors were refitted with a washable strip wallpaper with a 55 percent reflectance, greatly increasing the visual comfort of the area. Wallpaper was applied to cardboard and force-fitted into the door panels. This treatment is completely temporary—it can be removed by prying out the panels —and in no way will mar the finish of the apartment's cabinetry. A two-light, side-mounted strip was added above the sink with a shielding skirt, giving that work area greater illumination. A 40-watt deluxe warm white fluorescent lamp was added under the cabinet for counter top illumination. *Courtesy General Electric, Nela Park*

Soffit above the sink conceals two 40-watt deluxe warm white fluorescent lamps that produce sufficient light on the counter top and sink work areas. "Little Inch" units (15-watt) on either side light the counter tops. Deluxe white fluorescent is best for the woodwork and matches the incandescent over the range and eyeball units above the cupboards. *Courtesy General Electric, Nela Park*

Shallow storage cupboards in extrawide hallway are lighted by four small louvered eyeball units using 50-watt R20 reflector lamps. Aiming the units toward the storage cabinets not only makes the contents more visible but also accents the attractive color and finish of the cabinets. As an extra bonus, the passageway is amply lighted from the top "spill light." *Courtesy General Electric, Nela Park*

Some lighting points to remember

1. For any wiring or electrical work, including changing switches to dimmers, be sure all electrical current is turned *off*.

2. Consider the reflection of light from surrounding surfaces in determining whether you will be bothered by glare or a bright-dark contrast.

3. A light-colored ceiling will evenly reflect all light from it.

4. Nonglossy surfaces will diffuse and scatter light rays to give a pleasing overall illumination.

5. Always select "deluxe" tubes instead of standard warm or cool white tubes when using fluorescent lighting. A cup of coffee, for example, often takes on a greenish color with standard tubes.

6. Make sure all fixtures and fixture parts are U.L. (Underwriters' Laboratories) listed.

7. Rather than use extension cords, which may be hazardous, especially if the plug is not in the outlet tightly, replace cords with one that is long enough for the purpose.

8. To conceal wiring, run it along corners or molding, secure in place and paint to match. If it still looks too conspicuous to you, place a plant or similar object in front of it.

9. Before mounting fixtures, find out what wall and ceiling materials are. Different materials require different methods of anchoring.

10. Be sure that lamps or fixtures are not next to any combustible material which could be heated to an excess of 90 degrees Centigrade.

11. Beware of putting stress on wires by pulling too tightly or twisting them. Such stress may create wiring hazards.

12. Never support fixtures from wire supplying circuit. Use chain or some other material.

13. Use a grounding cord in areas near water, such as sinks, laundry tubs, etc.

14. To obtain most materials, contact a local building supply house, electrical distributor, or hardware store.

Plumbing

Perhaps the plumbing system you have now is sufficient for your needs. However, if you are installing a dishwasher or a disposer you will want to have a plumber check the waste line to be sure it is large enough and conforms to building codes. You will probably want to have him check the adequacy of the septic tank, if you have one, at the same time.

If you are planning a laundry in your kitchen, place it as near to the plumbing as possible. Similarly, locate your water heater and water softener system as close to the point of use as possible. Water cools off in long runs. Consult plumbing contractors for guidelines and estimates. And don't be afraid to bring your plumbing up to date. It is no economy to build a new kitchen around inefficient, outdated plumbing.

Heating and Cooling

If your heating system is forced hot water, consider "baseboard" heating panels set at ceiling height to gain maximum space at floor level. Set forced warm air registers into walls if floor installation is not practical. If the heating system is steam or hot water, consider hiding a radiator behind perforated metal if it does not cut heating efficiency. Put the radiator near the window or on an outside wall if possible, and avoid having heat directed right on you as you work.

As far as cooling is concerned, unless your home is centrally air conditioned and you've a thermostat in your kitchen, you might want to consider installing a room air conditioner in or near the kitchen for those days when your cooking load is heavy and the kitchen is especially hot. Real comfort, of course, depends upon proper capacity. To make certain you are choosing the right unit and that you have adequate wiring, it is a good idea to consult your electrician, local utility company, or some other qualified source, such as your kitchen dealer or designer.

CHAPTER 12

A Place for Everything

Like wiring, ventilation, and plumbing, storage is one of the "arteries" that keep a kitchen functioning. Even the most efficient kitchen with the most up-to-date appliances becomes inefficient when things are cluttered, out of place, or inaccessible. And yet this is precisely the predicament of most kitchens. They lack organized storage space.

Our modern storage needs are prodigious. There are more than eight thousand items in today's supermarkets, six thousand of which are foods—perishable, nonperishable, frozen, canned, packaged, bottled, bagged, and boxed. It is a good bet that a large percentage of these items —just how many depends on your family's life-style—will find their way into your kitchen. There they must be stored. In addition there must be a space for tableware, cooking tools, and, of course, the myriad modern appliances that make the kitchen at once more convenient and more exciting. Given this wealth of objects is it any wonder that things have a way of collecting on counters in your present kitchen, that many of your utensils are stored in inaccessible places, and that you are constantly bending, reaching, and fighting through other items to get to what you want.

There is only one way to avoid these pitfalls in your new kitchen. Plan now where you will store everything and then allow some extra space for things you will acquire in the future.

Think seriously about how you live and how you work. Do you entertain a lot? Are you an elaborate cook and have many utensils to store? What are your family's eating habits? For example, if they like cereal each morning but prefer to vary the kind from day to day you will need space for a lineup of boxes. Are you planning on a grill or barbecue in your new kitchen? Then you will want adjacent storage space for condiments, tongs, and a big platter.

Obviously you know your needs and preferences best and given sufficient time and thought can probably plan an ideal storage system for your new kitchen. On the other hand, kitchen specialists often know how to translate your specific needs into an efficiently organized kitchen. Their specialized knowledge and experience enable them to use space to the best advantage of you and your pocketbook. Once again, you may find the use of a kitchen specialist more economical in the long run.

Whether you decide to design your kitchen storage space yourself or turn to an expert, you will have to devote considerable thought to your life-style and work habits and to certain basics of efficient storage:

1. When planning each center, review all of your equipment to determine how much and what sort of storage you will need. As we said before, whenever possible store equipment and supplies at point of first use and do not hesitate to duplicate certain basic items such as measuring cups, spoons, and beaters.

2. Make sure that everything is within reach. Obviously this does not mean out in the open, though some people do like open shelves and

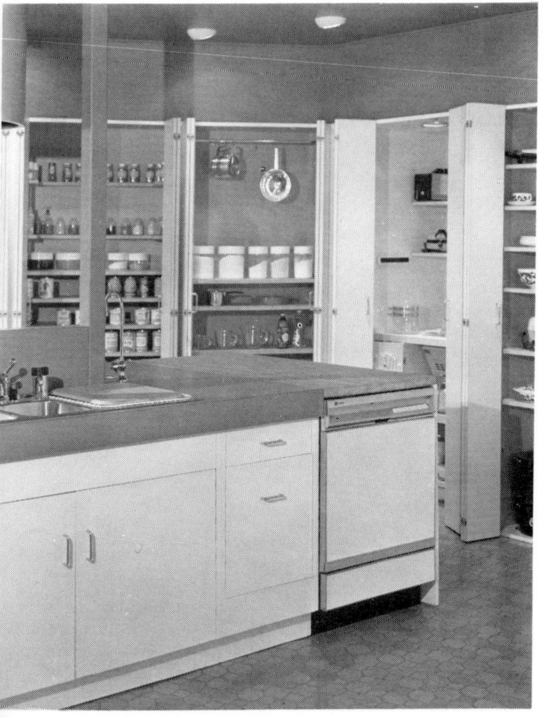

Both traffic and storage revolve easily around island work center. In this unique cabinet-type locker items for food preparation are easily accessible when needed and quickly returned to storage after dishwashing, since dishwasher is located right at hand. In this flexible storage arrangement, four different types of accessories for the pantry can be arranged in a multitude of ways to house all kinds of utensils, tableware, and food supplies: a U-shaped shelf permits clear visibility of canned goods or glassware, a shelf with built-in drawer may serve as a desk, workshelf, or bar, a regular shelf the depth of the unit (15 inches) accommodates large tableware, serving items, most small electrical appliances; an accessory rod stores hanging items securely and neatly. The pantry itself measures 3 feet in width, 15 inches deep, and 7 feet in height. All surfaces are covered in easy-to-clean laminated plastic. *Courtesy Maytag, Formica*

Hideaway niche reveals pull-out plastic flatware storage tray—conveniently located just above dishwasher. The 13-inch deep cabinet is designed for dinnerware storage and serving accessories. Twelve-inch counter in front provides ample space for working. *Courtesy Maytag*

Consider elevating the dishwasher. Convenience is the keynote in this dishwasher-equipped entertainment center. Built-in dishwasher has been elevated 18 inches for easier loading and unloading—an idea that would work with any dishwasher location. Within easy reach from the dishwasher is a custom-built pull-out cabinet for prompt after-party storage of dinnerware and serving accessories. Easy access to the "workings" of the dishwasher is gained by a removeable panel under the dishwasher, held in place with cabinet door catches. *Courtesy Maytag*

This center island features a portable appliance center on one side and closed-circuit television intercom master, radio and phone on the other side. Kitchen is illuminated by a custom-made ceiling fixture and undercounter fixtures that light the work surfaces. All are fluorescent. *Courtesy Westinghouse*

pegboard walls or beams from which to hang pots and pans. The point here is that something which is not easily within reach will mean either wasted time and effort or lack of use.

3. Keep items used most frequently, such as your coffee pot and toaster or certain condiments, in the front of the cabinet.

4. Think not only about where you will store things but how you will store them. There are cabinets of all sorts—wall, base, and special purpose units and accessories—that automatically organize kitchen storage and save space, clutter, and work. For example, think about cabinets with built-in planning desks, cutting boards, food files (today's version of the old-fashioned pantry), Susans, corner and blind corner Susans, flatware drawers, cutlery partitions, bread boxes, mixer accommodations, adjustable roll shelves, sliding towel racks, tote tray organizers, and even planter sections.

Cabinets may also be assembled with various components to resemble cupboards, sideboards, hutches, and china closets. If you have a variety of table and cookware and like to display special china and crystal these may be ideal for your needs. We will talk more about the variety of cabinets available on page 150.

5. Keep in mind that storage can also be decorative. How about a pegboard or wall rack for hanging cooking utensils? Or open shelves for displaying handsome crockery, cookware, baskets, and other decorative but useful items?

Now let's think about some of the specific things you will want to store.

• *Food and staples.* Where will you put those extra canned goods and staples you want to keep on hand? Is there enough space to stock up when foods and grocery products are on special sale? Would you prefer and do you have room for a separate pantry or do you want several special purpose cabinets built into the kitchen proper?

• *Small appliance cookery.* The average family owns a minimum of sixteen small appliances. Chances are that you own, or will own as your new kitchen takes shape, even more. Where will you store these fry pans, toaster ovens, blenders, mixers, can openers, knife sharpeners, juicers, meat grinders, and slicing knives, to name only a few? Will they be accessible when you need them, or will they be hidden away somewhere in the back of a cabinet or high above out of reach?

Island which divides kitchen from family room houses cooking top and special built-in wok for Chinese cookery. Stylized hood in brushed stainless steel provides amply for the removal of cooking odors, smoke fumes, and grease. Indoor-outdoor cooking capacity is perfect for entertaining and buffets. *Courtesy* Modern Bride *Magazine*

Keep in mind that the appliance which is inaccessible will soon become the appliance which is never used. For a perfect example of a kitchen with a creative storage plan which actually increases the efficiency of an appliance see page 146. This kitchen provides a special space to store a wok plus a built-in drawer for rice and a chopping block to prepare Chinese vegetables.

• *Appliance accessories.* In addition to providing convenient storage space for appliances, be sure to allow space for the important accessories that come with each appliance. There is nothing more frustrating than wasted moments spent looking for mislaid electric cords, instruction booklets, covers, or extra attachments.

• *Drinking.* Stop to think about it. If your family is like most, not an hour goes by without someone reaching for a glass—for a drink of water, soda pop, milk, or juice. And do you enjoy wine with dinner or a highball or two before? Consider a beverage center in your new kitchen. Provide space for the storage of glassware and perhaps a bar sink and undercounter refrigerator. You will find it an ideal way to cut down interference, confusion, and mess in the rest of the kitchen.

• *Cleaning.* We suggested earlier that supplies needed for dishwashing, silver polishing, and other cleaning be stored in or near the sink area and out of the reach of children. Think too about where you will store the many other cleaning products such as dish and paper towels, trash and paper bags, dusting and polishing cloths, brooms and dustpans, wax applicators, floor polishers, and a carpet sweeper, lightweight vacuum, or electric broom for quick cleanups. You will want most, if not all of these things, easily accessible in the kitchen. Keep in mind the tall broom cabinets designed for just this purpose.

• *Planning.* It is astonishing how quickly papers can accumulate in a kitchen. Bills, receipts, recipes, instruction manuals, product warranties, and lists have a way of getting stuffed into an extra drawer that soon turns into a "junk" drawer. Whenever you want something you will have to waste precious time digging for that particular piece of paper. A planning desk with some slotted storage and perhaps a file drawer or two will save time and needless headaches.

• *Outdoors wraps and indoor aprons.* Do you usually use the back door? If so where do you hang your coat when you come in? Where do the children put their coats and boots, bats and skates? Is there some place where you can hang an apron or two so that you can grab one in a hurry or produce one quickly for a helpful friend?

Designed for a paraplegic, this kitchen is both handsome and efficient. Lower drawers are recessed under counter tops to accommodate wheelchair occupant's knees. Flip-up doors on upper cabinets permit removal of cans and boxes from the shelves using long-handled grocer's tongs. Counter top is lowered for convenience as are the built-in ovens. Note that U-shaped work area leaves plenty of space for maneuvering wheelchair. Compatible with strongly grained wood and stainless steel trim and appliances is the quarry tile floor; it's 6 X 6 inch square. *Courtesy American Olean*

Above, left. The center unit for dishes is on roller shelves and can be opened up from either side. It's wonderful for storing dishes taken from the dishwasher and makes it easy to set the table. Cabinets on each end have a center divider. On the kitchen side are stored cocktail treats and condiments. On the dining room side, there's room for table mats, hot pads, and linens.

Above, right. Floor-to-ceiling utility cabinets in the upper left corner offer shelf space for food storage—a pantry corner right in the kitchen.

Right. Natural brick wall adds to the attractiveness of the kitchen and sets off the cooking center. Up-to-date appliances are surrounded by a country kitchen atmosphere with copper utensils and a cast-iron enclosed warming oven. To the left over pass-through counter and behind built-in mixer-blender are open shelves which house a delft collection. Pass-through closes the dining room off from the kitchen with French-style doors, paneled in mesh. Adjacent to the refrigerator next to the cooking center is a smaller sink for rinsing pots and pans quickly or washing vegetables and fruits which are stored in the ventilated cabinet below. Wooden chopping blocks are built into the counter on each side of the sink. The corner chopping block has slits cut into the surface for storing knives safely in a downward position. (See floor plan.)

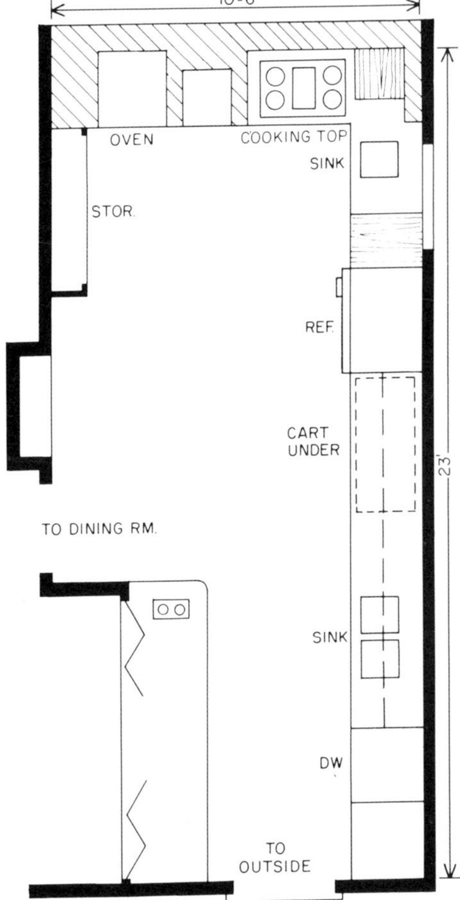

This kitchen was designed for large-and-small-scale entertaining. Obviously a carefully considered layout, the plan makes meal preparation and serving easy and enjoyable. Studying the plan, a wide counter top (lower left corner) serves not only as a mixing center with a built-in unit for a mixer and blender but also as a pass-through serving counter to the dining area. Beneath this counter are three storage cabinets. *All photographs courtesy* American Home *Magazine.*

Above, left. To the right of the refrigerator, under one portion of the counter is what appears to be open shelves. (See preceding photograph.) As you can see in this photograph, this is actually a mobile serving cart which can be wheeled about the kitchen for use in preparing meals or pushed into the dining room for serving at mealtime. This wall also contains wall and base storage cabinets, with unique undercabinet stainless steel storage bins for paper, foil, and plastic products. There is also a large cleanup sink. Notice the dishwasher is raised for ease of loading and unloading. Cabinets above give it a truly built-in look.

Above, right. Base cabinet under surface cooking tops is a pull-out unit for storage of pots, pans, utensils, and baking equipment.

Could this be today's version of tomorrow's kitchen? These mechanically operated kitchen storage cabinets are automated to "bring" to you the items you need. This unit, compact and efficient, is 7 feet wide. It has fourteen rotating shelves, each divided into three equal compartments. Storage space is equivalent to fourteen wall cabinets, 30 inches high by 24 inches wide. Should the power go off, there is a hand crank for emergency use. Base cabinets offer additional 12-inch deep fixed storage. In the three pictures following you will see the mechanics in action. *Courtesy Remington Rand*

•*Entertaining.* If you do a lot of entertaining, especially formally or for large groups, you will need specialized storage for large bowls, platters, serving pieces—all those infrequently used items that are essential when you entertain. And what about trays? Some are large, some small, some round, some rectangular, and all are difficult to store. Whatever your entertaining habits, think now about specialized storage space for these all-important aids.

Cabinets

Now that you have mapped out your storage needs, it is time to consider the cabinets you will select to meet those needs. Cabinets form the framework of your kitchen. Not only do they allow you to store, stash, hide, and organize but they add to the general appearance of your kitchen as well. There are several methods of building and installing cabinets.

Built on the site cabinets are installed as they are built. They pro-

vide storage space, but that is about all. Generally, they lack standards of construction and quality control. Shelves are rarely adjustable and materials are usually lower quality. Even if you are determined to spare no expense and have insisted on the best of every component, there is still no guarantee of perfection and considerable chance for error. Unless you have complete confidence in the carpenter—there are still some fine old-world craftsmen who take pride in their work—or are qualified to draw up your own specifications and make sure they are expertly followed, you will probably find the end result something less than satisfactory.

You may order your cabinets from an already *stocked or standard* line which will provide certain specialized conveniences, but may not fit your individual kitchen specifications. If the standard sizes do not fit your requirements, you may need fillers or units designed to "fill in" gaps. They may vary from one to three inches, or more. Moreover, you may want special design features which standard cabinets do not always offer, though most standard lines do carry a substantial number of special purpose cabinets. Standard lines cost less than custom-made designs and can be quite satisfactory. In a standard line of stocked cabinetry, look for the certification seal of the National Kitchen Cabinet Association. This means that the cabinet meets specific standards of quality. If you want certain extra accessories or special designs in molding and finishes, they will no doubt add to the cost. Sometimes you can change the knobs and exterior designs on your own once they have been installed.

You may also choose *custom-designed* cabinets, tailor-made to suit you and your specifications. With the help of your kitchen specialist, you can have a custom-built kitchen in standard-sized units or units built to your own personal specifications, such as base cabinets designed for oversized or undersized utensils or whatever your needs dictate. That's what makes them custom made!

Delivery for custom-made cabinets will take from six to eight weeks, perhaps longer, depending upon when the factory receives the order and can begin production. Stock cabinets will take from a week to ten days for delivery, and if there are any special orders or if the dealer happens to be out of stock on a particular cabinet, it may take a week or so longer to fill the complete order.

There are basically four cabinet materials from which to choose;

wood, metal, a combination of wood and metal, and *plastic.* Which material you select will depend on personal taste, cost, durability, ease of maintenance, and workmanship. In every material, there are degrees of quality and a wide choice of colors, finishes, hardware, styling, interior fittings, and flexibility.

Wood cabinets are probably the most popular. They are durable, and flexible as they can be built to fit any specifications. Sometimes warping can occur, but that should not be a problem if you have an adequate air conditioning system with some capability for dehumidification of the moisture of housekeeping and on excessively humid days. Stained finishes are easy to care for and can be touched up if scratches do occur. They are available in both soft and hard woods. Soft woods include pine, fir, knotty pine, knotty cedar, and hemlock. As the term indicates, they are soft and will scratch easily. Hardwood varieties include birch (probably the most common), oak, maple (popular for colonial styling), and walnut. All are strong, durable, and expensive. Fruitwoods such as cherry and pecan are also popular as well as cabinets made of beech, alder, ash, and Philippine mahogany. Some of the woods in teak and sandalwood are actually birch or particle board, printed and pressed with teak and sandalwoodlike finishes.

Metal or steel are also extremely durable but scratches, dents, and mars in the enamel finish are more obvious and harder to touch up. Metal cabinets can be repainted if you wish. Depending upon the design, the interior is sometimes more usable since the cabinet frame requires little space. Combination cabinets with metal storage units and wood doors offer the advantages of both types. The doors may have changeable panels of plastic, fabric, grillwork, or other materials.

Plastic cabinets come in many types, including melamine and polyester laminates, plasticized vinyls, and molded urethanes. High-pressure laminates are made of several sheets of heavy Kraft paper, the top sheet printed with whatever pattern is desired—woodgrains are popular—then covered with a transparent melamine plastic coating. It is usually $^{1}/_{16}$-inch thick, which is the dimension used for counter tops, though $^{1}/_{32}$-inch thickness is now available in some lines. This thinner coating is less expensive and quite suitable for areas that do not get heavy wear. Keep in mind that while plastic laminates are extremely durable and sturdy, they may chip under heavy wear or with abuse. They are heat-resistant, but not fireproof.

In addition to the variety of materials, cabinets come in many different styles. The one you select will determine, along with the various "wrap-ups" we will discuss in Chapter 14, the personality of your kitchen. Styles fall under the general headings of Modern or Contemporary, Colonial, Traditional, and Provincial. The style is determined by the design elements on the cabinet doors and drawers.

Colonial usually refers to Early American, knotty pine, or pegged styling. Designs include board-and-batten, V-grooves, and pegs. Another design with a recessed or a raised panel is often referred to as American Colonial, though it is really more of a formal Georgian motif.

Traditional as we stated above is often referred to as American Colonial or formal American styling. There are many variations of traditional, including a conservative, formal cabinet with raised, recessed, or superimposed panels.

Contemporary or Modern cabinets have a clean, sleek look with smooth lines. There are often no door pulls or handles on the drawers, but rather a cutout area under the bottom edge.

Provincial is usually French or Italian. Generally there are moldings on door and drawer fronts. French designs are smoothly curved and arched while Italian motifs are more ornate.

What is popularly known as the *Mediterranean* style (referring to the countries along the Mediterranean Sea) doesn't really fall into the provincial designs, though it is Spanish, Moorish, or Italian in feeling. It is usually dark in finish, heavy in design, and often quite ornate, though there are some styles that are more subdued in feeling.

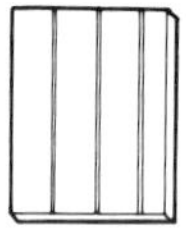

COLONIAL

TRADITIONAL

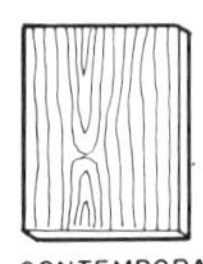

CONTEMPORARY

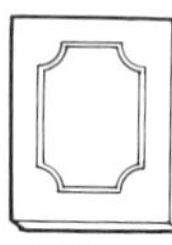

PROVINCIAL

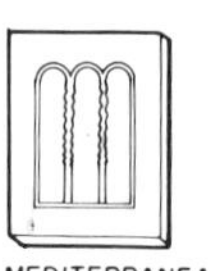

MEDITERRANEAN

Selecting cabinets

In choosing cabinet sizes always use the widest cabinet possible. It is more useful and economical. Cabinets less than 15 inches wide are practically useless unless for vertical storage, such as large trays and platters. The following guidelines are well worth noting.

•Stock cabinets come in widths from 9 to 48 inches in 3-inch increments. Base cabinets are usually $34^1/_2$ inches high and 24 inches deep. Wall cabinets are 12 to 13 inches deep.

•Quality hinging is important for convenience and safety.

•Sliding door cabinets limit accessibility since only half the cabinet is open at one time.

•Shelving should be adjustable for flexibility in storage.

•Sliding shelves are more usuable and convenient than stationary shelves in base cabinets.

•Make certain that drawers slide easily on ball bearings or by some other means, that they have automatic stops, and are removeable.

•Check to be certain that interiors are resistant to scratches, stains, and absorption of odors, and are easy to clean.

Special features that add convenience

All cabinets offer a vast array of special treatments for drawers, shelves, corners, and built-in appliances. Taking advantage of these convenient features will add immeasureably to the organization of your kitchen. Keep in mind that while some of these special features are standard, most are optional and will add to the cost. Depending upon how you work, however, they could well be worth the additional cost.

WALL CABINET EXTRAS

special corner cabinets
adjustable shelves
"see-through" shelves of metal or glass
shallow shelves for canned goods storage
step shelves
spice racks
cup racks
plate rail
cookbook shelf under cabinets

BASE CABINET EXTRAS

special corner cabinets
pull-out shelves (deep ones for casseroles, pots and pans; shallow ones for lids)
wide, shallow drawers for linen storage
waste storage (deep drawer equipped with plastic wastebasket)
"pop-up" mixer cabinet
bottle storage cabinet
pull-out table
special silver storage drawer
divided cutlery drawers
pull-out cutting surfaces
vertical file slots for trays, platters, baking pans
sliding towel racks

(base cabinet extras con't)

built-in flour and sugar canisters
bread box
pull-out ventilated bins for vegetables
sliding bars for hanging pan storage
sewing machine cabinets
canned goods storage

DOOR VARIETIES

sliding doors—glass, wood, metal, plastic
perforated hardboard doors
metal grillwork inserts
doors with interchangeable or reversible decorator panels
louvered doors, leaded glass doors
selection of finishes and designs
drop-down door to form a shelf or desk
inside-door mirrors
door storage for spices, cookbooks, and paper products
pass-through cabinets with doors on both sides

SPECIAL UNITS

full-height utility cabinet for storage of cleaning equipment
full-height pantry storage
moveable work bases
sit-down sink
towel-drying unit
storage "garage" for small appliances
storage "garage" for undercounter cart
island or peninsula serving bars
suspended wall cabinets
midway cabinets between wall and base cabinets
power unit built into counter top

Corner cabinets

Corners are real "bugaboos" in planning kitchens. Wherever cabinets meet in a corner, storage space is forfeited unless you provide a special cabinet designed to provide access to an otherwise dead corner. A 27-inch allowance for turning corners on both walls is standard, but there are some corner cabinets that require more space than that. Be sure to check the measurements of the cabinet you are considering and the kind of door opening provided. Here are several ways to handle wasted corner space.

•You can leave the corner open and provide shelves which are accessible by reaching through from the adjoining base cabinet. This is an inexpensive method of utilizing the space. Although it is inconvenient, it can be used for storage of infrequently used items.

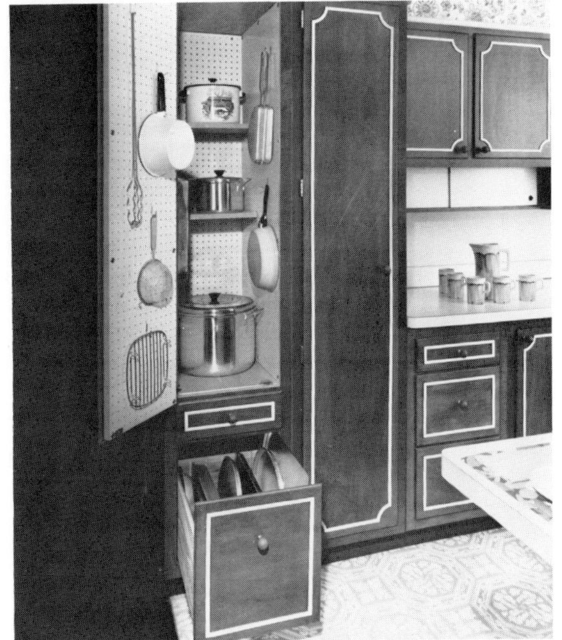

Left. Utensil storage cabinet has perforated hardwood panels at top to hang utensils, pots, pans, and other supplies on hooks provided with unit. Two adjustable shelves add storage convenience and divided bottom drawer is perfect for lids, cookie sheets, and pans. *Courtesy Wood-Mode*

Middle, left. Adjustable sliding trays hold a variety of essential pans and utensils and pull out for easy reach. Such a base cabinet is ideal when installed where most needed—near the range or food preparation center. *Courtesy Wood-Mode*

Below. Lid and cookie sheet storage cabinet is partitioned to hold things neatly and noiselessly. *Courtesy Wood-Mode*

Bottom left. Convenient hardwood pull-out chopping block. What looks like another drawer when closed is really this maple chopping block in disguise—great for preparing vegetables, meats, and sandwiches. The cabinet beneath chopping block is a concealed slide-out wastebasket unit. *Courtesy Mutschler*

Above, left. Base pull-out utensil cabinet with pegboard for hanging smaller pans and other items. Hooks are provided for this cabinet that's so handy near the range or cooking area. *Courtesy Wood-Mode*

Above, right. You'll love this pop-up mixer cabinet with fingertip control of moveable shelf for up, down, in, and out positions. Sliding tray gives extra convenience. Functional counter top above, to right, is a chopping block of beautifully grained wood . . . practical to use, easy to care for. *Courtesy Wood-Mode*

Right. This ingenious storage cabinet is designed with shelves that roll out conveniently and hold cans *in a horizontal position.* All the labels can be read at a glance and the last can is always a fingertip away. What a fantastic way to store cans and eliminate homemaker's headaches! It features eight pull-out trays and two adjustable shelves in the upper section. *Courtesy Wood-Mode*

Left. *Swingaway shelves.* Getting down on your hands and knees may be fine for keeping you in shape. But not for your temper, when the bowl or pan you need is way at the back. This swingaway shelf unit brings all the utensils right out into the open, for ready access, and it's easy to clean. Extra space inside provides "hidden" storage—narrow shelves which are the full depth of the unit but which pull out for easy reach. *Courtesy Mutschler*

Bottom, left. Corner cupboard with "pie-shape" cut-out pulls utensils to you, makes use of otherwise "dead" or hard-to-get-at space. Keeps everything at your fingertips. *Courtesy St. Charles*

Bottom, right. A hamper cabinet eliminates unsightly storage hampers in kitchen, laundry, bath, and similar areas. *Courtesy Wood-Mode*

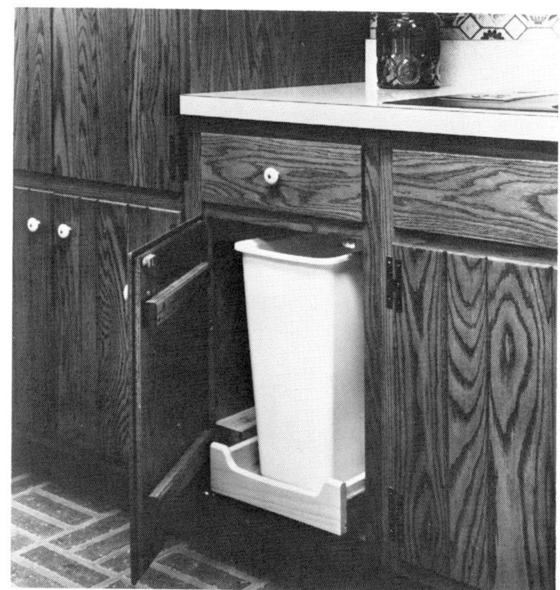

Above, left. A tilt-out waste receptacle with large, plastic waste container that is removeable. Handy for dry waste, it is clean, and, better yet, out of the way. *Courtesy Wood-Mode*

Above, right. Another neat way to bring to hand something you normally hide: a roll-out shelf for a trash receptacle near or under the sink. *Courtesy Rutt-Williams*

Right. Packaged food storage cabinet 18 inches wide, has many adjustable shelves with additional shelves in the doors . . . makes it easy to organize a variety of packaged items. Lower door rack holds taller bottles and jars and secures them behind rail. At left is a cleaning utensil cabinet which keeps these items right on hand but out of sight. Top cabinet holds a large number of cans, bottles, and boxes that contain detergent and cleaning supplies. *Courtesy Wood-Mode*

Above, left. Corner turn-out food storage cabinet with two shelves that work separately. What a nice way to use every inch of corner space. *Courtesy Wood-Mode*

Above, right. Here is what is called a minichef pantry —a base cabinet designed like a full-sized pantry. This fantastic cabinet holds an unusual number of cans and other packaged items. Center units have shelving on front and back and pivot to make contents easily accessible. Adjustable shelves in back of cabinet provide additional storage. *Courtesy Wood-Mode*

Left. Corner wall carousel cleverly uses all space in corner of top or bottom cabinet. Note leaded glass door, a nice change of pace. *Courtesy Wood-Mode*

Above, left. Corner Susan revolves to bring canned goods within easy reach wherever they're placed on corner-shaped shelves. Hinged door cabinet also accommodates corner. *Courtesy Rutt-Williams*

Above, right. *Waste Space Put to Work.* In this kitchen a "midway" storage unit fits between wall and base units. See-through sliding doors provide display space for preserves, glassware, crockery, whatever you want to keep close at hand. (Sliding wood doors are also available to keep canned goods, puddings, cereals, baby food, the sugar bowl, etc., out of sight.) The shallow depth of these midway shelves makes them especially suitable for canned goods, since more labels are visible than if cans were placed four or five deep on an ordinary shelf. *Courtesy Mutschler*

Right, middle and bottom. Spice problems? Here is a cabinet with three hardwood shelves on each side of a vertical partition, enough shelf space to hold a gourmet's assortment of spices and seasonings. The shelves are also sized right for baby foods, variety-pack cereals, or packaged *puddings and gelatin desserts. There's room* enough behind the swinging shelves to store other packaged foods. The entire piano-hinged unit *swings out for full accessibility. Courtesy Mutschler*

Left. No stooping or bending to find the can you want. This pull-out cabinet makes it easy. Canned food storage cabinet is cleverly designed with two-sided shelves that hold assorted cans, bottles, jars, and other receptacles. *Courtesy Wood-Mode*

Below, left. Chef's pantry with unbelievable storage capacity! It accommodates cans, boxes, bottles, and other containers in many shapes and sizes. Unique pivoting center units swing out to make contents completely accessible. Adjustable shelves behind one unit provide additional storage space. Longhandled cleaning utensils fit neatly behind the other center unit. Shelves on cabinet doors provide even more storage space in this compact, luxurious pantry. *Courtesy Wood-Mode*

Below, right. Base cabinet beverage storage houses divided tray for soft drinks, plain tray for other items. Located to left of refrigerator and near glass storage by sink, it is handy for ice cube accessibility. *Courtesy Coppes Napanee*

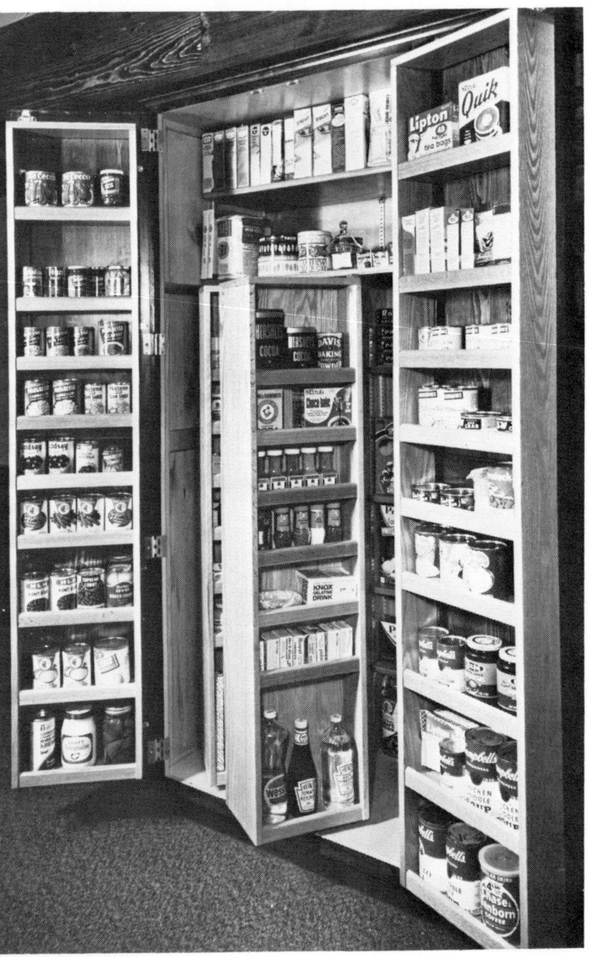

Left. Pantry storage cabinet with full-width shelf at top, three adjustable shelves in left section, and a three-shelf carousel in upper right section. Behind separate doors for base cabinet there are drawers for utensils of all shapes and sizes plus three full-width pull-out trays to store lids and shallow pans. *Courtesy Wood-Mode*

Below, left. Combination vegetable-waste storage cabinet. Divider baskets below are excellent for ventilated nonrefrigerated vegetable storage of onions, potatoes, while pull-out drawer above houses plastic container for dry waste. *Courtesy St. Charles*

Below, right. Fruit and vegetable cabinet has tote trays that are easily removed to carry to food preparation center or for cleaning. Pull-out feature provides easy, quick access. *Courtesy Wood-Mode*

Left. Another storage wall, designed as part of a beverage center, utilizes 36-inch wide, 13-inch deep utility cabinets with adjustable shelves. Everything is within easy reach, yet everything has its place. Specialized storage such as this, with a place for each item, helps to cut down on wear and tear, also breakage. *Courtesy St. Charles*

Above, left. This handsome hutch, which can be constructed from the same cabinets used in the kitchen, is just the answer for china, crystal, flatware, and linen storage. Wide, shallow trays store linen wrinkle-free and where they are quickly accessible. *Courtesy St. Charles*

Above, right. Specially lined tarnish-proof drawers in base cabinet house silver hollowware and flatware. *Courtesy St. Charles*

Left. Practical is the word for this custom-designed storage wall located at one end of the kitchen near the entrance to the dining room. Completely outfitted with specialized cabinets for linen, silver, glassware, china, and other entertaining accessories, this storage center also serves as a pantry counter for the placement of foods to be served in the dining room or for parties elsewhere. Also excellent for a kitchen buffet! *Courtesy St. Charles*

Right. To the right of the storage wall is a 24-inch deep utility cabinet with slide-out shelves—perfect for large, flat accessories. Stationary shelves above ideal for large bulky items. *Courtesy St. Charles*

•Try a lazy Susan cabinet (turntable) with a diagonal front. Inside the cabinet, revolving shelves are attached to a center shaft which spins in a full circle. This usually requires from 36 to 39 inches of wall space from the corner.

•A half-moon revolving base cabinet is designed with a cabinet door which forms a right angle and has circular shelves attached that swing out into the room as the door is opened. It requires from 36 to 39 inches of wall space.

•Swing-out shelves with one or two half-circle shelves attached to a door are excellent; they pull out when door is opened.

•Install an undercounter water heater where feasible and when necessary.

In addition to the variety of specialized cabinets and cabinet features available, consider these four special storage ideas. Your kitchen expert can work any of them into your kitchen plans and give you an estimate of the cost. With the exception of the first idea, all can be built for around $75.

1. Select a cabinet with handy roll-out shelves. Make sure it is large enough to hold every one of your appliances. Fit it into a continuous line of cabinets in an island, peninsula, or a wall arrangement to maintain the clean, uncluttered look in your kitchen. Install an outlet panel to operate several appliances at once on the top of the cabinet or on a nearby wall. Presto, you have your own appliance center where everything is within fingertip reach.

2. A jog in a wall around a chimney provides an excellent place for storage. Appliances stored on open shelves can be used on a counter equipped with plug-in stripping.

3. An appliance cart makes it easy to cook anywhere in or outside the house. Three ideas worth copying include the sliding doors, built-in edge around cart top, and built-in outlet.

4. Here a storage cabinet is flush with a built-in oven. Perforated hardboard over the counter holds hang-up appliances.

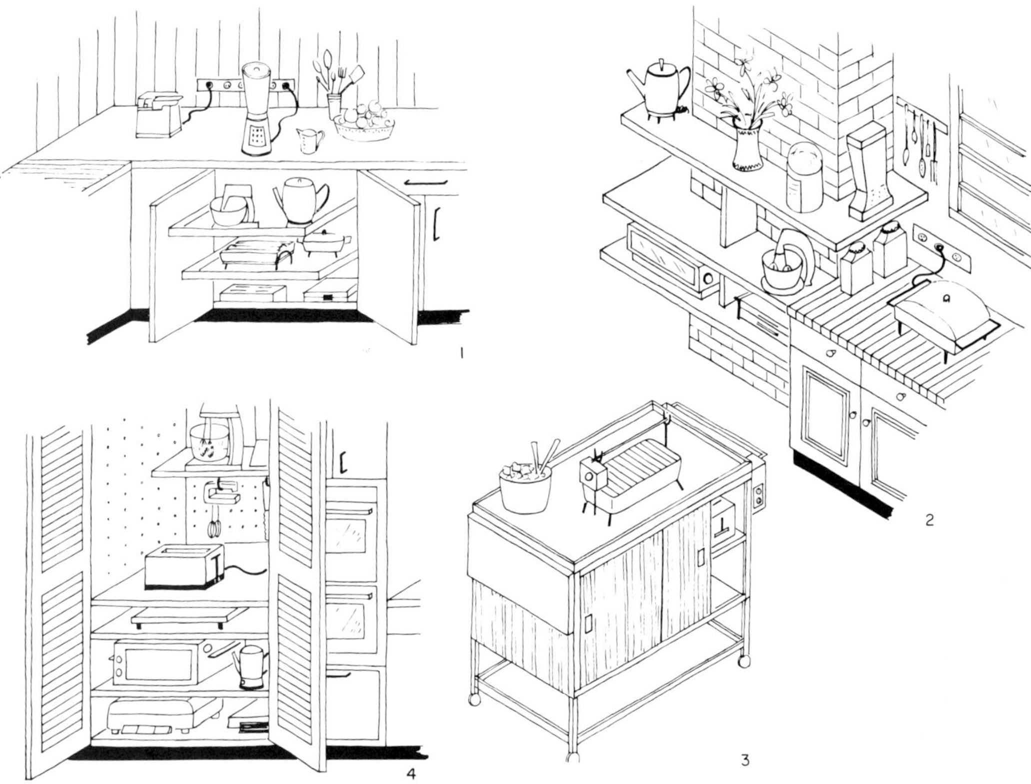

Soffit Treatments*

While you are thinking about cabinets for storage, think about the variety of uses you can make of soffits as well.

1. To use area above cabinet as storage, use Cap 8 molding as shown and slip 1/4-inch material in slots as sliding doors . . . plywood, glass, plastic, masonite, etc.

2. Soffit built after cabinet is installed usually has front face flush with front frame of cabinet. Scribe molding is used over joint. Cove might be used at ceiling, if desired.

3. Extend soffit as shown using fluorescent fixture to provide lighting for work area. Panel could be extended to provide general lighting as a lighted ceiling.

4. Alternate to example #2 uses Cap molding at top of cabinet and at ceiling instead of cleats.

5. Front face of soffit should be approximately 4 inches in back of cabinet front frame. Cap 8 molding supplies ledge for plates.

6. Soffit can be extended in this fashion to provide lighting for counter work using high-hat fixture.

7. Soffit built before cabinets are installed, extends beyond cabinet face. Cove molding is needed under soffit and may also be used at ceiling.

*Illustrations courtesy IXL-Westinghouse.

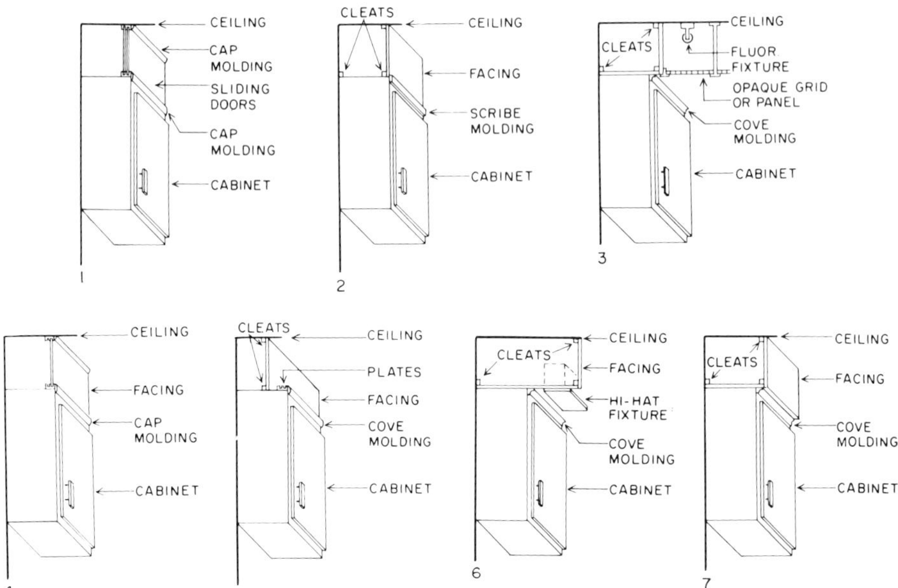

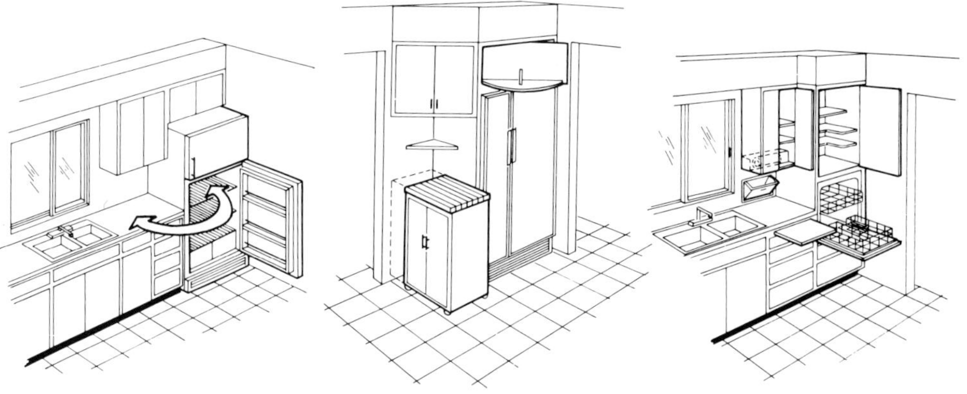

Storage Sketchbook*

Placement of the refrigerator

If your refrigerator has a right-hinge door, place it to the right of the adjacent work center, so that the door opens away from the counter for easy loading and unloading. Do the opposite for a left-hinged door.

Double-duty counter with over-the-refrigerator storage

Make the base cabinet into a moveable cart and locate it next to the refrigerator as a work center. On casters, you can use it in other areas. Install a wood chopping block as a counter top for convenient chopping, mincing, and dicing. Use the space above the refrigerator to store infrequently used items. A half-round shelf which swings out for fingertip access is a handy solution. Or install vertical dividers spaced 5 inches apart for such items as cookie sheets, baking pans, muffin, and cake pans.

Raising the dishwasher

Whoever heard of raising the dishwasher? We have and recommend it if you find stooping and bending a problem. It can be raised conveniently from 6 to 12 inches above the floor. Build in a special cabinet above it with U-shaped shelves to house china and glassware.

*Illustrations courtesy Kitchen Planning and Storage Ideas for Balanced Power Kitchens.

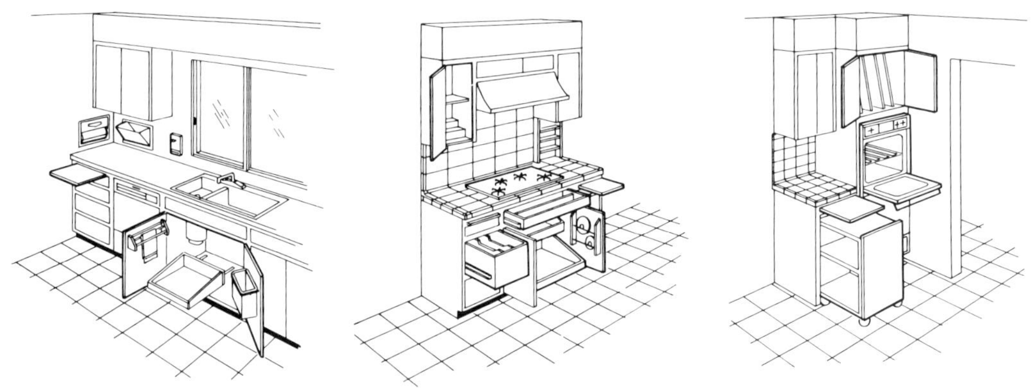

A special cleanup center

Consider this oversize sink area. Useful for large, bulky items that will not fit in the dishwasher, it also includes such conveniences as a garbage disposer, built-in paper towel dispenser, trash chute, built-in can opener, pull-out cutting board, towel-drying rack, undersink pull-out shelf, and a door-mounted trash container. Below: The same kind of installation with a trash compactor.

Specialized range center

Special purpose storage can make the range center more functional —divided drawer, slide-out pan shelves, lid racks, slotted drawer, and spice shelves. Full extension roller hardware gives easy access to these deep drawers and pan shelves.

Built-in oven area

Set back far enough so its door does not open into the doorway, this built-in oven is well planned for narrow passages. Note the slotted cabinet above the oven, heatproof ceramic tile counter, pull-out board, and an undercounter cart that makes sensible use out of a small space.

Moveable island

Construct a storage cabinet on wheels. Make it from one large or two small base cabinets, install casters underneath and design it to slide beneath the regular counter top. (Use lower base cabinets to allow room for sliding in and out.) A laminated hardwood top is excellent for both food preparation and serving. Use it as an island, at the end of a counter, or on the patio—wherever you need it.

Specialty roll-out shelves

Design a compact undercounter pantry with roll-out shelves. A variety of shelf heights accommodates large and small items. It is a good idea to use heavy duty hardware that will support a large supply of canned and packaged foods. Keep in mind that both wall and base cabinets can be made more functional with cabinet and shelf organizers. You can purchase a variety of dish racks, spice shelves, lazy Susan turntables, and pull-out shelves that make items easily accessible. Pull-out drawer cabinets and shelves eliminate stooping and bending, not to mention hunting for items you need quickly.

Custom-planned storage

Suit the storage to the need. Wall cabinets with adjustable shelves, half shelves, step shelves, and shelves on doors provide various storage needs. Fixtures installed either below the wall cabinet or recessed under the step-shelf supply counter lighting. Pull-out cutting board gives you extra space, yet allows easy access to drawers beneath. Install pull-out shelf racks in base cabinets for accessible storage. Note drawer dividers for separating cooking tools. Some dividers available for flatware. Spices and small utensils are within fingertip reach in midway units installed underneath wall cabinets and enclosed with sliding glass doors.

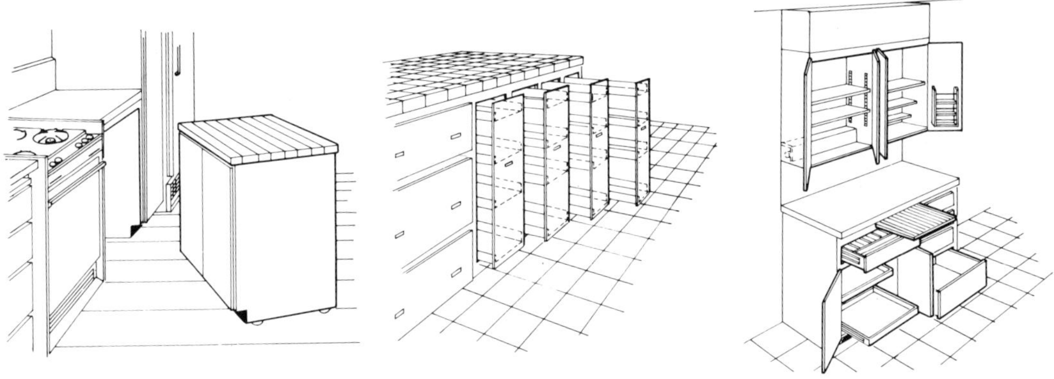

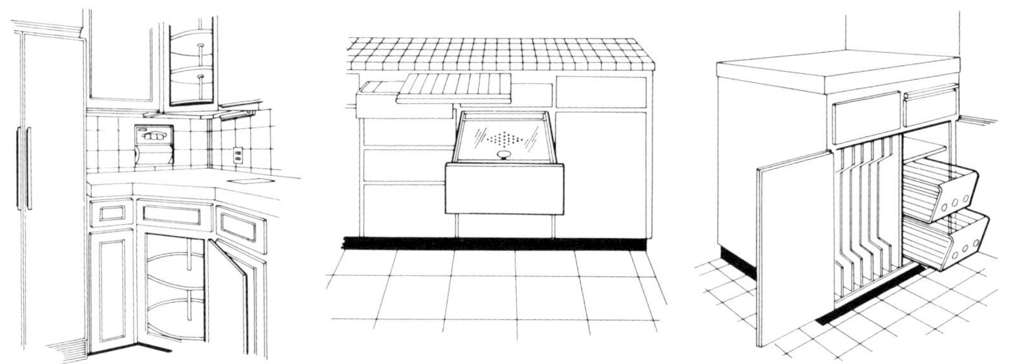

Corner storage

•Revolving shelves above and below the counter top enhance the convenience of corner storage. A small undercabinet light brightens the corner and the built-in mixer-blender along with a recessed paper dispenser are convenient features.

•The "notch"-type revolving shelves allow you to stand closer to the corner to reach the lazy Susan shelves in the upper cabinet. Midway cabinets below wall cabinet are excellent for spices as is the rail above the counter.

•Half-circle shelves attached to the cabinet door swing out and make use of dead corner storage. Raised lip on shelves help to hold stored items in place.

•Hard-to-reach corner storage next to the dishwasher has been put to good use with half-round, swing-out shelves. Pivots are attached to the cabinet frame so each shelf swings out independent of the cabinet door. Ask your carpenter how to make them, or if he can design something similar for you.

Bread storage

With the increased interest in bread making, it might be very worthwhile to consider installing a bread box. Near the bread board it's a good idea to make sure one drawer will fit the metal bread drawer bins available. This frees the counter area usually required for a bread box.

There are drawer bins available for sugar, flour, rice, and other similar items.

Tray and unrefrigerated food storage

Divided storage for trays and large platters makes them more accessible. Pull-out ventilated bins are ideal for storage of potatoes, onions, etc. They come in a variety of sizes.

Unusual sink storage

Use shallow, tilt-out, and waterproof bins to hold plate scrapers, dish mops, cleansing pads and sponges.

Towel bar and deep drawer storage

Pull-out towel bars in a small cabinet keeps them accessible and dry. No need ever to throw a wet towel into a linen hamper! Note the deep drawers that are excellent for pots, pans, large sacks of flour, sugar, grain, rice, etc.

Small appliance storage

•Enclose space between wall and base cabinets as a garage for small appliances. Install adequate number of convenience outlets inside for operation of appliances. Cover "garage" with roll-down folding, sliding doors, or lift-up panels.

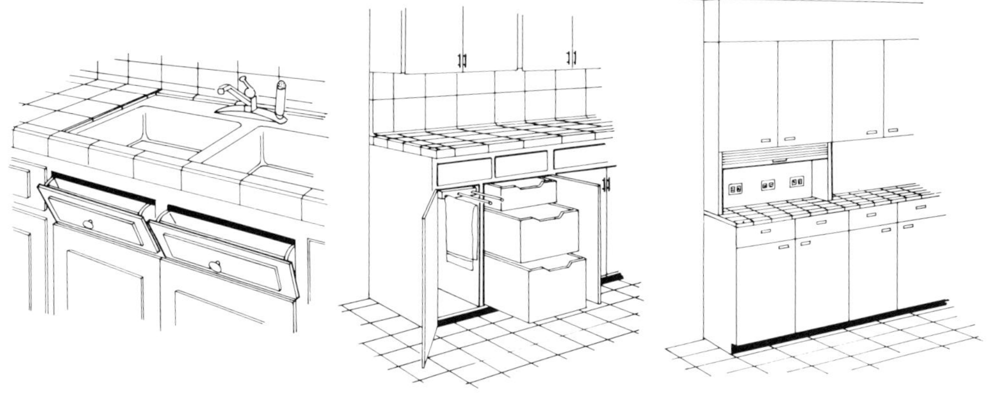

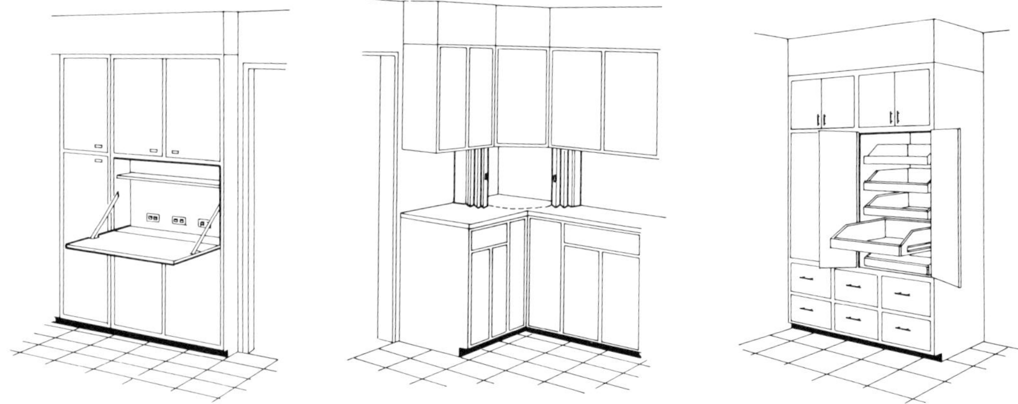

•Design a drop-down counter as a small appliance center, again installing enough convenience outlets for convenient operation. The idea is applicable for a planning desk, gift-wrapping area, or sewing center.

•Utilize a corner area as a small appliance center. Excellent for appliances often used on the counter such as a mixer, blender, toaster, or coffee maker. Folding doors make an excellent coverup.

•A pantry cabinet normally used for canned goods makes an excellent small appliance center. Pull-out shelves provide easy accessibility.

Remodel a closet—make it a walk-in pantry

Convert a closet or build a small room and line it with shallow shelves. Add doors with shelves and a light and you've your own indoor

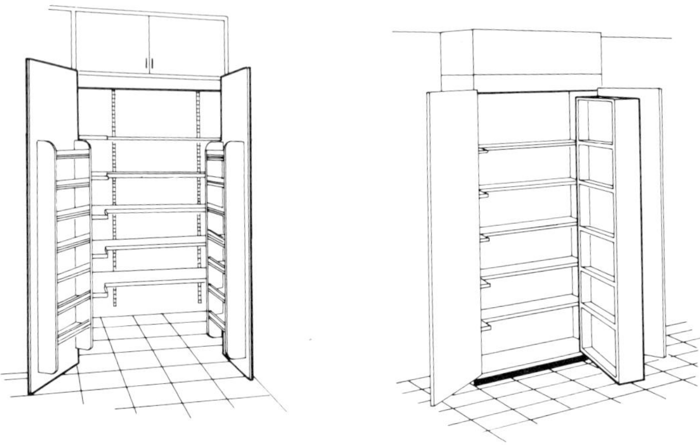

market. Make sure shelves are adjustable to accommodate varying package, can, and jar sizes.

A secret pantry

This special swing-out pantry has storage shelves on both sides. Each shelf boasts a raised lip to hold objects in place when unit is being turned. Open the door completely and you'll find shallow shelves behind it—one-can deep.

A wall pantry for entertaining needs

Here is a floor-to-ceiling pantry, built against a free wall. It has adjustable shelves and provides ample storage for all your "Sunday" best dinnerware, crystal, flatware, and linens.

"Permanent-press" linen closet

If you have the space and you dislike pressing already ironed or no-iron linens before you set the table, build yourself a special closet for hanging linens. This floor-to-ceiling 6-to 12-inch deep cabinet utilizes large diameter closet poles to support linens.

Wine storage

A wine and beverage rack made from clay and cement pipes or decorative blocks is convenient and inexpensive. Locate it in an area with cool room temperature.

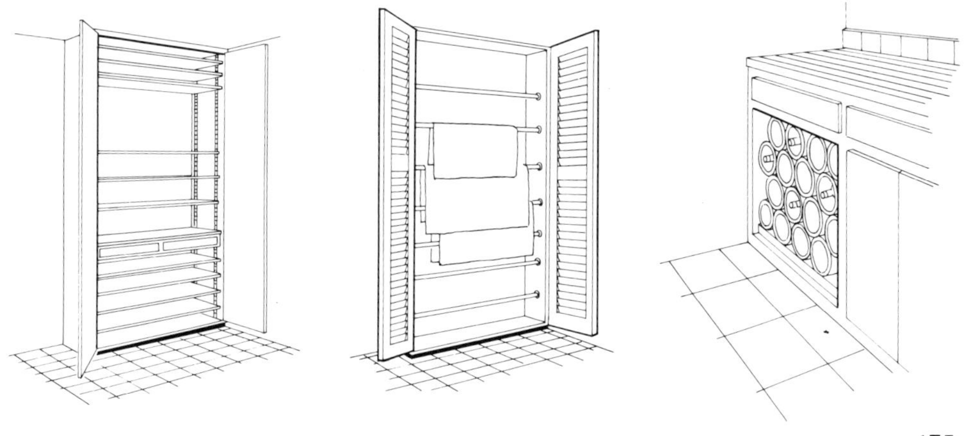

CHAPTER 13

Appliances and Equipment

Your appliances can be enormous aids or implacable enemies. Oven temperatures that are dependably undependable and refrigerators that need constant defrosting turn kitchen chores into pure drudgery. The newest appliances make life at once easier and more complex, for along with convenience comes a more exacting, sophisticated route to shortcut living. Self-cleaning ovens, microwave ovens, ranges that cook with cool, smooth top surfaces, no-frost refrigerators, and programmed laundry equipment cut your time and effort, but also make demands upon your knowledge and skill in their use.

Once again think carefully about your particular life-style. Which appliances and which features will you continue to use after the novelty wears off? Are your needs likely to change in the near future?

If you are remodeling in stages decide now what you plan to buy at a future date. That way you can install base cabinets now that are the same size as the appliance you intend to buy. When the time comes you will be ready to slip out the cabinet and replace it with a new appliance. Be sure to provide whatever plumbing or wiring requirements will be necessary in anticipation of the new appliance.

What about built-ins? They give a kitchen a chic, streamlined look, but in some cases have certain drawbacks. A built-in oven and separate cook top, for example, take up more space than a freestanding range. Built-in appliances on the other hand allow you more flexibility in planning in that you can place your cook top in one place and the oven in another.

There are many possibilities in built-in equipment. For example, you might need a dishwasher now, but do not want to go to the expense of building it in. In this case, you might purchase a convertible model, use it as a portable now, and build it in permanently at a later date.

In some cases it is possible to achieve that built-in look with freestanding appliances, thus saving space and money. Freestanding appliances have taken on such a sleek look these days, with squared off corners and thin lines, that many of them actually look built-in after they are installed.

Whatever your preferences in new appliances, be sure to shop the market. Look for features that are meaningful and useful to you rather than those which are merely "new fangled." Make sure to check the appliance specifications against the space you have available and be certain that you can provide the proper installation requirements such as electricity, plumbing, and gas. Is the appliance durable? Will it be difficult to clean? Is it the appropriate model for your work habits and your family's needs?

Above all, check the reliability of your dealer and manufacturer. Read the guarantee and warranty thoroughly and ask about any terms that are not clear to you. Check to see who will service the appliance and if there are any hidden costs such as delivery and installation. Always look for seals of safety and certification that tell you an appliance has been tested for safety, performance, and durability. Such seals will be the UL seal of the Underwriters Laboratories, Inc., the AHAM certification seals of the Association of Home Appliance Manufacturers, and the blue star seal of the American Gas Association.

If you are using a professional kitchen dealer or a specialist who will take over your entire job of remodeling, he will, of course, be responsible for seeing to it that all the above terms are clear to you and will spell out who is responsible for what. Nevertheless, it is imperative that you take the responsibility as a good consumer to follow through yourself. If you are doing the remodeling yourself, all the more reason for you to check on these details. See kitchen template for appliance sizes available, page 214.

Before you begin your shopping expedition, you might like to have a copy of *The Handbook for the Informed Consumer*, written by the Major Appliance Consumer Action Panel. It supplies the details of purchase, use, and care of major appliances. Write to MACAP, 20 North Wacker Drive, Chicago, Illinois 60606. The booklet costs under a dollar and will prove invaluable.

Ranges

Whether you choose gas or electric will depend upon your installation requirements, which you prefer to cook with, what is available, and, of course, the cost. Both generally provide the same features and cooking ability, but some cooks prefer the instant shut-off of heat in a gas range, while others opt for the retained heat capability in electric units.

Electric ranges require a 208 (for some metropolitan areas such as New York) or 220/240-volt line. It depends upon location. Gas ranges require a gas line and a 115-volt circuit for lights and controls.

There is a wide selection of types and designs of ranges from freestanding models with one or two ovens and broilers and eye-level designs with one oven on top and the other below the cooking surface to built-in surface cook tops and separate built-in single or double ovens. There are slide-in or drop-in models in freestanding design that can be set between cabinets to give a built-in look and stack-on models that can be set on a counter top or a special base cabinet.

As I said above, an oven and cook top installed side by side are space eaters. The smallest combination of 48 inches is 18 inches wider than a freestanding 30-inch range and 12 inches wider than a 36-inch range. However, you might save space in a particular area by installing the oven in one center and the cook top in another. Separate installation gives you the option of having one cooking surface and two ovens or vice versa, depending on your cooking habits.

Built-in ovens in either gas or electric can be installed in several ways. Cabinet manufacturers provide special cabinets for built-ins. Many come with a special wraparound cover and can be stacked onto a base cabinet or counter. Ovens can also be installed directly into and flush with a wall. Built-in ovens come in a variety of combinations including a single oven, oven and separate broiler, oven and warmer, or two ovens in a single frame.

Range tops may be installed directly into counter tops. There is even a model which fits into the counter and folds back when more counter space is needed. Depending upon the number of burners or units, ranges fit into cabinets from 15 to 48 inches wide or even larger.

Ranges may be installed in an island or peninsula and do not necessarily have to fit into a cabinet. The space below may be open or it may be used for storage. The range may be installed next to the built-in oven or in another area of the kitchen.

You alone determine where and how your range will be installed. If you are less than 5 feet, 4 inches tall, install the range top at a height of 32 to 34 inches. If you are average height, a counter height of 36 inches is comfortable. If you are taller, raise the height of your range top a bit. To determine the best heights for you, see page 218.

Ovens and ranges, both freestanding and built-in, come in a variety of models with many new features. You can have a top in a variety of sizes with controls either on top or on the front panel. Some models have a temperature-controlled burner or unit. A new design is a smooth ceramic or glass cook top. Once again this new model comes in both built-in and freestanding ranges.

The most outstanding breakthroughs in oven convenience are the automatic self-cleaning and continuous cleaning models. In a self-cleaning oven the soil is cleaned during a separate high heat cycle. With continuous-cleaning models oven surfaces are specially treated to clean during the cooking operation at normal temperatures. Usually this method of cleaning is not as effective as the automatic self-cleaning type, but it does provide a presentably clean surface if you don't mind a few stains. If such surfaces are scratched, efficiency may be impaired.

Other features include automatic oven timers, clocks that let you "cook without watching"—the oven turns on automatically and turns off when the food is cooked—rotisseries, automatic meat thermometers, warming shelves, grills, cook and hold settings, thermostatic controls, speed broilers, infrared gas broilers, warning or signal lights, infinite heat controls, and changeable decorative door panels.

A built-in oven, like a range top, should be geared to your height and work habits. Most cooks prefer an installation that places the oven door between 1 and 7 inches below the elbow when open. (These measurements will vary depending upon whether oven is gas or electric. Many women prefer 3 inches below elbow height and the top surface of the fully opened door of an electric oven.) *Electronic ranges and microwave ovens* (high-frequency cooking) cut cooking time literally to seconds for some recipes, minutes for others. Microwaves penetrate the food and produce heat within which does the cooking. The food gets hot, but the oven and utensils stay cool. You can purchase one as a complete range with a surface cooking top and a conventional oven or as a built-in oven and tabletop range. Microwave ranges usually require 220/240 volts, although some may call for 110/115 volts in which event cooking time is increased.

Refrigerator/Freezers

These fall into two categories, the combination refrigerator/freezer with two separate doors and the conventional one-door model with an inside frozen-food storage compartment. The combinations are available with the freezer on top, at the bottom, or with the two sections located side by side. The freezer compartment in a conventional one-door model maintains temperatures from 10 to 15 degrees F. and is used only for making ice cubes and very short time storage of commercially frozen foods. In two-door combinations, the freezer is a true freezer which maintains temperatures from −5 degrees F. to +5 degrees F. It can be used to freeze foods. Some must be defrosted manually, others are automatic. The most popular design is the freezer which never forms frost.

These new models with their added convenience do increase running time, noise level, and operating costs. It is possible now to determine how much any new refrigerator or freezer will cost to operate by checking the energy consumption figures when you buy it. To compute the average operating cost you multiply the KWH (kilowatt hours-per month) figure by the energy cost on your electric bill.

Popular refrigerator features include specialized storage compartments for meat, vegetables, fruit, butter, cheese, and eggs; adjustable shelves; removable interior parts for easy cleaning, exterior dispensers for ice cubes, crushed ice, water and beverages; casters or rollers for easier floor cleaning; lighted interiors; quick-chill compartments; automatic ice makers or add-on ice makers; powersaver switches that let you reduce power consumption and operating expense; and special decorative front panels.

Size is an important factor in your selection. How large a refrigerator do you really need? Fresh food storage compartments should provide approximately 8 cubic feet for a family of two and 1 cubic foot for each additional person. Add 2 cubic feet if you do a lot of entertaining. The freezer space should provide approximately 2 cubic feet per person.

Be sure to check kitchen and ventilation space required, door and hallway clearance for delivery, and whether the kitchen plan requires right- or left-hand door openings. Some models have reversible doors.

Freezers

There are two types—the chest and the upright. *The chest freezer* requires the most floor space, stores larger, bulkier packages, and usually requires manual defrosting, although newer ones are available in no-frost models. The initial cost of this model is less. Small models, some with counter tops, may fit at the end of a counter and provide additional work space. If you plan to install wall cabinets above the freezer, be sure to account for the lid opening. Larger models can, of course, be located in other suitable areas, such as basements and pantries. Sizes vary from 32 to 72 inches wide by 27 to 32 inches deep; height is 36 inches.

The *upright freezer* requires less floor space and packages are more easily accessible. It is available in both manual and no-frost models.

If you have a space problem, there are *compact* freezers available in top-opening chest models and front-opening upright models. If kitchen space is not a problem, a good rule of thumb in selecting freezer size is to figure 6 cubic feet per family member. Keep in mind, too, your shopping habits and amount of freezer space in your refrigerator.

Always ask whether or not the warranty provides for food loss. If it does, check in what amounts and under what conditions. Popular freezer features include signal lights to indicate whether current is on or off or the temperature is too high, automatic reset mechanism or motor protection device; adequate drainage for easy water removal on no-frost models; removable basket or adjustable shelves; counter-balanced lid on chest types; separate quick-freeze sections; lighted interiors; easy-to-read controls, and rollers or casters to slide the unit out for easy cleaning.

Garbage Disposers

They will handle food waste with dispatch, by grinding it small enough to be flushed away quickly and effectively. There are two types—the *continuous* feed and the *batch* feed.

The *continuous-feed* model is turned on and off by a switch which enables you to add waste while the disposer is in operation, feeding it slowly until all the waste has flushed away. A rubber backsplash over the opening keeps waste and water down.

The *batch-feed* type requires a cover which activates the grinder. Waste is put into the disposer, the cover is locked into position, and the grinder is activated to grind one "batch" at a time.

Check to see if there are local city ordinances forbidding the use of a disposer and make sure your sewage system is capable of handling the residue. Check on installation costs. Installation of continuous feed models is higher, but purchase cost is usually less. To economize on installation, install the disposer at the same time as the dishwasher. Ask about acoustical installation for sound control.

Popular features include heavy-duty motors, high-bulk cutters for husks, corn cobs, etc.; grind wheels and shredders made of corrosion-resistant materials corrosion-resistant parts; antijamming features; circuit breaker or automatic reset switch to prevent overheating of motor, and an overload reset to prevent overloading.

It is possible to have a disposer with a septic tank system, but the septic tank must be properly designed and sized for your family. To determine the correct size, check current FHA Minimum Property Standards for septic tanks. Septic tank regulations for disposers, dishwashers, and washing machines require a:

- 750-gallon tank for a two-bedroom house
- 900-gallon tank for a three-bedroom house
- 1,000-gallon tank for a four-bedroom house
- 250-gallon additional capacity for each additional bedroom

Dishwashers

These are available in freestanding, built-in, portable, and convertible types. Convertible models can be used as portable units and may be permanently installed at a later date. There are also undersink models and dishwasher eye-level range combinations with the dishwasher where the lower oven would normally be.

Popular features include laminated plastic or wood tops on freestanding models; a variety of washing cycles, including short wash, prerinse, rinse-hold, scrub, gentle, and soak; racks designed for flexibility in loading; booster units for raising water temperatures; automatic detergent and rinse agent dispensers; convenient cord length and cord storage facility for portable and convertible models; handles and casters on portable units; stop switch; cycle indicator; varying water distribution patterns; spray arms; impellers; and rust- and scratch-resistant door liners.

Ask your plumber to make sure the drain is adequate for both dishwasher and disposer when in use at the same time.

Trash Compactors

This is the latest addition to the family of kitchen appliances. It has the ability to compress trash to one-quarter its original volume. About half the width of a dishwasher—15 to 18 inches—it requires a 115-volt circuit and is powered by a 1/3 horsepower motor. The trash is compressed into neat packages, weighing about 20 to 25 pounds. A water-resistant, polyethylene-lined Kraft bag fits into place inside the compactor and contains the trash until it is full enough to be sealed and carried out for pickup. Available in freestanding or undercounter models, it crushes most food waste or garbage, including cartons, plastic bottles, glass, and metal cans. However, it is best for dry trash and does not replace the garbage disposer. The unit contains deodorizer sprays to control odor. Each time the compactor compresses, the deodorizer is activated.

Water Heaters

Your choice is either gas or electric, which, of course, depends on your fuel supply and preference. Electric models require a 220/240-volt circuit; gas models a gas line. In both gas and electric two types are available—*the standard storage* type and the *quick-recovery* model. The heating capacity of the quick-recovery heater, equipped with extra-quick heating features, is greater than that of the standard storage model. Sometimes a smaller quick-recovery type will provide the same convenience as a larger storage-type model.

Water heaters vary in capacity from 30 to 100 gallons. To determine the right one for you, consider the size of your family and their needs. How many baths or showers are taken at one time? What are your laundering habits? How many appliances requiring the use of hot water, such as dishwasher and washing machine, will be in use at one time?

While most water heaters are not usually located in the kitchen, often a small model may utilize wasted corner space. If you have a small water heater and plan to add a dishwasher for the first time or perhaps a compact washer, you might want to consider installing a supplemental water heater in the kitchen, either undercounter or in a corner.

When installing a gas water heater locate it as close as possible to a vertical vent for combustion products and good air circulation. In any event, wherever you locate any water heater, be sure to provide access to the drain valve so that you can drain accumulated mineral deposits when necessary, especially if you live in a hard water area. While these deposits will not really harm the tank or decrease heating efficiency, they may create a small reduction in the storage capacity over long periods.

Built-In Equipment

As I said before, built-in appliances give your kitchen a sleek look with a custom-built personality. They know few limitations and can be adapted to an individual user's measurements and installed in many unconventional ways.

I have already discussed built-in ovens and ranges in some detail. You might also want to consider built-in refrigerators, freezers, dishwashers, laundry equipment, and other conveniences such as keep-warm ovens, griddle and barbecue grills, built-in can openers, and toasters. A refrigerator and freezer may be installed side by side, one on top of the other in sizes designed for such installation, or at opposite sides of the room. Be sure they have adequate ventilation space and a clearance of 3 inches all around for air circulation. Dishwashers, washers, and dryers may also be built-in in a number of different ways. Discuss the possibilities with your contractor.

Built-ins come in a variety of colors and finishes. Some of the most popular finishes are bright or brushed stainless steel and antique copper.

Sinks

Although we do not normally call a sink an appliance, it really functions in that capacity. There are so many styles and designs with unusual convenience features, it would be less than accurate to call them anything else.

Sinks are available in stainless steel or porcelain enamel. Porcelain enamel on cast iron offers a variety of colors and styles. Stainless steel is durable, improves in patina with age, and requires little care. It costs more, but the prices will vary according to the gauge of steel and the content of nickel and chrome. An 18-gauge is heavier and better than a 20-gauge. Chrome gives it durability and nickel makes it corrosion-resistant. When you see two or more figures in relation to steel, such as $^{18}/_{8}$, it means that the mixture is 18 percent chrome and 8 percent nickel.

There are single, double, and triple bowls and all sorts of combinations from corner designs to those with center sink compartments for disposer installation. Hospitality or deep bowl bar-type sinks with gooseneck faucet assemblies are excellent as second sinks in kitchens and in bar installations for family rooms or dens. See page 33.

There are many styles of faucet assemblies, but the single-lever designs that mix the water to your desired temperature seem to be the most popular. Popular sink features include a built-in food center either to the right or left side, a retractable spray for handy rinsing, soap or lotion dispensers, remote control drains, and hardwood cutting boards that fit over the top.

In a two-bowl sink, it is wise to have one deeper than the other. Although experts have suggested that if you have a dishwasher, a single-bowl sink is adequate, two bowls are always more efficient and convenient. For example, you can use one for cleaning vegetables or berries while the other one is used for normal meal preparation.

What to Do If You Have an Appliance Problem

If you have a problem with one of your major appliances, there are a few things you can do to resolve it satisfactorily:

1. First, doublecheck the electric plug, fuses, operating controls and consult your instruction manual to see if there is something you can do on the spot to correct it.
2. Next, check with your dealer or servicing agency to correct it.
3. If you cannot resolve the problem locally write or call the manufacturer with all the details, stating the exact problem, the appliance, and model number, name of the dealer, date of purchase, etc.
4. If you feel this will not solve the complaint, write MACAP (The Major Appliance Consumer Action Panel), 20 North Wacker Drive, Chicago, Illinois 60606.

CHAPTER 14

Kitchen Wrap-Ups

The mechanical components—appliances, proper wiring and plumbing, sufficient storage, properly organized—that you choose for your kitchen are what make it run efficiently, but the materials in which you wrap it all up are what finally give it the image you have in mind.

The wide variety of new materials and furnishings with easy-care features such as washable wall coverings, no-wax vinyl flooring, and soil-resistant kitchen carpeting, often makes selection a confusing matter. Your choice should be guided by durability, cost, ease of maintenance and resistance to heat, soil, and grease.

On the following pages you will find a complete evaluation of all kitchen furnishings including ceiling treatment, wall coverings, flooring, counter tops, window treatments, and color possibilities. Study them carefully before shopping the market.

It might make your selection easier if you pick one of the major components first and then work around it, selecting and choosing items that match and complement. Keep in mind that it is possible to assemble your entire kitchen with a "total look." Coordinated wall covering and flooring, matching appliances and housewares, and stylized cabinetry make it easy to give your kitchen a "coordinated" theme.

Counter Tops

It is the counter top that ties your entire kitchen together and connects the work centers into one integral unit. The counters cover such a major portion of the kitchen area that their importance cannot be minimized.

New Materials Bring Elegance

Here is a new approach to kitchen decorating—an atmosphere of elegance that is achieved simply by the use of new materials and color. The unique design components that make it attractive and workable include:

•Nylon kitchen carpeting—quiet, resilient, moisture-resistant, and so easy to clean.

•Walnut cabinets—warm and mellow hardwood kitchen cabinets with walnut exteriors; the refrigerator door is paneled to match.

•Metal cabinet handles—sleek, black, and contemporary.

•Fiberglas masonry to simulate a brick wall adds texture and color. It comes in 4 X 8-inch nail-on sheets. Lightweight, it is simple to install, easy to clean, and heat-resistant.

•"Cane" window detail—panels of plastic black mesh on acrylic sheets encased in wood frames offer an unusual window treatment. These frames slide up under the dropped ceiling line for access to the counter storage area. Panels snap out for cleaning windows. (For an inside kitchen installation the panels can enclose artificial lighting.)

•Black appliances—a sophisticated touch, to say the least.

•Laminated plastic counter tops—cool green, easy to clean, and so attractive.

•Decorative lighting, normally used as living or dining room fixtures, adds a final touch of elegance.

•Drink dispenser installed in a ventilated closet. A touch of a button and you've got hot or cold water for preparing beverages or soups.

Courtesy American Home *Magazine*

Simplicity and superb efficiency characterize this long, narrow kitchen. At left, the grill, cook top, broiler, sink, and dishwasher are housed in a counter topped with maple cutting board. The opposite wall lines up refrigerator, built-in ovens, and a generous array of storage cupboards. Daylight enters through the large window over the sink and the top of the Dutch door, augmented by ceiling fluorescent panels. Flooring is ceramic tile, whose random-textured surface and walnut glaze are easy to clean. Highlighting easy maintenance is ceramic tile on walls. *Courtesy American Olean*

Not only do they serve as the runway and landing strip for all your kitchen activities but they play a leading role in the decorative scheme as well. Color choice here is most important as the counter top is one of the first things you see when you enter the kitchen. Along with the color selection of your appliances, counter tops determine the entire color scheme of the kitchen.

Keep in mind, too, that the counter tops take the brunt of all kitchen activities and must therefore be selected on the basis of durability, cleanability, and resistance to stain and spotting. There are two basic counter top materials from which to choose: laminated plastic and ceramic tile.

Laminated plastic is a high-pressure laminate such as Formica, Micarta, and Textolite. It is highly durable, easy to clean, and resistant to heat, staining, and moisture. However, it can be damaged by extreme

This corridor kitchen, with utility room adjacent, is all wrapped up in loveliness. Besides the convenience of colorfully designed appliances—side-by-side refrigerator, electronic oven, dishwasher, trash compactor, and drop-in range—the parquet flooring, enameled woodwork, bright floral wall covering and light-colored counter tops add warmth and charm. Other special touches include open shelves over the refrigerator for artful objects, wine rack, shuttered windows, ceramic canisters, and wooden cooking tools on the wall. *Courtesy Hotpoint*

Corridor kitchen goes supergraphic in design and decor. Ultramodern, the clean, sleek lines make this kitchen easy to work in and keep clean with washable, wipeable surfaces —laminated plastic counter tops, cabinets, and vinyl tile flooring. Dropped ceiling, decorative hanging light fixtures, and recessed down lights add warmth. *Courtesy Hotpoint*

Two Kitchens with a Graphic Approach

In this kitchen color takes over to separate the main work area from the eating area by means of a supergraphic that zigs up the door to the basement, swerves across the ceiling, and dashes down the swinging porthole door to the laundry room (not shown). Flooring is sheet vinyl, cut to desired widths, cabinet fronts are plastic laminate, and the door and ceiling designs are painted on. *Courtesy Mary Osborne; Photographer, James Brett*

This corridor kitchen reflects the talented artistry of the owner who wanted to display her skill in practical ways —hence the graphic designs and stylized illustrations on the kitchen cabinets. Sliding doors keep the designs in view. Again, ample use of white helps to reflect the light on counte tops and surfaces. *Courtesy* American Home *Magazine*

heat and will burn if you are not careful. It is available in a glossy finish or a matte finish. While the smooth or glossy surface is much easier to keep clean, the matte finish is glare-resistant. A $^{1}/_{16}$-inch thick grade is best for counter top applications. Anything thinner, such as $^{1}/_{32}$-inch, though less expensive, is recommended only for vertical applications such as wall paneling.

Laminated plastic tops may be *self-edged* or *post-formed.* The more popular *self-edge* design is flat with a squared off edge of the same material. It also has a 4-inch high backsplash, also self-edged, though you can make backsplashes as high or low as you like. Many prefer not to use a backsplash but to carry the plastic finish up the wall to the bottom of the wall cabinet. Since the wall is then easier to clean, this application is especially practical in areas where a good deal of mixing and cooking takes place.

The *post-form design* is one complete, slightly curved sweep from the bottom of the front edge to the top of the backsplash. I find it an obstacle to smooth work flow, and, in my opinion, not as attractive as the self-edge.

Ceramic tile is another popular counter-top material. You will find it used mostly in the West and Southwest areas where the Spanish and Mexican influences are popular and in areas where Country Provincial is prevalent.

There are many colors and designs in ceramic tile. It is heatproof and durable, though not chip-resistant. One prime disadvantage is that it increases dish breakage and the grouting between tiles may be hard to clean.

Insert materials used for cutting surfaces or as landing areas for hot pots and pans are becoming increasingly popular. They include:

• *Stainless steel* which is heatproof, durable, and easy to clean and care for. It is also expensive. Stainless steel is especially useful near the range and sink areas.

• *Wood,* either laminated or natural, is excellent for cutting, kneading, and rolling out pastries. It is especially durable and moderately priced, but is limited in heat resistance. Though not difficult to clean, it does require regular care and mut be oiled periodically. Its appearance looks "used" and "spotty" in short order.

• *Glass ceramic or marble* is extremely heat-resistant and is excellent for kneading, rolling out dough, and for candy making. The glass ceramic surface, but not the marble, can be used for cutting as well.

Look what wallpaper can do to spark up an old kitchen! And it can be done on a shoestring. Simple shelves over the sink provide easy-to-reach storage; paper towel dispenser and can opener flank the sink where they are needed most. *Courtesy* Modern Bride *Magazine*

Wallpaper-covered plywood provides a frame for the refrigerator, makes it look built-in. Design is echoed in valance board above window. Note how birdcagelike light fixture complements the "canary" design in the wallpaper. Useful accessories are stored atop cabinets—a practical idea. *Courtesy* Modern Bride *Magazine*

Open-plan kitchen takes advantage of the view. Storage concentrates in base cabinets with the exception of cabinets over and next to the range, providing a pleasant, practical change of pace. Eating area captures view of the garden. Cafe curtains open up for view, pull together for privacy, as do the window shades. Sliding windows on sink side open up pass-through to patio. Note container of wooden cooking utensils next to range—functional yet attractive. *Courtesy* Modern Bride *Magazine*

Geometric, tilelike design of wallpaper and the ceramic tile counter top create a south-of-the border aura in this cheerful kitchen. Much of the charm lies in its striking decor—the contoured eating area, wallpapered ceiling, Mexican light fixtures, and the clever curtain treatment. Eating area, in a niche of its own, leaves plenty of working room in the kitchen itself. Hutch of cabinets houses dinnerware. *Courtesy* Modern Bride *Magazine*

Right. A study in checks and bold lines, here we find that shelving takes the place of wall cabinets. Besides providing a decorative note this arrangement also puts items within fingertip reach. The double drainboard stainless steel sink-in-the-center-of-things offers a large expanse of cleanup area as well as extra counter space. Table in the center of the room doubles as work counter when not used for dining. Bentwood chairs add traditional touch. Note how table appointments color-coordinate with cabinets and brown and white floor tile. *Courtesy* Modern Bride *Magazine*

Left. Remodeled kitchen with a sprightly touch—cabinets were painted blue and white, ceramic tiles were applied to wall area, and a new slate blue plastic laminate counter top was installed. White porcelain enamel sink blends nicely with white touches in kitchen. Pull-down light fixture over the table provides spot lighting for work or dining. *Courtesy* Modern Bride *Magazine*

There are many varieties of design and color in counter-top materials. Keep in mind that an overall pattern with a small design appears as a solid color and will keep its appearance longer than a solid color. However, solid colors are often more dramatic and vivid and less apt to clash with strong designs in flooring and wall covering.

Floor Coverings

Since you spend so much time in the kitchen, it would be wise to select a comfortable, easy-to-care-for surface underfoot. Time and motion experts urge us to do as much of our kitchen work as possible sitting down, but the number of tasks that can be done in this position is limited and most of our work is still done while standing.

Suffice it to say that long hours of standing on a hard, uncomfortable floor are one of the major factors that contribute to body fatigue.

Exactly what does comfort in a kitchen flooring material mean? The flooring you choose should provide some firm cushion and resiliency and absorb the shock of your footsteps as you move about the room. It should also be safe for you to walk on; in other words, level, smooth, and not slippery.

Maintenance is another factor in your selection. It should be easy to clean and require little care. There are many new wet-look, no-wax vinyls available now which keep their new appearance indefinitely. On the other hand, you may choose a pattern in vinyl flooring or tile that does require waxing. Make sure you find out what care is necessary to maintain its sheen. Or you may prefer the ease of vacuum cleaning a kitchen carpet to that of waxing a floor. These are all questions you must ask yourself before you make the choice. Remember, too, that whatever kind of flooring you select, the color will be a major factor in determining the color scheme of the entire kitchen. Like the counter top, the floor is one of the most noticeable parts of the kitchen. Generally there are three categories of floor coverings—smooth or resilient, hard, and soft.

Smooth or resilient surfaces are the most popular. *Vinyl*, available in tiles or sheets, is probably the winner in this category. It is the most expensive, but there are varying grades and qualities. Its gauge and thickness determine the cost. Easy to maintain, it is highly resistant to grease and alkalis.

With luxurious elegance and exquisite taste, this small kitchen is designed for generous storage and maximum convenience. U-shape in plan, the butcher's block serves as a work island and a pivot around which all activity centers. Homey touches of center rug, specially designed window shade, paintings, and table appointments make it inviting. White porcelain knobs on cabinets are traditional in feeling. *Courtesy* Modern Bride *Magazine*

Sheet vinyl comes in two forms. *Inlaid,* the most durable, carries the design or pattern throughout the vinyl layer. A less expensive and less durable type is *rotovinyl.* It has the design printed on a vinyl sheet which is then coated with a transparent vinyl layer. It comes in a variety of designs. Some sheet vinyls are cushioned with a sponge backing which makes them extremely resilient and easy to stand on.

Solid *vinyl tile* is generally expensive and luxurious. Like sheet vinyl it is easy to maintain, resistant to grease and alkalis, durable and especially easy to install. You can probably do it yourself if you desire. Both sheet and tile flooring come in the wet-look no-wax finish.

Vinyl asbestos tile is fairly inexpensive, easy to install (you can do it yourself, as with vinyl tiles), durable, and easy to care for. It is extremely resistant to moisture, grease, and alkalis.

Linoleum made from cork and linseed oil is inexpensive, durable, and fairly easy to maintain, though not as easy as vinyl. It should never be installed over concrete subflooring. Variety of pattern and color is limited.

Asphalt tile is probably the least expensive, though it does come in

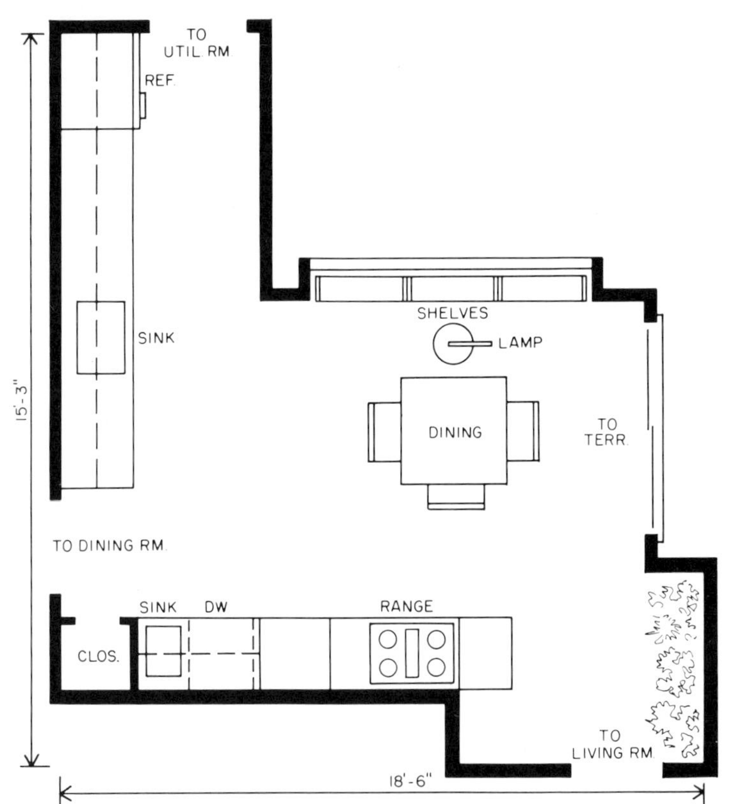

Wickered étagères recessed into window area provide a "just-right" setting for greenery and herb growing . . . a perfect background for the eating area. Sink and cleanup area to left is sleek, stark, functional. Butcher block table at end of counter at left provides excellent work surface and landing counter for buffet food. This kitchen lends itself nicely to kitchen entertaining. No-wax vinyl flooring adds a decorative as well as practical footing. Noteworthy appointments include lamp, artichoke plates, wall clock, and wicker chairs. *Courtesy Armstrong*

a variety of colors. It does not resist oil or grease well and is a poor choice for kitchens.

Cork or rubber tile, though resilient, sound absorbent, and durable is also not recommended for kitchens as it is not resistant to grease, oil, and solvents.

Hard surface flooring is durable, elegant, and offers a wide variety of designs and textures, but it is uncomfortable and hard to work on for long periods of time—and short ones, too, for that matter! *Wood,* natural and warm in feeling, was not recommended for kitchens for years because it was hard to take care of. Today there are new finishes and coatings that have improved its maintenance qualities and resistancy to water and stains. For a hard surface, it is fairly resilient. It is also expensive and even though the finishes have been much improved, it is still harder to maintain than vinyl. You may find it so attractive, however, that whatever work is involved in caring for it will be worth the effort. If you do select wood, consider using area rugs at places where you stand for long periods. Be sure they have nonskid backing to avoid sliding.

Ceramic tile, marble, quarry tile, flagstone, terrazzo, stone, and brick, all natural materials, make handsome floors, but they are uncomfortable underfoot, and require lots of care. Many people prefer not to wax these hard surfaces, but they take on a soft, mellow patina if you do. Beware with these materials, however, for if you drop anything made of crystal, china, or glass you've lost it forever.

Soft surface floors or kitchen carpeting, the newest product in kitchen flooring, is here to stay. Though fairly expensive, it is extremely soft and resilient underfoot and very comfortable. It reduces kitchen noise and clatter with its sound-deadening qualities and reduces breakage. Make sure that the carpet you select is recommended for kitchen use. Most of it is broadloom, though it is available in carpet tiles as well. These do have the advantage of being replaceable if a section is burned or stained. One disadvantage of carpet tiles is that they may loosen around heavy traffic areas. Some kitchen carpeting is cushioned with a foam rubber base, which means it is moisture-resistant and needs no padding. Others are jute-backed and will require some type of padding if you desire resiliency. Jute-backed carpeting is not moisture-resistant.

Materials available include nylon and propylene, which are resistant to abrasion and stains, resilient, and easy to clean. Propylene or

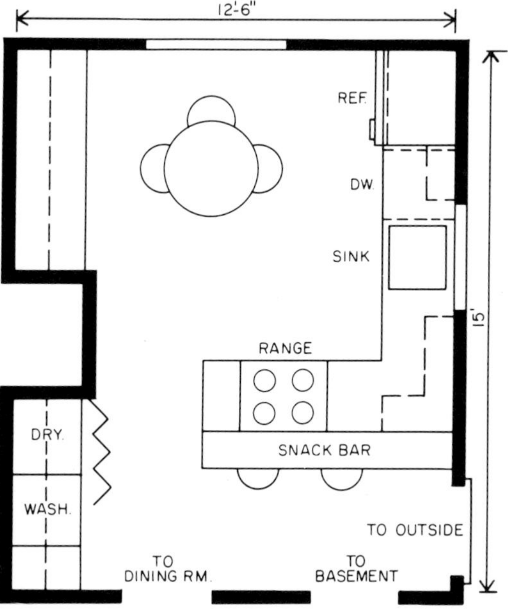

Beautifully designed eating area is striking with wall covering used in window shade and as door panels on buffet wall. Bentwood chairs and pedestal table are substantial and decorative. *Courtesy Bill Margerin Studio*

Olefin is moisture-, stain-, fade-, and shrink-resistant, though not as resilient as nylon. Rayon is really not recommended as it is highly stainable.

Walls, Wall Coverings, and Ceilings

The treatment of your kitchen walls and ceilings can wrap your kitchen in loveliness or leave it dull and lifeless. What you do with them must be decided early before any of the remodeling takes place. There is such a wide selection of materials for walls and a variety of treatments for ceilings that it requires more than just a snap decision. They should coordinate with the rest of the room, be easy to maintain, and resistant to wear and care. Let's consider walls and wall coverings first.

Paint allows you a wide choice of colors to work with. If you cannot find a ready-mixed color you like, it is always possible to have it mixed to your specifications. Make sure that you select either gloss or semigloss for easy maintenance. It is washable and thus easy to clean off kitchen grease and other soil. A good quality paint properly applied will be quite durable. However, areas such as those around light switches, convenience outlets, and door knobs may wear off in time. Paint will not offer any variety in textures and pattern unless the painter attempts to treat it in some way to achieve a textured design. One treatment that is fairly easy is to wad up a sheet of newspaper and daub the painted wall while wet. This does give it a mottled look that can be quite attractive if done well.

Wall covering may be plain wallpaper, plastic-coated paper, fabric, or vinyl-coated fabric. If you feel that you may want to remove the wall covering in time consider the strippable variety which is fabric-backed vinyl. Paper-backed wall covering must be removed by steaming which can be an expensive process. It is not a good idea to select a plain uncoated paper for the kitchen, because soil accumulates at a fast rate and paper is grease absorbent. Plastic-coated papers or vinyls are best as they are either wipeable or washable. Always ask for care instructions and select the easiest to maintain. It is usually true that the more expensive the covering, the more durable and easy to maintain it will be. Fabric or cloth, such as grasscloth or burlap, is lovely. The texture is subtle, but also highly grease and oil absorbent and not really recom-

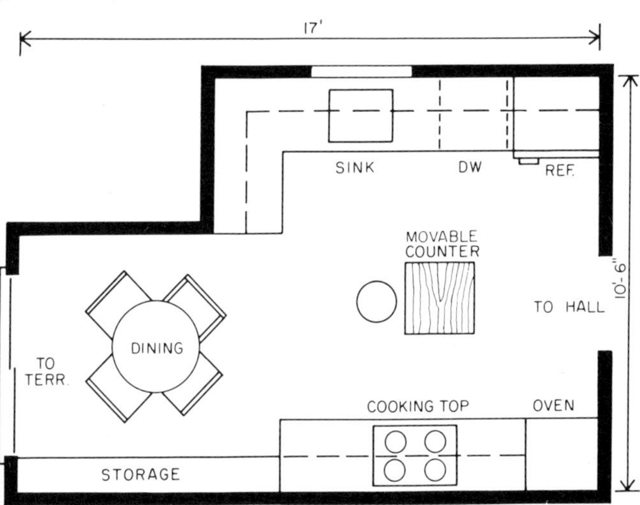

This kitchen in a vacation home is practically maintenance-free with its wood shingled walls and random pine floor. Round pedestal table with butcher block top, wicker armchairs, and enameled shelves are functional touches. Colorful cabinets with plastic laminate counter top are complementary to wood tones, especially cheerful in a kitchen setting. Indoor-outdoor capability makes this kitchen especially workable and convenient. *Courtesy Bill Margerin Studio*

Floral wallpaper with matching fabric for curtains and stool cushions literally "make" this kitchen. It's amazing what a little ingenuity, lots of color, and an eye for combining designs can do when you want to remodel for peanuts.
Courtesy Bill Margerin Studio

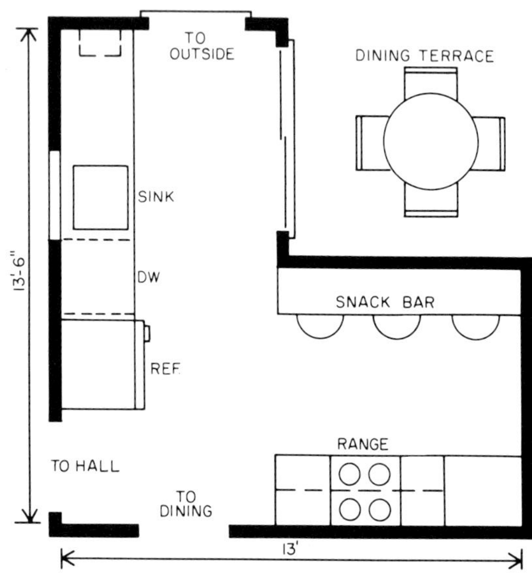

mended for kitchen use. Vinyls that resemble grasscloth and burlap combine their attractiveness with grease resistancy and durability.

Wall paneling which is highly durable and easy to maintain is becoming increasingly popular. It offers warmth and texture and is relatively easy to apply. It acts as an excellent coverup for badly damaged walls. Materials include natural wood, plastic laminates designed to resemble wood, and hardboard in a variety of baked-on finishes and textures. Your choice will depend upon your tastes and how much you want to spend. Paneling is moderately priced and, as mentioned, most are easy to care for and soil-resistant. Textured surfaces, however, do tend to attract and hold soil. As for natural wood, it is warm and attractive, but bear in mind that many of the laminates look so much like wood that it's hard to tell the difference. If you want the feeling of marble or travertine, leather, stone, brick tiles, tapestry, or murals they, too, are available. These synthetics look almost like the real thing, but are much less expensive.

Ceramic, plastic, or metal tiles are excellent for kitchen use. Ceramic tile is available in many colors, designs, and patterns. Some are smooth and glossy; others have texture and depth. They are resistant to soil and grease, especially food acids, and are hard to scratch because of their surface glaze. They are washable and rarely if ever need waxing, though waxing does lend a soft patina and is recommended for tiles in areas with much water and grease. Plastic tiles are not as soil-resistant or scratchproof and plastic seems to have the ability to attract soil while ceramic does not. Metal tiles are attractive, though highly vulnerable to scratches. They are washable and might be a wise choice around cooking and mixing areas.

Bricks and stone are attractive and unusual in pattern and texture. In some remodelings homeowners have come upon lucky finds as papered or paneled walls are removed revealing a hidden treasure of brick or stone. Needless to say, many a mind has been changed in midstream, though we constantly warn you against this expensive habit, with such lucky finds. Be forewarned that brick and stone are porous and highly soil- and grease-absorbent. If you apply brick or stone to a wall, it may be necessary to add extra support for the wall as these materials are extremely heavy. If you like this effect, you can find many imitation bricks and stones that closely resemble the original. Usually made of plastic, they are light in weight, easy to clean, and less than a half-inch thick. Price is tricky, but generally the more you pay, the better the quality.

Ceilings reflect light in the kitchen and should be relatively light in color. Almost anything that you apply to a wall can be applied to a ceiling. It is becoming increasingly popular to carry an overall wall covering design, especially one without definite pattern direction, to and over the ceiling. Such a treatment can give your kitchen a completely self-contained feeling and create an illusion of almost any mood—geometric and mod, a flower garden or forest, even of sky and water. This treatment does make your kitchen seem smaller though.

A suspended ceiling is ideal for covering up an old, ugly, or cracked ceiling or for lowering one that is too high. One advantage is that a suspended design allows you to install recess lighting into designated squares or to install fluorescent fixtures into the ceiling itself. The actual suspended ceiling is then composed of translucent plastic diffusers that help to spread and soften the light uniformly and without shadows.

Beams are popular in kitchens with a provincial, colonial, or country decor. Old, stained wood beams, once a part of the support of the structure, are much too hard to install and extremely expensive. What's more, there is no need for using heavy wooden beams these days. There are new lightweight beams, arches, or cornices fabricated from foam plastic and stained to resemble the real product. These can also be finished or painted to match any color scheme.

Ceiling tiles and panels may be installed as part of a suspended ceiling, applied directly to the ceiling, or on wood furring strips. In a kitchen where noise is a real problem, acoustical tiles may be a good solution; however, being porous, these tiles are extremely susceptible to absorbing soil and grease. They are virtually impossible to clean but the regular use of a vacuum cleaner attachment will help reduce soil accumulation. If noise is a major problem, you may be willing to overlook the cleaning difficulties.

Some ceiling tiles are now available in vinyl plastic finishes and are easy to clean. Most ceiling tiles, whether acoustical or not, absorb some sound. Look for the many new designs and varieties on the market in textures, patterns, and even in panels that fit together to form a solid look.

Noise

While we are on the subject of floor, wall, and ceiling covering, let's talk a bit about noise. The kitchen is one of the noisiest rooms in the house. Dishwashers, no-frost refrigerators, disposers, exhaust fans, and possibly laundry equipment all depend upon a variety of moveable parts that whir, hum, buzz, and worse. A concerted effort is being made in the appliance industry to minimize these noises without affecting the efficiency of the machine, and many new appliances are much quieter than their early counterparts. To make your new kitchen as quiet as possible, consider the following:

•Use cushioned vinyl floor coverings or kitchen carpeting to help muffle sounds.

•Whenever possible use acoustical materials on ceilings and walls.

•If you are at the building stage or involved in major structural remodeling, consider building sound conditioning into the house.

•Make sure that pipes and ducts are well insulated.

•When purchasing, check the sound-deadening features provided in new appliances such as disposers with rubber mounts and rubber hose extensions, wraparound insulation on dishwashers.

•Support noise-making appliances such as disposers and dishwashers on pads to control vibrations.

Windows

All the better to see out of? Or to hide? Think seriously about the role windows play in your kitchen. Do they provide light and ventilation or are they poorly situated and virtually useless? Do they bring the outdoors in or draw your eye to an unpleasant scene such as the dark shaft that so many apartment kitchens open onto?

The window treatment you select goes a long way in determining the mood of the entire kitchen. You can choose to diffuse the light in an overly sunny kitchen or open the view to allow you to baby-sit while you cook. The important thing is to determine exactly what it is you want your windows to do for you. Only then can you decide on a particular window treatment. Here are the several accepted methods and how they work.

The mood and look of a country kitchen was deftly translated to city life. It carries an illusion of spaciousness with a compactly constructed floor plan, plus a luscious color scheme of bright blue and white, with brilliant touches of lemon. Springboard was the three-dimensional look of Portuguese tile in a delphinium and white wall covering that conceals a built-in storage wall, its pattern played off against the vinyl print that covers the ceiling in the same color combination.
A hardy, antique drop-leaf table in front of one wall doubles as dining and work area, while the projecting beam diagonally opposite is host to an antique fruitwood table with drawer space engineered for flat silver. Fresh and trim, and as successfully planned, is the window treatment that relies on a glass fiber mesh shade. This unique shade cloth deflects heat and cold, and lends privacy without obscuring the view. Trimmed with a band of violet blue nylon velvet and framed with glossy white shutters, the shade is as completely scrubbable as everything else in this delightful cooking center. *Courtesy Window Shade Manufacturers Association*

In remodeling, the designers carved out a charming kitchen-dining area, dressing the window in a bright chevron print of sunlit yellow, orange, and lime that makes the room look cheerful, rain or shine, night or day. The window shade was a do-it-yourself project, easily produced with an iron-on lamination method, and the cafe curtains (that cover an air conditioner in cool weather) were made to match. An old brick wall, right, roughhewn but painted white, accommodates an unusual collection of antique tin canisters, many finished in the same mellow, yellow-into-orange and red tones.
This small but charming space is bounded at the entrance by a decorative—and handy—wine rack built onto the wall of a closet otherwise allotted to a complete laundry. On the opposite side of this room, the "L" of the kitchen peninsula contains double-faced storage, with room for pots and pans kitchen-side, and for linens facing the dining room. *Courtesy Window Shade Manufacturers Association*

Azalea and tangerine plaid wall covering and stripe shade make charming and inexpensive go-togethers in this walnut-finished kitchen. The azalea and white, vinyl-coated shade was topped with a plaid-covered valance, and its border finished with decorative trimming—one row in the deeper raspberry of the counter and another, wider one, in the orange of the gay wall covering pattern. This nylon velvet trimming is as washable as the shade itself, and the matching tab pull adds a definitive touch that is brightly practical! *Courtesy of Window Shade Manufacturers Association*

In this kitchen, the designer helped a discontented city dweller remain part of the scene, even when she cooked. To accomplish this, the forty-five-year-old kitchen was given an up-to-date turnabout, moving the eating area in front of the old, double-hung windows, and setting the appliances U-shape along the back walls. In this way, the cook can be part of the conversation group at all times, in the best farm-fashion. Tilelike wall covering in turquoise and gold established a provincial atmosphere for the round butcher block table, flanked by rush-seated chairs. The window treatment concentrates on shades in a compatible, pastel celery green that allows glare-free light. The shades' white-fringed classic hem shapes are very much in the mood of the decor, and white curtain ring pulls add extra pretty and practical touches. Even the "ship's lantern" chandelier is nostalgic. The birch counters of the kitchen section are topped with sunlit yellow laminated plastic. This happy, carefree kitchen-dining area would be at home in suburb or exurbia, but just happens to be set right in the middle of a great big metropolis! *Courtesy Window Shade Manufacturers Association*

Indoor-outdoor kitchen gains its privacy with woven wood blinds in handsome shades contrasting to drapery panels. L-shaped kitchen divided from family sitting area with peninsula counter is excellent for serving buffet parties indoors or out. Note how brick-design vinyl tile indoors blends with real brick on patio. *Courtesy Del Mar Woven Wood*

Curtains, of course, are the usual solution. They add warmth to your kitchen and help to absorb sound. Kitchen windows are perhaps the easiest windows in the house to dress. You can buy curtains ready-made, make them yourself, or have them made. And you need not limit yourself to the usual curtain fabrics. Almost any fabric can be used to match your decor. Today most fabrics are treated for soil, heat, and sun resistancy, and are washable with permanent-press, no-iron features. Keep in mind that many fabrics may be coordinated with matching wall covering and even flooring.

Window shades can be used with or without curtains and are extremely decorative as well as functional. If you can dress up your window with a shade and avoid using a curtain, you will find the window easier to keep clean. Window shades, no longer merely plain and practical, can play a big part in kitchen decor and provide shade and privacy at the same time. Available in a wide variety of colors, patterns, and textures, they have washable surfaces and can be opaque to shut out light or translucent to let it in while shutting out glare. One type is laminated to enable you to iron on any fabric. You can also paint or stencil on designs to match another pattern in the room or add fringe, trim, and other decorative features.

Blinds, Venetian and otherwise, can be vertical or horizontal. They come in almost every color, the slats can be made to any width, and have both decorative and functional values. It is possible to apply wallpaper or wall covering to some blinds to give your kitchen a uniform look. Many have unusual trims and are excellent for controlling and directing light.

Shutters and *folding panels* or *screens* also help to control light and provide privacy. While they are washable, they might not be easy to clean, since they tend to attract soil and grease.

Window coverups are happy solutions to unsightly or poorly placed windows which you don't need. If you have such a window and do not plan structural changes to remove it, then hide it. Consider using the window for a plant and herb garden, a niche for hanging a painting or object of art, or as a place to display a favorite collection.

If you need more light and do not have space for a window on the wall, consider a *skylight.* Use a translucent material, plastic or glass, that lets in light, but holds out glare.

Color: Your Best Asset

Color has invaded the kitchen. Appliances no longer have to be white or floors dark in order to be functional. Now there is color in everything from appliances to accessories, floor coverings to ceiling treatments. Use color in your new kitchen. Let it enhance and complement the food you cook and serve. Let it bring your table to life and set a mood. Use it to warm or to cool, to hide or to accent, to cheer or to soothe. Use it for any purpose you want, but use it!

How to use color

Get to know colors and what they do. The *cool* ones are the blues and greens; *warm* ones include yellow, orange, and red. As for black, white, and gray, they are neutral and and take on the mood of colors used with them.

Pick out your favorite color and make it the predominant one in your color scheme. Use it for the walls, the counter tops, or the floor. Then, pick out several other colors that harmonize, blend, or complement.

There are generally three methods of combining color: the *monochromatic* uses several shades or hues of one basic color; the *secondary* uses colors that are next to each other on the color wheel, usually three of them; and the *complementary* combines two opposite colors on the color wheel. One of the colors should dominate the other and the second should be used for accessories or accent themes. Whichever method you decide to use, create! Experiment! Try swatches of color together using pieces of carpeting, wall covering, paint chips, and fabric.

We have been talking mainly about solid colors, but you may want to consider pattern and texture in developing your color scheme. Pattern adds variety and texture adds dimension. You need all three—color, pattern, and texture—to create an aura of loveliness in your new kitchen.

Most patterns and textures have a predominant color. Make sure it fits into the rest of your color scheme. And, remember, planning is all-important. Think about what you want to do with color before you make a single purchase whether it be an appliance, an accessory, cabinets, counter tops, wall covering, or flooring.

CHAPTER 15

How to Measure and Draw Your Plan

Now, Mr. and Mrs. Draftsman, you are ready to draw your plan! Don't be afraid to tackle the job. It's tricky, but not as tricky as you might think once you get into it. And think of the pitfalls you will avoid later if you measure and draw a rough plan now.

Even if you plan to have a professional do the entire job from start to finish, drawing your own plan is important. The specialist will, of course, take his own measurements and draw his own plans, but your rough sketch will tell him clearly and intelligently just what you have in mind for your new kitchen.

Of course, if you plan to do the work yourself, drawing a plan is essential. You will probably want your cabinet dealer to check the plan in this case. Many appliance and cabinet manufacturers offer kitchen-planning kits with templates and scaled ruler and graph paper.

You will need:

•A rigid measuring tape of flexible steel. Avoid the cloth kind as there is a possibility the tape may have shrunk.

•A sharp pencil

•Graph or blocked paper that is scaled 1/4 or 1/2-inch to the foot, an easy scale to use.

•A scaled ruler

Taking Measurements

1. Accuracy is essential!

2. First, draw a freehand sketch, showing the general floor plan of your kitchen, beginning in one corner and including all four walls.

3. Now take measurements and write them on this rough plan. At the risk of repetition, be accurate. It will make a big difference when you begin to fit in cabinets and appliances of specific sizes.

4. To get overall measurements measure each wall at counter height (36 inches above the floor) from corner to corner.

5. Take individual measurements, from corner to window, then window including trim. Do the same for doors. Continue taking measurements this way around each wall. Be sure to include all walls, windows, doors, openings, and obstructions. Always include casing in door and window measurements. The following diagrams will indicate how to measure doors and windows.

6. Measure distances from windowsills to floor. Indicate swing of door and where door leads.

7. Indicate kind of heating and mark any radiators, registers, wall gaps, enclosing pipes, and trimmings.

8. Mark location and indicate height of plumbing, gas, and electrical outlets. (It is wise to mark the location of plumbing in basement, if

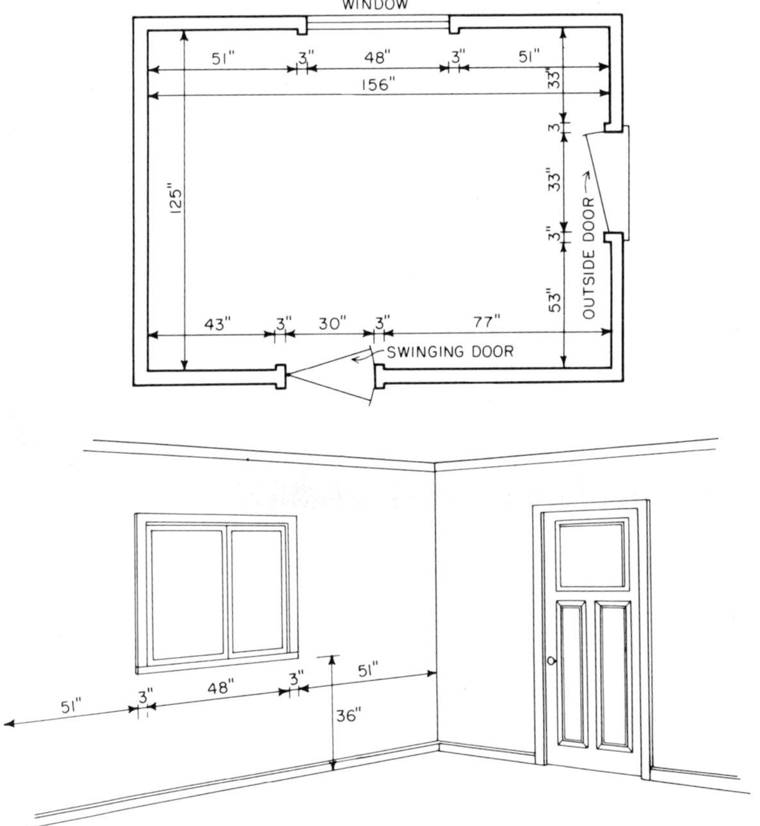

you have one, as well as in the kitchen. Understanding the nature and length of pipe runs now can save costly mistakes later.) Indicate areas for possible venting of range and dryer if you plan to install laundry in kitchen.

9. Take notes on the following: height of ceiling (finished floor to finished ceiling); orientation of room and wall (south, southeast, etc); present appliances—sizes, doors, hinges, etc.—and appliances you plan to buy.

10. If you plan on making structural changes note load-bearing wall which cannot be moved. In changing walls or windows mark sizes of adjoining rooms, hallways, or porches which have a bearing on the plan as well as the width of walls and partitions.

11. Check all your measurements. They should total the entire wall size.

Your Scaled Drawing

1. Use the template on page 214 to plan your kitchen.

2. In drawing your plan use the following symbols which are commonly found in architectural drawings. They will be helpful in interpreting your drawing to your dealer or contractor.

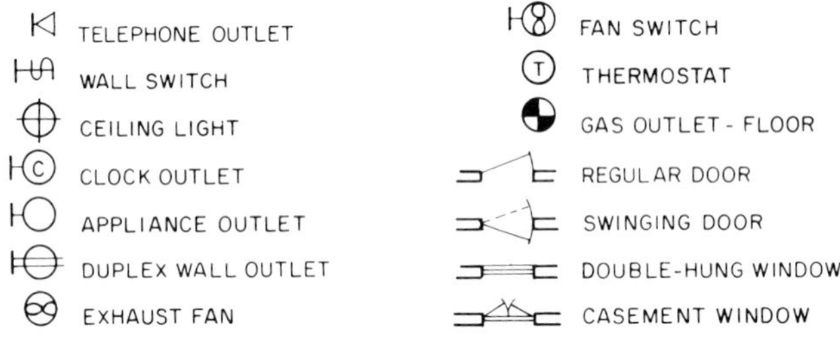

3. Decide on the shape of your plan according to the various kitchen shapes discussed on pages 36–37 and then locate your sink, range, and refrigerator centers as directed on pages 21–30. (Remember, the refrigerator is best located on an outside wall for good ventilation and the door should swing *away* from the counter and range.)

4. Next position other appliances such as dishwasher, trash compactor, ice maker, etc.

5. Plan remaining work centers.

6. Indicate location of electrical outlets. Plan lighting now.

7. Next, draw in your cabinets. The floor plan will indicate base cabinets first. Use your template to draw wall cabinets over the base cabinets.

8. Don't forget that you are not limited to walls. You can sketch in an island or peninsula to accommodate equipment, too.

9. Don't be afraid to move your plan around or change things several times. That's what the template is for. Consider whether a small structural change, like altering the size of a door or window or relocating it, might give you a better plan.

10. Be sure to note floor-to-ceiling height and distance from floor to bottom of windowsill. Write this information beside your kitchen plan and take it with you when you go to purchase your cabinets.

A Review

1. Consider the number of people who will work and eat in the kitchen.

2. In planning storage space, allow a total of 6 square feet of shelf space for each person. Add an additional 12 square feet of shelf space if you entertain a good deal.

3. Provide a minimum of 10, preferably 11 to 14, linear feet of base cabinet storage and 10 linear feet of wall cabinet storage.

4. For counter space, provide 18 inches by the refrigerator on the latch side; 36 to 42 inches for the mixing area; 36 inches on the right side of the sink, 30 to 32 inches to the left of the sink (if you have a dishwasher 24 inches may be adequate), and 24 inches on both sides of the range, if possible.

5. In planning counter and storage space, corners present certain problems. Where a counter turns a corner, allow at least:

- 9 inches between the edge of the sink and the turn of a counter
- 14 inches from the center of a cook top to the turn
- 16 inches from the latch side of a refrigerator to the turn
- 12 to 14 inches on each side of the corner turn to any fixed appliances. This will permit you to install a corner base cabinet with either fixed or revolving shelves.

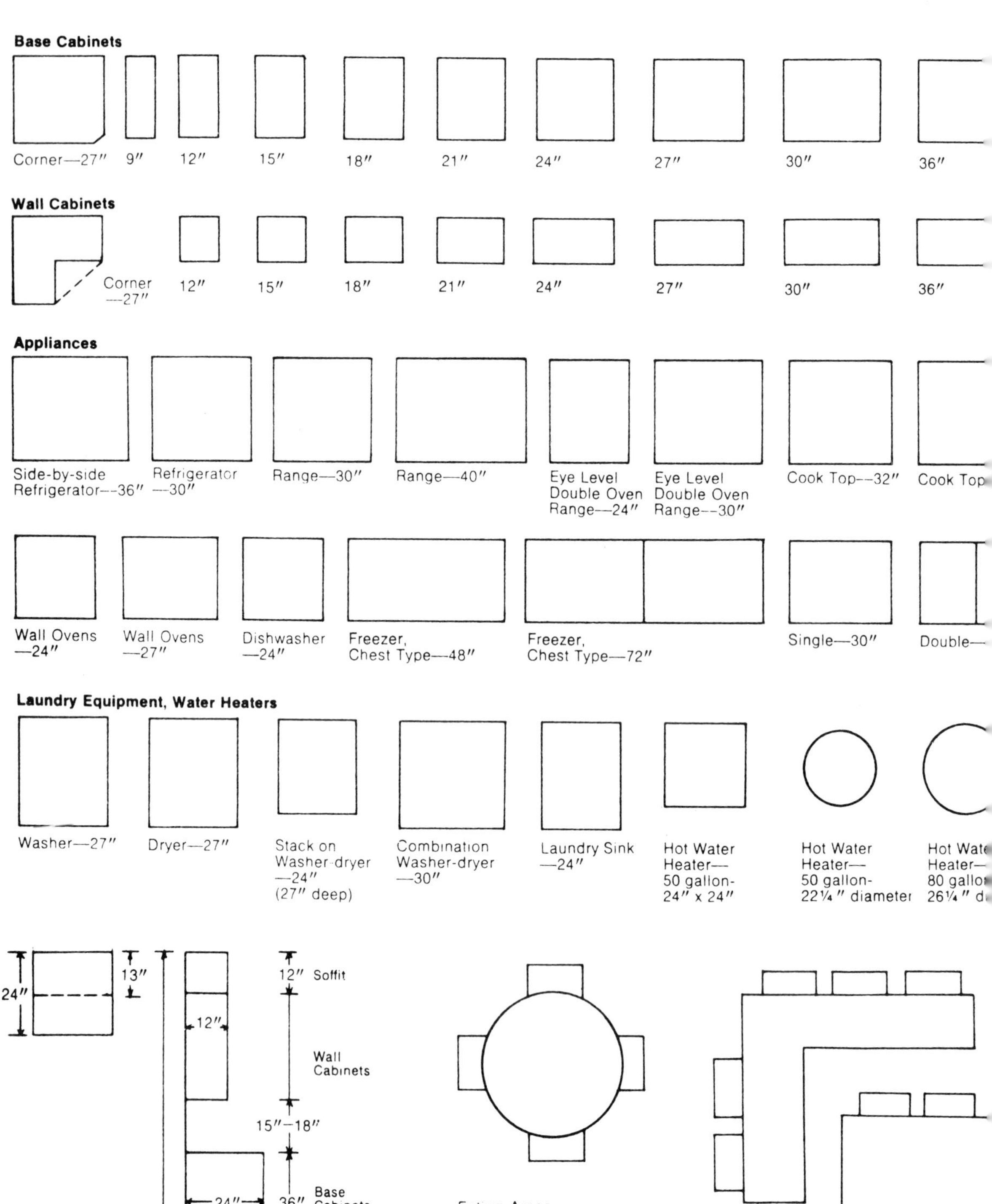

Use this scaled template to plan your kitchen. Cut out or trace the appliances and cabinets from the guide. Then place the guide over the graph paper and use it as a stencil.

Note: Some products may vary slightly from these general measurements. Check the specific sizes with your dealer. Mark your plan lightly, as you may want to change it several times before making a final decision. *Courtesy Electric Energy Association*

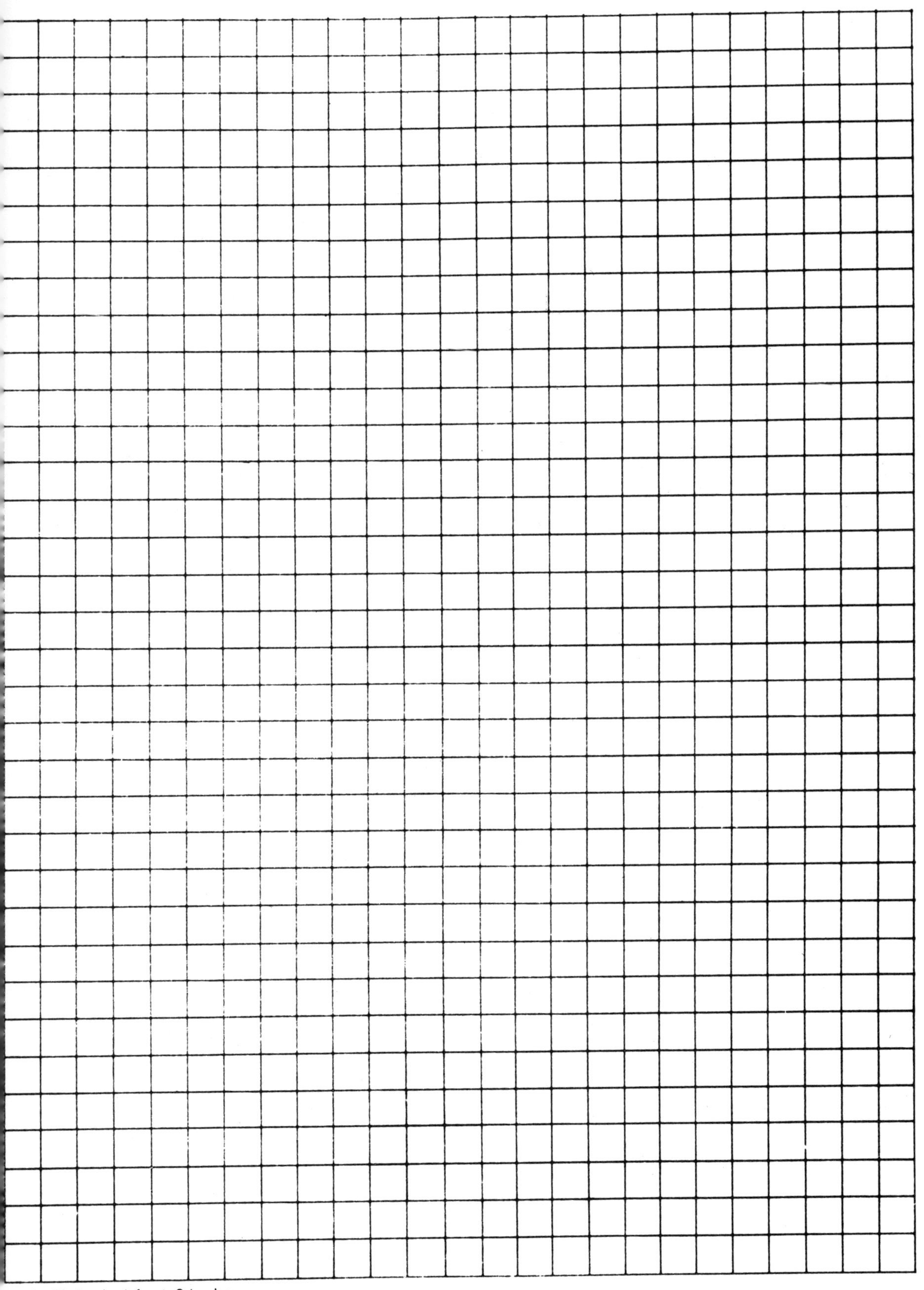

scale ¼ inch-1 foot-0 inches

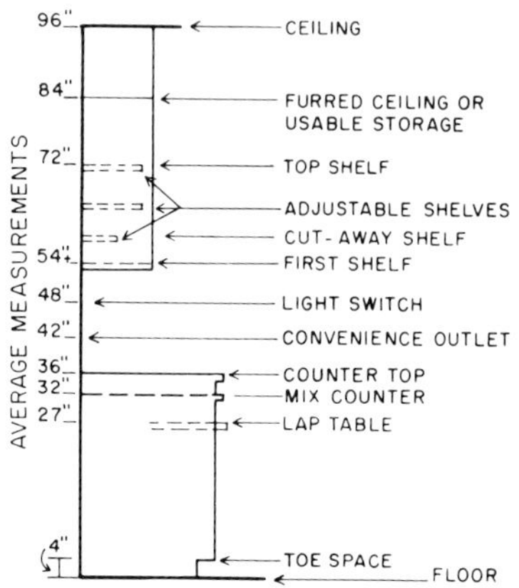

6. Allow 27 inches of space on both walls to turn a corner.

7. In order to work efficiently and comfortably, certain clearances are recommended. FHA requirements include spacing wall cabinets 15 inches above counter tops. Eighteen inches is the maximum. In the area between base and wall cabinets, you may want to use shallow (6 to 7 inches deep) midway cabinets. Hang them just below the wall cabinet. They are great for spices, herbs, and measuring equipment.

8. The backsplash attached to counter top should be at least 4 inches high or it can cover entire wall.

9. Wall cabinets range from 30 to 33 inches high.

10. Most base cabinets are 34½ inches high and counter tops are 1½ inches high, totaling the standard 36-inch base cabinet including counter top height.

11. Base cabinets have a 4-inch kick space.

12. Base cabinets used for kitchen desks or buffets are 28¼ inches high—with 1½ inches counter top making a total of 30 inches.

13. Overall cabinet height is usually 84 to 87 inches from floor. To get maximum use out of the top shelf in wall cabinets hang them so that the top is no more than 72 inches from floor. If storage is inadequate or limited, consider building "dead" storage for infrequently used seasonal items. See page 168 for soffit treatments.

14. Tall utility cabinets are 84 inches tall with a depth of 12 or 24 inches.

15. Cabinet widths range from 12 to 42 inches in 3-inch increments.

16. Allow 4 feet of clearance between opposite work areas and 3 feet for passageways.

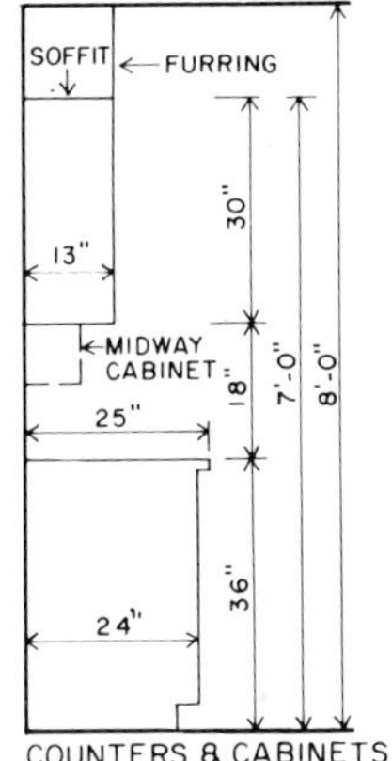

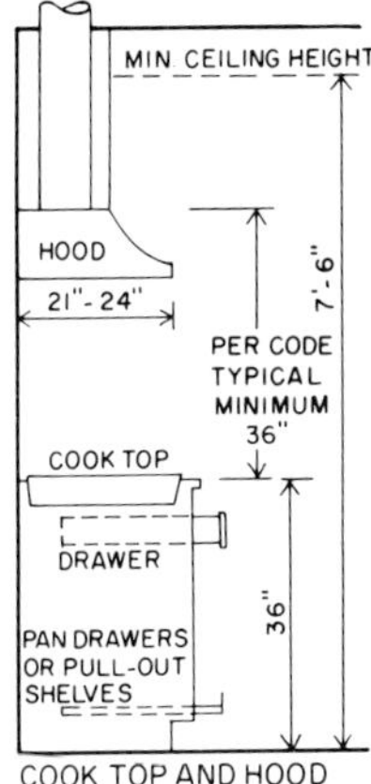

Good Tips on Designing Your Kitchen

1. If possible, avoid layouts which route household traffic through the work area.

2. Try not to isolate appliances, but if you must, provide adequate work space in that area.

3. Insist on elevation drawings from your kitchen designer to help you visualize cabinet heights and the overall balance of the plan. These drawings will give you a good idea of how things will eventually look.

4. Plan pull-out or revolving shelves or drawers in base cabinets and adjustable shelves in wall cabinets.

5. Work should flow in one direction—for right-handed people from right to left; the opposite for left-handers.

6. Counter surface between work areas should be continuous, if possible.

7. Avoid separating counters by doors.

8. When planning centers try to use work areas for more than one purpose.

9. Allow enough space for people to walk around one another easily (about 3 feet) and, if more than one person at a time usually works in your kitchen, enough space for them to work at adjacent centers forming a right angle (about one foot extra for body thickness).

10. Provide space between the wall and side of an appliance or cabinet so that you can open the door to more than a right angle. Otherwise you will be unable to remove drawers or shelves for cleaning.

WORK WITH EASE AT THE RIGHT HEIGHT

Women's sizes aren't standard.

Counter heights should fit YOU.

So should the height of the sink, range, and oven.

COMPLETE THIS CHART TO SEE HOW FAR FROM THE FLOOR YOUR WORK SURFACES SHOULD BE

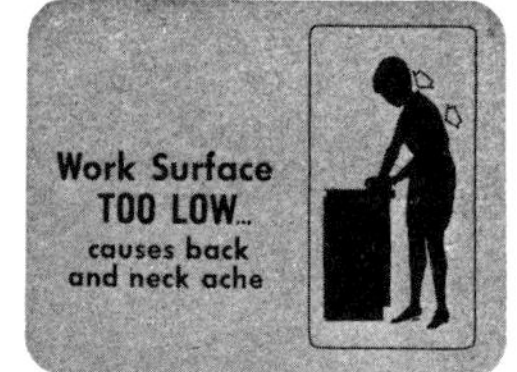

		Your elbow height	minus	Distance below your elbow	equals	Best distance from floor for YOUR Work Surface
Elbow	**Counters** *For most activities.* Examples: serve food stack dishes make sandwiches		–	3 inches	=	
	Counter or Pull-out Boards *For work requiring force or long handled tools.* Examples: mix batter by hand, chop nuts, knead bread, and beat with an electric portable mixer.		–	6 to 7 inches	=	
Have someone at home check your elbow height again when you are wearing the shoes you usually work in.	**Sink rim** *For hand washing of dishes or preparing fresh vegetables.*		–	2 to 3 inches	=	
Bend your arm as shown above.	**Cooking surface of Range** *For most activities.*		–	3 inches	=	
Measure the distance between the floor and your elbow.	*If working with long handled tools.*		–	6 to 7 inches	=	
	Fully opened oven door *For lifting in and out of oven.*		–	1 to 7 inches	=	

11. Visualize appliance and cabinet doors open to be sure they do not present traffic bottlenecks or safety hazards.

12. Avoid boxing in a work surface. Wall ovens, tall appliances, and floor cabinets on both sides of a counter confine your arm movements and limit you in placing utensils and supplies.

13. Remember to allow for plumbing if you choose a refrigerator with an automatic ice maker or plan to install a separate ice maker.

14. Plan the number and location of electric outlets for small appliances as well as major ones.

15. Plan lighting so you can see clearly as you work.

16. Plan space and location of windows for safety. Never place a gas range below a window because the breeze may extinguish the flame or pilot light.

17. Plan space now for trash, can openers, hanging dish and hand towels, clamping a manual food grinder, and for a kitchen stool and cart if you have them.

18. Consider activities other than meal preparation and cleanup that place demands on your kitchen equipment. For example, is your sink commonly used as a source of water for drinking and washing hands, for plants and flowers, for cleaning jobs and washing clothes, and for fixing food and water for pets? If your children generally use the kitchen sink to get drinks and wash their hands, you may want to plan the sink location so that they can reach it without disturbing your work. A second sink may be a practical addition, or a second source of water with only a small basin for drainage may be the answer.

19. If you want to sit for some jobs, you will need to plan the design of the work area so that you can work comfortably when seated. Your elbow must be above the counter and your legs need space under it.

Note: Some compromises will always be necessary because of space, money, room arrangement or other limitations. Your written list of priorities will help you choose the alternative which is best for you.

Some Typical Problems and How to Solve Them

In drawing your rough plan, you may have come up against some common problems. Perhaps you have radiators and pipes where you can see them, walls and windows where you don't want them, no wiring or convenience outlets where you need them most, plumbing in the wrong place, insufficient ventilation, or any one of a hundred other common difficulties. Structural changes can be expensive, but sometimes these changes are easier than they seem at first and more economical in the long run. We have listed here some of the more common problems and some of their possible solutions.

If you have a door in the wrong place or one that you don't want at all you can do several positive things. If the passageway is unnecessary, you can remove the door and fill in the wall. If you want to get rid of the door but preserve the passageway, you can open it up into an arch. Or you can move the passageway completely. Simply remove the door, fill in the wall, and cut a new opening where you do need it.

Perhaps you do not have to move the door at all. Sometimes a simple change in door style will eliminate the obstacle. There are sliding types which may require some structural work since they require a slot in the wall into which they can slide; two-way swing doors; louvered French-style doors, and two-part Dutch doors. Shop around for the right style for your particular problem.

If pipes are a problem, you can box them in by extending the wall out and around the pipes. In this case you will need to cover that area with paint or wall covering to match the wall. You can also move the pipes into the wall by making a niche in the wall for the pipes, cutting the pipes, and directing them into the wall area with elbows. You will then have to fill in the wall and repaint or cover it.

If you have an unsightly chimney flue, you can camouflage it or make an issue of it. Cover it with plastic brick or wall board or paint it a bright color to give it some interest.

If wiring needs to be changed, consult an electrician. It may not be a major job. (See page 127 for more on wiring.)

How about windows? The same rules apply to windows as to doors. You can move a window from one place to another or you can replace it with one of a different type—smaller or larger, casement or pane, jalousie or sliding—whichever solves your problem best. (See window treatment on page 205.)

Radiators are one of the most common problems, particularly in older homes. Fortunately radiator problems are perhaps the easiest to solve. You can *cover them* with perforated metal, which allows air circulation for adequate heating, and paint them to match your decor. You can remove a radiator entirely (if you don't need the heat) or move it to another location (in which case you should still cover it) or you can replace it with a low baseboard unit that is more inconspicuous. Of course, you will need a free wall for this type of installation. You will have no radiator or baseboard problem if you have heating and cooling systems that can be adjusted without too much expense to include the kitchen.

If you want to make a kitchen larger by combining two rooms you will need to remove a wall, perhaps more than one. Do exercise caution here as some walls support the structure itself. This means they are load-bearing walls and are not moveable, unless some provision is made for additional support. Making such an important structural change requires a skilled tradesman such as a building contractor or a carpenter who knows what he is doing.

If you want to make two rooms out of one, such as blocking off a separate area for a laundry or utility room, you will have to *add a wall.* Although this is a comparatively easy job, it still requires some skill as you may need to add wiring or bring a plumbing line through to the opposite side.

Counter tops may be raised or lowered to suit your height. To raise a counter top put plywood or boards of appropriate thickness on the floor under the equipment. To lower a counter use a lower base cabinet.

CHAPTER 16

Do-It-Yourself Kitchen Remodeling

We spoke briefly about the dangers of do-it-yourself jobs in Chapter 10. If, however, after all my warnings you are still determined, let's consider the procedures and a few of the problems. As I've said before, you will need some talent for carpentry and a certain facility with building tools.

There are two methods of do-it-yourself remodeling. You can build and install your own cabinets. (In this case you will probably need specific directions and a good deal of help. Both can be found in a book entitled *How to Build and Buy Cabinets for the Modern Kitchen* by Robert Stevenson (Arco Publishing Co., 1974). On the other hand, you may want to buy cabinets and install them yourself and at least two cabinet manufacturers I know of, perhaps more, offer illustrated booklets on do-it-yourself remodeling. It is this second plan which I will consider in this chapter.

Study the rules thoroughly before you begin. Give yourself as much time as possible and use it. Know exactly how you want your new kitchen to look and talk with as many professionals and skilled tradesmen as you can before you begin. (Check carefully to determine fees connected with any type of consultation; and make certain you know what is included in the fee—what you will be getting for your money.) Above all, study this book from stem to stern before you start and familiarize yourself with the mechanics of installing a new kitchen, and the design and operation of appliances. Fortify yourself with a basic education in electricity, plumbing, lighting, and ventilation. Delineate exactly what you can do and what someone else should do. Some national and local codes require that licensed tradesmen such as electricians and plumbers do certain technical jobs. Ask the manufacturer or local cabinet and appliance dealer for installation instructions and any special tools required for the job—and whether or not you will affect warranty terms if you install an appliance.

According to do-it-yourself experts, your first step is to arm yourself with good quality tools. I have listed the basic tools which you will need to start work.

- sturdy metal tape measure or a 6-foot folding ruler
- carpenter's level (4 feet)
- Phillips head screwdriver
- regular screwdriver
- claw hammer
- crowbar
- electric drill (1/4-inch) and bits
- magnetic stud finder
- plane
- wood saw
- metal saw
- scribe tool
- two C-clamps
- 1-3/4-inch and 2-inch wood screws
- metal screws (if you're installing metal cabinets)
- T-square
- L-shaped metal angle braces with screws
- glue
- touch-up kit (wood or metal)
- spray finish to match wood
- plaster stick or patching plaster
- medium and fine sandpaper (000 and 0000 or 3/0 and 4/0)

The Planning and Ordering Stage

1. Take accurate measurements of your kitchen and draw a rough plan. (See Chapter 15.)

2. When you have selected your cabinets, ask the dealer to go over your plan and help you with the details. If there are any questions get the answers now. Many dealers will have a kitchen design book available either from the cabinet manufacturer or the appliance manufacturer. Ask for one and study it thoroughly. When you have made all your decisions, place your orders; then make a delivery and work schedule.

3. Check plumbing and electrical needs with plumbing and electrical contractors. A plumber will check the condition of your present system and do any of the plumbing work necessary such as removal of the old sink and installation of the new, removal or relocation of a radiator, and installation of the dishwasher, disposer, and washer. Have an electricial contractor check the adequacy of your wiring, suggest changes, and do any electrical work necessary. Follow the same proce-

dure for metal work and any ducting and ventilation that should be done.

The Removal Stage

1. Whether you are doing the work yourself or hiring outside contractors, the first step is to remove the range and refrigerator and reconnect the refrigerator in another room.

2. Next, remove the counter tops. You will find that they are securely attached to the base cabinet and you may need an assist from a crowbar to lift it off. If you are not planning to change the sink, it will have to be disconnected to remove the counter top.

3. Remove the wall cabinets and then the base cabinets. In dislodging both you will need a claw hammer to remove the nails and a crowbar if the hammer does not work.

4. Remove any baseboards from walls where you plan to install new cabinets.

5. If you plan to install a new floor, remove the old one, at this point.

The Installation Stage

1. To install new floor covering, first cover the old boards with plywood, baseboard, or a material recommended by the floor-covering dealer.

2. Level the floor by shimming low spots with scrap lumber or shingles.

3. Now you're ready for the preparation phase of installing the base cabinets. If you are not installing a new flooring, step back and take a close look at the present one. If it is not level (few floors are) find the highest point. (If it seems hard to find a high point in the floor, lay a 6-foot piece of lumber across a high spot and against the baseboard or wall. Using a level, make the board perfectly flat and draw a line on the baseboard or wall. If you continue to do this around the room, you can readily spot the high point.) From there measure 34½ inches up the wall and draw a horizontal line. This, then, is the top height of your base

cabinets. Now measure 84 inches up the wall from the same high point in the floor and draw another horizontal line. This is the top height of your wall cabinets. See page 218 for desired heights.

4. Repair any rough spots on walls with patching plaster or plaster stick. Sand the finished wall. If you have uneven walls with high and low spots, shim out to the highest point so the cabinets will be level.

5. Using a stud finder, search for the wall studs. Attaching the cabinets to them will assure you of a firm support. They are usually located 16 inches apart, from center to center.

You may also locate the studs without a stud finder. Tap the wall with a hammer until you hear and "feel" a solid sound. Check the area by driving in a thin nail. Then find the center of the stud and measure 16 inches to right and 16 inches to left, to find the other studs.

6. Many like to begin their installation in one corner. However, if you have not leveled the floor, install the first base cabinet at the highest point and let that be your gauge for the remainder of the cabinets.

7. Installing the first base cabinet to the wall studs is comparatively easy. Drill small holes through the top of the back horizontal frame of the cabinet and into the wall until you just hit the stud. Insert screws securely. Rubbing a little bar soap on the screws makes the job infinitely easier.

8. Install remaining cabinets in the same way.

9. Keep checking cabinets with the level and shim whenever necessary.

10. Make a tight joint between cabinets by drilling two holes in the vertical frame of one cabinet, just inside the door and just into the vertical frame of the adjacent cabinet. To hold the cabinets together use C-clamps. To protect the finish of the cabinet cover a piece of fabric between clamps and frame. Secure frame with screws.

11. Install dishwasher and range. If it seems as if you have to force them, plane the frames of the adjoining cabinets.

12. In order to place the wall cabinets properly, it is usually better to install the base cabinets first. However, this does pose a problem in that you have to stretch across the base cabinets to install the wall cabinets or place a flat surface over the base cabinets and work from there. To make it easier to handle the wall cabinets, especially if you are working alone, construct a T-support to hold the cabinets. Use a 2-by-4 for the top of the T and a smaller piece for the vertical support. If you

put in the wall cabinets first, the vertical support must be longer to reach the floor.

When installing the wall cabinets start with a corner cabinet, if possible. The top of the cabinet should be placed at the 84-inch line I mentioned earlier. Again, following the instructions for your particular cabinets, drill holes from the inside and into the studs, then insert the screws. Avoid turning them too tightly at this point in case you must make adjustments later. Continue, following this plan, until all cabinets are installed. Check periodically to be sure every installation is level. Make sure to check the evenness of the wall and shim out the back edges where necessary. When you have finished, make a tight joint between the cabinets as you did with the base cabinets.

There will probably be a space between the top of the wall cabinets and the ceiling. In many older houses ceilings are higher than 9 feet, but in newer homes they are usually 8 feet high. This open space is generally closed in with a *soffit.* The face of the soffit is usually flush with wall cabinets and you may close off the space entirely or make the face of sliding doors, in which case you will have extra storage space for infrequently used items. In some cases the soffit is extended over the wall cabinet and serves to house "down lighting." (See soffit treatments, on page 168.)

13. Now you are ready to install the counter tops. You may have the cabinet dealer make up the counter top or hire a special fabricator. It is wise to install all your cabinets then have the fabricator come to your home and measure for the counter tops. In this case he will be completely responsible for the fit. (See counter tops, page 186.) If you plan to do the installation yourself, study the instructions for installing your particular brand. Generally the base cabinets have corner braces with a center hole. Drill up through this hole into the bottom of the counter top, then insert screws. If you have the fabricator install the counter tops, ask him if he can install the sink. Otherwise, have a plumber do it and make the necessary connections. Note: If you find openings behind the backsplash due to uneven wall, try installing quarter-round or cove moldings.

When you have finished, check to see that your installation is completely level. If not, then make whatever adjustments are necessary. If you have a touch-up kit from your dealer or cabinet manufacturer, cover up the scratches or make any minor repairs.

CHAPTER 17

Now the Work Begins

Assuming you have done your homework, sifted through your clip files, shopped around, gotten estimates from everyone—kitchen dealers, individual contractors, appliance dealers—and decided who will do the job, what next? Here in sequence is a picture of how your new kitchen will take shape.

Dealer Responsibility

If you have opted to have a kitchen dealer with all his specialists do the entire job—he may have all the technicians on his staff or he may subcontract to individual tradesmen—he will be responsible for the end results. This provides a certain security in that all the work will be coordinated through one source.

After you have shopped around and know what each specialist has to offer and what his services include, invite the prospective dealer to your home.

During his visit, he will, in effect, interview you, asking all the questions you have asked yourself in the early planning stages. Because you have asked yourself these questions and because you have a rough plan of what you would like your new kitchen to look like you are better prepared to answer his questions. The person who comes to your home may be the designer himself, but more likely it will be a salesman trained in kitchen design. He will take all the information, including measurements and your special requests back to a designer who will prepare a finished plan for your estimate and discussion.

During this "interview session" you will be discussing generalities in price, ideas, and desires. Only after the designer works with the actual facts and true measurements will you know exactly what to expect and what the price will be.

When the estimate is ready, it is time for the final meeting, probably in the dealer's showroom. Here you will see the final floor plan and perspective drawings, discuss specific details, and look at samples and swatches of materials, color, and fabric. This is the time—before you sign the contract—to ask any and all questions you have on your mind. This is also the time to make changes and adjustments. After you sign the contract it will be too late. In other words, now is the time to alter the plan and customize it to your own specifications and budget! Establish the work schedule at this meeting; when do they plan to start and finish the kitchen? Determine how you will make the payments.

Now that you have made all the changes you want to make, have no more questions to ask, and have read the contract carefully, it is time to sign.

The next step is up to your kitchen dealer. He will order all the materials, subcontract the necessary tradesmen, and make the final arrangements to begin the job. How long that will take depends to a large extent on how complicated your kitchen plan is, how many kitchen installations are ahead of you, and what kind of cabinets you have chosen. If you have ordered stock cabinets, which the dealer will obtain from a local factory warehouse, he may be able to begin within a week to ten days. If you want custom cabinets, that will take from six to eight weeks or longer.

Your Responsibility

Your dealer will let you know when he is ready to start. Immediately before they begin delivery and work empty the kitchen of everything—food, utensils, dishes, and anything that will be in the way of the workmen. Cover up nearby furniture. Put masking tape over cracks and openings around inside doors. Dust has a way of settling on everything in its path.

Plan to use the kitchen as little as possible while the work is in progress. If you can, take some of your meals with friends or neighbors and make this the time you take the family on several inexpensive restaurant outings! Kentucky Fried Chicken, a McDonald's hamburger, a Burger King Whopper, or Arthur Treacher's Fish and Chips are a boon to the kitchenless family.

If you do have to cook at home, consider using your electric skillet, saucepan, or portable oven. A hot plate is not a bad idea either. Keep in mind convenience foods and shortcut cooking.

Try to obtain a work schedule from your kitchen dealer. It is important to know what they are planning to do on each day, such as shutting off the electricity, gas, and water. And don't panic! Keep in mind that there is water in the bathroom or laundry.

Unless you have an important question about the work that is taking place, try to avoid talking constantly to the workmen. A cup of coffee is nice, but they do not want and cannot afford the time for a coffee klatch. Remember, they are on a schedule. Don't steal your own time, for that is what you'll be doing if you take up too much of theirs.

As we said earlier, make your changes before you sign the contract. Don't expect the workmen to take on extra chores such as installing a hook or an adjustable shelf in your bathroom.

Make sure that the designer or kitchen dealer is there the first day to supervise the work as it begins and that he is there when the job is finished to go over every detail with you. Do not make the last payment until you are completely satisfied that everything you have contracted for has been done to your satisfaction.

When the Work Begins

Gear yourself for a messy, dusty job for a few weeks. If you do, it won't get on your nerves—or at least not as much. Remodeling is never an easy job. Everything you remove from your kitchen has to go somewhere. Try to organize it in some way to reduce clutter and so that you can put your hands on certain things when you need them.

Your house will seem like U.S. Highway 1 while the work is underway. The number of workmen coming in and going out will seem endless. There will be carpenters, cabinet installers, plasterers, electricians, plumbers, appliance service men, flooring specialists and painters. Of course, there should be someone from your kitchen dealer on hand at all times to supervise the work. And just remember, though it all seems hopeless now, in no time at all you will have a brand new kitchen, one so marvelous that it makes every moment of mess and headache seem worthwhile.

CHAPTER 18

Putting the Frosting on the Cake

Now that your kitchen is a dream come true and you are ready to set up housekeeping again, let's wrap it up as the gift package it surely is. And don't skimp on the finishing touches. Your new kitchen deserves the best.

The final touches are those special items that put your personal stamp on the whole job. These are the things that give the kitchen its personality. Make them special, but don't overdo it. Clutter is neither attractive nor efficient.

Sometimes the best accessories are the functional tools and utensils you use every day. Here are some of the most popular ideas for dressing up a kitchen.

•Cooking utensils—copper, cast iron, brightly colored enameled or whatever suits your fancy—make super accessories. Hang them from hooks and racks so that they are easy to reach, but out of the way of traffic.

•Potted and hanging plants and herbs are attractive inside, window boxes outside.

•Fill empty wall space with pictures, prints, plaques, and paintings of colorful fruits and flowers or any other subject of interest to you. If you have expensive oil paintings in the kitchen, make sure your ventilating system keeps grease-laden fumes to a minimum.

•Colorfully decorated plates and mugs are especially suitable for kitchen decor.

•Canisters, spice racks, cookbook stands, and wine racks are as handsome as they are helpful.

•Select accessories that highlight your kitchen decor. If you have a kitchen with French Provincial styling, hang a series of French prints or arrange attractive cheese plates on a plate rail.

If your kitchen has a "country look" arrange your wooden spoons and similar utensils in a milk can replica or a wooden jam bucket. Display some antique cooking tools.

•Don't forget that kitchen clocks and calendars are both decorative and functional.

•If you want a modern look, there are all sorts of handsome Plexiglas storage units and canisters that show off or enhance the ingredients stored within, such as spaghetti, macaroni, rice, and dried leaf herbs.

•Put your creative thinking to work and you will come up with all kinds of handsome accessories to add the finishing touches.

Just one last tip—putting the final touches on a room is like putting jewelry on yourself. After you put it all on, take one piece off. It's easy to fill your kitchen with "pretties" that do nothing but clutter and gather dust. Be selective in your choice and then step back and take one long, critical look. Chances are you will take one piece out!

CHAPTER 19

Planning Your Laundry

Whether it is a corner of the kitchen, a nook in a bath, an unused closet, or a full-scale utility room, a laundry should be planned to give the most working convenience for the space available. When there isn't much room, consider such space savers as stacked washer and dryer units, compacts that fit into closets, and even washer-dryer combinations. But remember no matter how compact your equipment, in a laundry as in a kitchen, you will need work and storage space.

Size and Location

Where you will locate your laundry and how elaborate it will be will depend upon the location of your plumbing, the amount of space you can afford, and your family's needs. If you are planning a major workroom, allow a minimum area of 8 × 10 feet, though a washer and dryer can be installed efficiently in a space as small as $5^{1}/_{2}$ × 10 feet—or even less as in the case of compacts, stackables, and combinations.

Think not only about how much space you have but what sort of activities will go on in the room. Do you want nothing more than a place to wash, dry, and sort clothes? Do you need a full-scale utility room with a place to iron, an area to hang garments after ironing, a drip-dry closet, a "mud" room for hanging outside wet gear and sports equipment, and a place to wash up, perhaps even shower? Did you have in mind an area for sewing, potting, planting, flower arranging, gift wrapping, and other hobbies? If you have the space, you probably have the need for a room for at least some of these activities.

Where you put your laundry will depend not only upon where the available space is located and which activities you plan to do there but where your sources of plumbing and water heating are located as well. Adequate water, ventilation, gas, and electric lines, all of which will be discussed, are essential.

Before you decide what size laundry you will plan and where you will locate it, consider some of the essentials that go into an efficient laundry.

Space allotment. No matter how small your laundry is, you will need some space to sort clothes, pretreat stains, and fold clean laundry. A sink close by and a counter top or table are essential.

Cabinets, hampers, and storage. Soiled clothes waiting to be washed? Clean clothes waiting to be ironed? Where will you store detergents, laundry aids, and stain-removal supplies? Don't forget a place to hang those permanent-press items which should be removed and hung as soon as the dryer stops tumbling.

Plumbing requirements. The availability of plumbing for a washer and ventilating for a dryer is vital in deciding where to put a laundry. And while you're thinking about plumbing, check the capacity of your water heater. Is it large enough to deliver an adequate supply of 140°F. to 160°F. water for laundry and still take care of other household needs? If your water is objectionally hard, consider installing a water softener.

Energy requirements. You will need a 20-amp, 120-volt circuit for your washer, a 30-amp, 240-volt circuit for an electric dryer or a combination electric washer-dryer, or a 20-amp, 120-volt circuit for a gas dryer in addition to a gas connection. You can use this same circuit for your iron.

Lighting. Good overall lighting, plus spot lighting for work areas, is essential for efficiency and safety. For close tasks such as ironing, sewing, and stain removal use 150-200-watt incandescent bulbs. For short work periods, one 40-watt or two 20-watt fluorescent deluxe warm white tubes (or deluxe cool white, if you prefer) should be adequate, but for prolonged periods use two 40-watt fluorescent tubes. Make sure all lighting is glare-free.

Flooring, counter tops, walls, and decor. Easy-to-care-for flooring and wall surfaces are essential in a laundry and, of course, you will want to make the decor as pleasant and attractive as possible. As for materials and finishes for counter tops, wall covering, and flooring, the recommendations for kitchens apply to laundries as well.

Laundry Equipment

The equipment you buy will depend upon the space you have available and your family's needs. Obviously if you have only a spare closet or corner of a bathroom you will want to think about compacts and stackables. On the other hand, if space is not a problem and your family is large, think about oversized or extra-large equipment.

Washers. If you are buying a washer, look for the greatest washing flexibility your budget can afford. By flexibility I mean a selection of wash and rinse water temperatures, of wash and spin speeds, and of washing cycles—normal, permanent press, extra rinses, and extra washes. You will find that the great variety of fabrics in today's laundry necessitates almost as many washing methods.

Check out washer convenience features available. Are you interested in bleach and fabric softener dispensers that allow you to add everything at the beginning of the cycle? Do you want programmed controls that make the decisions on water temperature and washer speed for you? With these you need only push a button for the type of clothes you are washing. Lint filters, positive water fill, off-balance controls, safety lid switches that prevent the lid from opening during spin cycle, and water-level selection are important features.

You will find a variety of washer capacities on the market with many large oversized washers to meet the demands of large families, king-size linens, and washable blankets and knitwear. Keep in mind, though, that a large capacity washer does not mean less sorting for you. No matter how great the capacity of the washer, certain items cannot be washed in the same load.

Compacts. If space is at a premium and you do not have large wash loads or mind washing more often, consider the compacts. Though they are pint-size units, they have maxi-size features. There are provisions for regulation of water level and variations in temperature and agitation speeds. Compact dryers are available to match these washers. Ask your dealer about them. Be aware, though, that they are compact units and will not do the large wash loads you expect standard units to handle.

Dryers. If you are buying a dryer, ask if it has a cool-down period which provides several minutes of tumbling without heat at the end of the drying cycle. This feature minimizes wrinkling and is especially important for permanent press. Look also for an electronic dryness control. This is an electronic sensor that feels the moisture in your clothes and turns the dryer off automatically at the proper time.

Other dryer convenience features include a selection of speeds, fast for towels and heavy fabrics, gentle for delicates, and special cycles including permanent press, damp-dry air only, or heat only. Ultraviolet lamps in the dryer give a fresh, sunshine smell and you can even buy a dryer that will sprinkle your clothes. Dryers, too, have larger capacities to dry the same large load you washed together.

Most dryers should be vented to the outdoors. If the location of your laundry makes that impossible, there are dryers that need no venting. These use cold water to condense vapor and then drain it away. They do need plumbing connections, however.

Combination Washer-Dryers. Though these units are not now currently available, they do keep coming on the market—and going off—because of the low demand. However, as we said earlier, if space is tight, you can consider either compacts, stacked units, or a combination which provides great washing-drying convenience in a minimum of space. Combinations do not have all the features listed above, but they do have the most important ones. Regardless of what you purchase, be sure qualified service is available.

Water Heating and Conditioning

Water Heaters. Asking a few very important questions in your search for a new water heater can save you money and aggravation in the long run. Look into which fuel—gas or electric—is most suitable for your requirements and check operating costs for each. Ask if there is an "off-peak" electric rate available, which could help cut down on operating costs.

How large a unit do you need? Since family habits vary so widely, there is no hard and fast rule about what size will be adequate. There are two types available—the *standard storage* and the *quick-recovery.* As mentioned on page 183, the quick recovery type often provides as much if not more hot water than the standard storage since stored water tends to cool quickly. When choosing between the two types, consider all your present needs—bathing, laundry, dishwashing, cooking, etc—as well as your future needs as your family grows and your habits change. For specific sizing recommendations ask your dealer or write to the Gas Appliance Manufacturers Association, 1901 North Fort Meyer Drive, Suite 900, Arlington, Virginia 22209.

Be sure to check installation requirements, gas supply, and venting needs before buying. A 240-volt circuit is necessary for electric models and a gas line for gas models. As for venting, gas water heaters should be located as close as possible to a vertical vent for the combustion products and where there is a free circulation of air. For economy and efficiency locate any water heater as close as possible to hot water outlets. For some homes, depending upon the size and location of pipe runs, it might be wise to consider two water heaters.

Wherever you locate the water heater, make certain it is accessible for servicing and cleaning. Installations should be made in accordance with the manufacturer's instructions regarding clearances and adherence to any local plumbing codes. Be sure to study the instruction book thoroughly before installation for any tips relating to your specific brand. Gas heaters should carry certification of performance and durability and both gas and electric designs should be certified for safety.

Water Softeners. For a continuous supply of soft water consider the installation of an automatic water softener. Softened water makes housekeeping and laundering easier and produces better results.

A water softening appliance removes the hardness minerals through ion-exchange resins contained within the unit. When these resins reach saturation they are recharged with salt which you obtain from a water softener dealer. How often you have to recharge the unit depends upon water hardness and the amount of water used.

If you are considering a water softener, it is well to consider softening both your hot and cold water lines. Though it is possible to soften only the hot water line, this procedure is usually less efficient since for many tasks cold water is mixed with hot water. Whether you choose to soften one water line or both, never soften the outdoor water supply which is used for gardening and sprinkling.

There are three ways of acquiring a water softening system—you may *buy* one, *rent* one, or *subscribe* to a service in which case the dealer will, at specified intervals, exchange the used unit for a fresh one.

Now that you are familiar with the variety of equipment available, let's consider the best place for your laundry.

This step-saver laundry is located in a small passageway between bedroom and bath areas in a California home. It collects the dirty laundry right where it accumulates. Installed in a compact space dryer, it stacks on top of the washer. In the bathroom area, laundry equipment is near plumbing connections. *Courtesy* American Home *Magazine*

Since the bulk of the family laundry accumulates in the bedroom-bath area, a laundry wall in the bedroom can save considerable time and energy. One wall of this bedroom contains all the elements needed for a laundry, plus wall cabinets for the storage of laundry supplies and linens. Concealed behind folding doors, paneled to match the wallpaper, is the washer and dryer with a deep bowl stainless steel sink. Undercabinet lighting makes seeing easy. Laundry backs up to bathroom wall for ease in plumbing connections. *Courtesy Maytag*

The Bedroom-Bath Area vs. the Kitchen Area

When you stop to think about it, you realize that the bedroom-bath area is where the bulk of the soiled linen and clothing originates. A separate utility room somewhere midway between the kitchen-dining and the bedroom-bath areas is ideal for saving steps. On the other hand, if yours is a two-story house you may prefer having your laundry in a separate utility room near the kitchen as most of your household work centers there.

A separate room, no matter where it is located, should have ample space for a washer, dryer, storage, ironing equipment, and a sink for pretreatment of fabrics. Some provision should be made for drying hand washables, hanging items still damp from the washing machine that you don't want to dry automatically, and for light mending and repairs. Any other activities will require more space.

In the kitchen

Many people prefer the laundry area in the kitchen. While this is not necessarily the best arrangement, it does mean that you can combine household tasks such as meal preparation and laundry. It can also be an advantage in that it is near an active source of plumbing, thus cutting down on long pipe runs and installation costs. If the laundry is located in the kitchen, try to separate it from the cooking area with a peninsula, partition, or perhaps a planning desk.

In the bathroom

If you have the space, the bathroom can be an ideal location for a laundry area. Materials and finishes used in bathrooms withstand high humidity and like the kitchen, plumbing is close at hand, thus reducing installation costs and long pipe runs. If your space is limited, keep in mind the stackable designs and compact washers and dryers we discussed above.

In a hallway

If you cannot find the space elsewhere and have extra space in a central hallway, consider a laundry there. Conceal it with louvered doors and install an exhaust fan to take care of moisture and humidity.

The basement

There are several advantages to a basement laundry. A basement usually provides plenty of space. In addition, plumbing and other utility outlets are located there. The main drawback in this case is that you will have to tote the laundry up and down stairs. In many older homes clothes chutes were built in. If you are remodeling an older home where a chute exists you have no problem, but it you are considering installing one, keep in mind that building costs are high.

The family room

If you have no other space, installing a laundry in the family room might make good sense. It allows you to combine activities such as family visiting, television, and doing the laundry.

Try to conceal the laundry equipment somehow with louvered doors, a partition, or a room divider. Noise could be a problem and may limit the times you can use the equipment. Some provision should be made for venting also.

In a closet

If you are using portable equipment, use the closet for storage, but if you are considering permanent installation in a closet, you must make some provision for venting and plumbing.

In a garage, carport, or breezeway

These are satisfactory locations if there is no other space available. They let you take advantage of what is normally wasted space, but though these spots are advantageous in warmer climates, they are most impractical in colder ones.

In an apartment

In any laundry, some provision must be made for plumbing standpipes and drainage facilities. Ask the apartment management if this is possible. If so, consider the possibility of installing compact machines permanently, or if you have the space, standard size units. If you don't plan to stay in the apartment, compact portables may be your answer or even standard-size washers available in portable models.

This proves that you don't need much space to install laundry equipment. In less than 36 inches a washer nests behind kitchen peninsula and a portable dryer is cleverly mounted on the wall next to a miniwall cabinet. *Courtesy Maytag*

Cabinet on one end of a kitchen wall opens to reveal compact laundry appliances. Top supplies extra counter space for kitchen or laundry duties and drawers provide additional storage. Portable washer rolls to nearby sink for doing the laundry; portable dryer tumble-dries average washload (about half that of standard-sized models) in 45 minutes or less. An adequately wired 115-volt outlet close by and louvers in the back of the cabinet permit use of the dryer in such a confined space. Outside of the cabinet no special venting would be required. *Courtesy Maytag*

Left. There are some new features in this compact, five-foot laundry closet which bear some thought. In addition to an automatic washer and a dryer that has been elevated for greater convenience, the laundry includes storage below the dryer for soiled laundry, generous space for laundering aids, lighting, and easy access to utility connections. Bifold doors conceal the work area, yet provide adequate ventilation if appliances are in use. *Courtesy Maytag*

Below, left. Recessed unit in a storage wall highlights louvered doors, open shelving, and a handy sorting bin located under sink area. Additional storage for linen and cleaning supplies is in closets to right. *Courtesy Maytag*

Below, right. When you've no other place for the laundry equipment, consider putting a compact washer and compact dryer, one on top of the other, under a staircase. It is a good idea to locate it near existing plumbing connections, for example, adjacent to a bath or kitchen. *Courtesy Frigidaire*

Handsomely elegant laundry bar in a den features copper appliances and walnut folding doors. One would never know that such a functional unit would be concealed in a major public area of the home. Note clever combination of bar sink, undercounter refrigerator, and accessories for entertaining.
Courtesy Maytag

Decorative laundry wall is the epitome of organization. Sorting baskets help sort laundry into loads, shelf above provides excellent storage for seldom-used items, open shelves to right house laundry aids and cabinet below, besides increasing storage, supplies needed counter space. Note how wallpaper is repeated on cabinet doors.
Courtesy Maytag

Laundry niche recessed at one end of a family/recreation room. No room to enclose area with folding or louvered doors, however, wallpaper and gay floral decals on cabinets make it a focal and attractive part of the room. Shelf above laundry equipment and indirect lighting add to convenience. Family sorting bins, on right, help to keep family clothing organized. *Courtesy Maytag*

This laundry at the end of a family room (or it could be located in a long narrow hallway) permits dovetailing of laundering and other daily activities. Flanking the washer and dryer is a pull-out hamper and a base cabinet, both of which provide counter space for working. Concealed behind louvered doors entire unit looks like a storage wall when closed. Programmed laundry equipment takes the guesswork out of washing and drying. *Courtesy General Electric*

The Separate Utility Room

The ideal solution is a separate room devoted to laundering and similar activities. In my opinion a dream come true would be a glorified utility room where the sewing machine could be left open, the ironing board out, and everything else that doesn't have a home in another part of the house could be located. I would call it a "clutter room" where I could be disorganized in an organized way. Oh, for a room where everything has its place and there is a place for everything and if you can't put it back in its place, it won't matter because you can close the door on "current clutter."

Another spinoff from a utility room might be called a "cleanup room," which could include the laundry, a shower, a "drip-dry" closet, a place for potting and flower-arranging, and a tile floor with a drain for hosing it down conveniently.

Having a separate utility room usually means having enough storage space, counters for working, and ample facilities for plumbing, water heating and softening, electricity, and ventilating. When a water heater can be installed near the laundry area—either in it or immediately below it—it cuts down on plumbing costs, shortens hot water pipe runs, and reduces temperature loss.

Center Planning

Just as in the kitchen where each appliance and particular activity determines the work center, so each step in the laundering process designates the work center. Center planning, even if a given center serves more than one activity, allows you to group supplies and equipment together logically. Remember to allow for work and storage space in each center.

Activities which require their own work centers include storage of soiled items, sorting, pretreating, washing, drying (automatic and line), folding, hanging, ironing, water heating, and, if you have space, sewing and mending, gift wrapping, potting and flower arranging, and hobbies.

Storage center

Soiled clothes, linen, and other items should be stored in ventilated hampers, bins, or baskets. Storage of soiled items may be more conven-

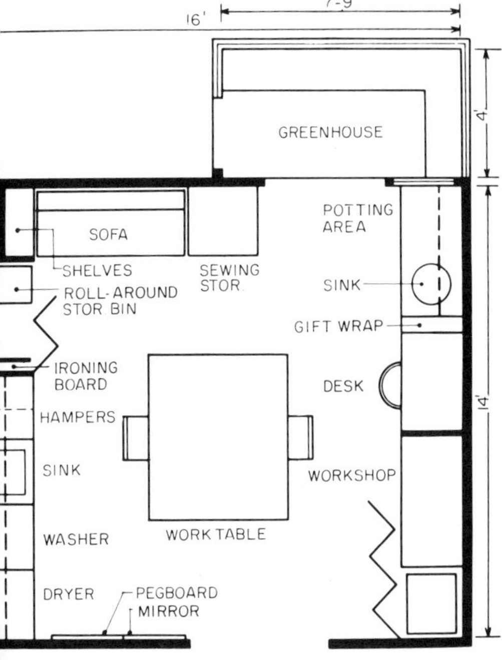

What Every Home Needs Is a "Clutter Room"

Every house has clutter. Busy clutter, like the sewing in the living room, model airplanes on the dining room table, potted plants in the kitchen sink. And it's usually there when unexpected guests arrive! The solution—a clutter room, a purposely planned, all-purpose room that's a catch-all you can shut the door on. I've been campaigning for the clutter room for a long time. My ideal is the expanded laundry area shown here, and it includes just about everything you can think of. It's a room to tell your builder about when you build your next home. Yes, it costs more, (but not much more) and may mean giving up "wasted" space. But no doubt it will become one of the most important rooms in your house!

This is the ideal clutter room plan. It has a complete laundry, space to sew, wrap gifts, arrange flowers, paint pictures, refinish furniture, turn a lathe, collect stamps, pot plants, store odds and ends, etc. And best of all, it has a door so you can leave the ironing board up, the wash half-sorted.

For many of us, the ideal laundry is still the complete separate room. A room where you can leave the ironing board up and let the unironed laundry wait until you're ready to iron it; where you can spread out and organize your storage so you know exactly where everything is; where you've room left over for other activities. In the photographs following, the gleaming laundry equipment belongs in the home of a laundry engineer who gets to try out all the new products before they hit the market.

In this laundry, the homemaker wanted white walls (because she could never tell when her clothes were really white in her last laundry, painted yellow) and loves the sparkle the red equipment adds. *Courtesy* American Home *Magazine*

Here is the drip-dry laundry closet—it has a shower floor with drain and infrared light. Closet is great for rainy-day gear as well as drip-dry laundry. *Courtesy* American Home *Magazine*

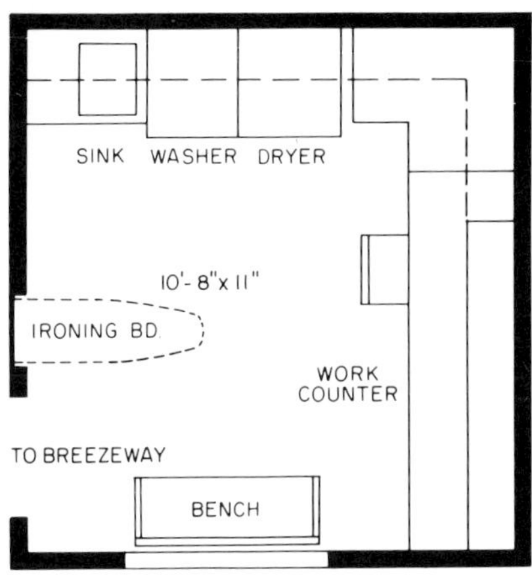

Here, furred out lighted soffits in the utility room deliver light where it's needed. The multipurpose room requires generous amounts of light at each work area. Deluxe warm white fluorescents, closest to color of incandescents, create a warm environment. *Courtesy General Electric, Nela Park, Lighting Division*

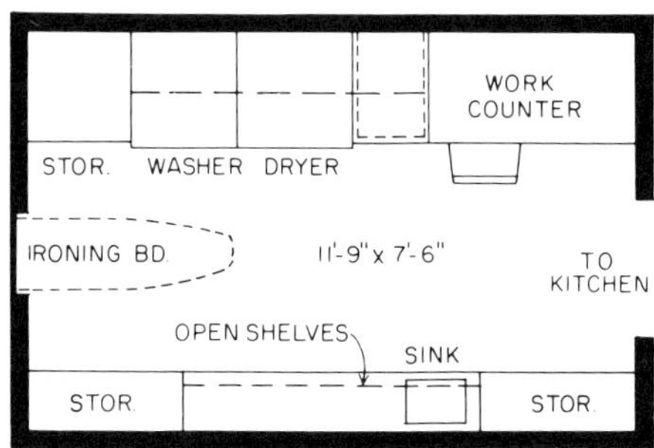

This patchwork laundry shows you what can be done in a small amount of space. The roll-out bin to the right of the washer and dryer can be pulled anywhere your laundry collects. Stash the soiled clothes in the bin, then roll it back to the laundry room where multicolored drawers store the laundry until washtime. With four drawers you can sort your whites, colored clothes, wash 'n wears, and delicates. And each drawer has holes drilled into its side walls and bottoms for ventilation.

The locked cabinet above the roll-out bin stores detergents and laundry products up out of the reach of children. And for offseason clothes storage, there's a cedar lining added to the large cupboard above the soiled clothes drawers.

When the clothes are clean and folded, they get popped into the patchwork-papered cardboard storage boxes. From there, family members claim their own clothes and return them to their original storage places.

Since patching and mending is often done in connection with the laundry, this area incorporates a sewing counter with pegboard behind the work surface adding still more storage—this time for sewing equipment, patterns, and notions.
Courtesy Maytag

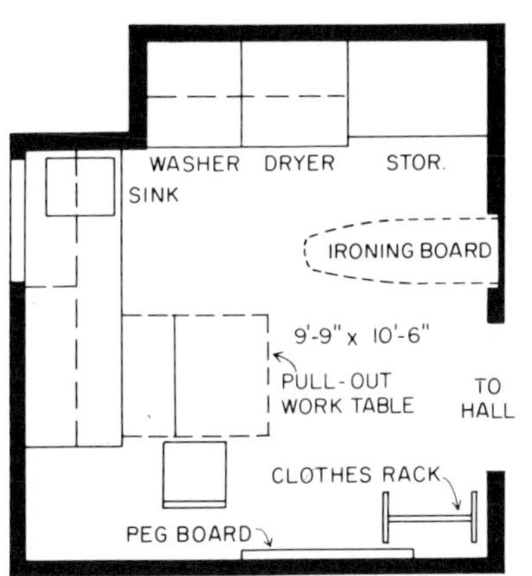

Combination sewing room/laundry is a pleasant place for anyone to work. Bright yellow enameled cabinetry, white walls, and fluorescent lighting fixtures make this a light, airy room. Sewing-work table slides back when not in use; pegboard-lined cabinet doors help to organize sewing supplies. *Courtesy Maytag*

Sewing machine cabinet conceals everything behind cabinetry and keeps machine out of sight when not in use. When folding leaf is extended you have a working surface of 39 inches. *Courtesy Wood-Mode*

ient for you at point of use—or rather disuse—either in the bathroom, bedroom, or kitchen, or you may prefer to bring them to the utility room where they may also be stored under the counter near the washer or on shelves above the laundry equipment. (See illustrations on pages 241–248.)

Some homemakers sort clothes just before laundering; others prefer to sort them as they become soiled. If you use the latter method and have the space, devise some means of dividing the various wash loads. A series of medium-sized hampers designed to fit under an open counter might be a good idea.

Sorting and preparation center

Here you will sort and pretreat or repair any clothes before you launder them. For proper preparation of laundry a sink is essential. A counter 25 inches deep, 42 inches wide, and a standard 36 inches high (lower if you are short, higher if you are tall) might house the sink and serve as a work area for pretreating, stain removal, and sorting. If you do not have room for a counter, a folding or drop-leaf table is a space saver and will serve the same purpose.

Here cabinetry in the laundry even conceals a built-in sewing machine that easily pulls out for mending chores or major projects by the seamstress of the house. This is such a wonderful way to organize what is usually a cluttered, unattractive area. There's abundant cabinetry for necessaries—even an open-mesh door on the drip-dry cabinet! *Courtesy Wood-Mode*

This laundry shows how you can custom-build a base cabinet to conceal bins for soiled linens. Unit is part of a sink cabinet that is also very handy next to the washing area. *Courtesy Wood-Mode*

The home laundry can be attractive as well as functional with new rustic cabinets. The cabinets provide ample storage for laundry aids and keep them out of sight and free from dust. This complete laundry center also doubles as a sewing area with abundant drawer space to organize supplies. *Courtesy Westinghouse*

Laundry in a greenhouse—another way to locate the laundry near to but not in the middle of heavy-duty areas. Greenhouse was attached to the main dwelling where a window, enlarged to make a doorway, gives easy access between the kitchen and the addition. *Courtesy Maytag*

If you do not plan a separate sewing center in your utility room, find a convenient niche in which to store a sewing basket. You will also want some cabinet space above the sink or at least out of reach of small children for the storage of stain removal and laundry supplies.

Washing and drying center

Obviously this center includes the washer and dryer with adequate storage for all your laundry products including:

- soap and detergent
- bleach
- water softener (packaged, if no automatic system)
- fabric softener
- starch
- presoakers
- bluing
- tints and dyes

Besides the necessary electricity and plumbing, drainage must be provided in this area. This center should be next to or near the sorting and pretreating center.

A well-planned laundry will allow ample space for each appliance and work center. Most laundry equipment—washers, dryers, and combinations—measure from 25 to 27 inches deep, 36 inches high, and about 27 to 30 inches wide. A standard washer and dryer require about 30×30 inches of floor space for each unit. An automatic washer, dryer, or combination and adjacent work areas require a space approximately 4 feet wide and 30 inches deep. To install an automatic washer and dryer side by side plus adjacent counter space, allow about $5\frac{1}{2}$ feet in width and 30 inches deep. If a washer and dryer face each other, allow 48 inches aisle space between them. Three feet is the absolute minimum. If you do have a combination washer-dryer or stackable units you will need an area 3 feet by 30 inches which will provide space for the equipment and a folding laundry basket or cart. A nonautomatic washer with stationary laundry tubs requires $6\frac{1}{2}$ feet $\times$ 8 feet of space.

If you do not expect to have a dryer, plan for adequate drying lines. It is important to plan for 2 feet of passageway in front of the line. One load of clothes requires about 40 to 50 feet of line. Several types are available, folding or umbrella types mounted on a center post and disappearing lines that unreel and lock in place are two popular types. Drying racks are also available for use in bathtubs or small areas; they provide excellent indoor drying space and serve as a good rack for ironed items.

For folding and hanging items that are taken from the dryer, provide a counter adjacent to the dryer and a rack for hanging permanent-press items. The rack may also be used for hanging ironed items.

The ironing center

Here you must allow space for an ironing board, an iron, an electrical outlet, and storage of items to be ironed. There are built-in ironing boards, but one stored in its own niche is far more practical. If you install the electric outlet forward of the spot where the ironing board will be used at a height of about 4 to 5 feet, the board will act as a cord holder. Look for some of the new and convenient ironing cupboards and holders that house and organize all the ironing gear in one spot. Remember to provide a place to hang or lay ironed items. Include a chair or stool here also if you sit down while ironing.

Sewing center

If you plan to include a sewing center in your utility room, you will need space enough for a sewing machine, ironing board, storage for sewing supplies, items to be mended, a dress form, and a place to hang unfinished garments. Four feet should be ample for a sewing machine, either a cabinet type or a sewing table and portable machine. If you do a great deal of sewing, you will want space for a cutting table or counter. A table top 36 × 72 inches, a moveable counter with a drop leaf, or a portable folding table are good solutions. A moveable counter 20 × 27 inches with a drop leaf provides a 40 × 72-inch cutting table.

You will need some drawer space and the drawer depths should vary from 3 to 9 inches. Use the shallower ones for cutting equipment and small items and the deeper ones for patterns, fabrics, and items to be mended. Dividers help to organize storage.

Work Flow

Work is much easier and more efficient if it moves in one direction. First you remove the clothes from the hamper to be sorted, then on to the sink for pretreating hard-to-remove stains, on to the washer, dryer, and to the center for hanging, folding, sprinkling, and ironing. If you are right-handed, the smoothest work pattern will move from left to right; for left-handed persons from right to left. Keep in mind that transferring clothes from the washer to the dryer is easier if the dryer door opens away from the washer.

CHAPTER 20

The Kitchen of the Future

If you are putting off remodeling until that day when everything you ever wanted in a kitchen is available, don't! The day of the perfect kitchen will never come. If you want to remodel, do it now. And just think, today is yesterday's future. That dream kitchen is nearer than you think.

Do you remember just a few short years ago when it was projected that soon you would be able to slice your turkey electrically? And the electric knife was born! The engineers prophesied a solid-state infinite speed control blender, a self-cleaning oven, a programmed digital read-out computerized range, smooth, glass ceramic cooking surfaces with electric units and gas burners underneath to supply the heat, cool cooking surfaces that heat the pan and food, but not the range top, a commercial ultrasonic dishwasher, a transistorized paging "beeper" for the kids, and a sonuswitch which turns on an electric appliance in response to a preset sound. All that and more is available *now*!

If tomorrow became today so quickly, what exciting new developments can we expect in the next few years? What will the kitchen of the future be? Perhaps it will be a *food studio*—a room in which to create rather than to work, an area made up of multipurpose appliance units in attractive furniture cabinets. What will they be like? How will they work? Why don't we join that future homemaker working in tomorrow's kitchen? Let's watch her as she prepares a dinner party.

Before she begins party preparations, she will prepare the children's dinner—a matter of selecting their menu from an assortment of frozen, prepared meals stored in a combination food freezer-electronic oven and setting the proper controls. The foods she selects will auto-

Kitchen for a Solar Home. What's unusual about this kitchen and adjacent patio dining area is that they're part of an energy-saving solar test home built by a leading university. It stresses energy-conserving appliances. The patio's bronzed glass skylight filters out most of the unwanted solar radiation, while an array of solar panels on the roof—partly visible at the upper right—collects the sun's energy to meet year-round heating, cooling, and hot water needs. *Courtesy Westinghouse*

matically be transferred from freezer to oven and made piping hot and ready to eat at the dinner hour.

On to the *bake center* to prepare a delicious French pastry. The bake center is probably a compact 3 feet wide. It contains a built-in mixer (we have that now) with infinite speed controls, a refrigerator drawer for eggs, milk, butter, etc.; a small oven for baking; and storage for mixes, spices, flour, and sugar. The storage shelves are moved up and down by a foot control or pushbutton so she can conveniently remove and replace items without reaching. (We have that now, too—see pages 150–151.) The basic parts of the pastry will be quickly prepared from mixes, and she will add the creative flavor and decorative touches that make it uniquely her own.

From a special vegetable refrigerator compartment in her *food preparation center* she will take out fresh greens for the salad. This area also has a sink with a garbage disposer that uses laser beams (high-intensity light beams) to disintegrate *all* garbage and a chopping surface counter with special recharging storage compartments for cordless, automatic knives and mixers. Once the salad is ready for tossing, she will whisk it to the cold-storage compartment of her serving cart.

Last stop is the *custom cooking center* (see how the work center theory will evolve into even greater efficiency than we have described on pages 21–30) to prepare the *pièce de resistance.* Her surface cooking is done on a smooth cook top with only buttons or designs to indicate where to put the pans. (We have that now, too.) Food is cooked by induction which means the heat is transferred directly to the utensil and the rest of the cooking surface stays cool. A hood over the entire cooking center quickly removes smoke, odors, and fumes by catalytic action. Here, too, she will store and use her specialized cooking appliances such as a rotisserie, barbecue grill, and automatic cookers with stirring devices. Once ready, the hot food will be stored in the "keep-warm" compartment of her serving cart.

As our young homemaker moves through the kitchen, she will stow all the used utensils in a *robot cleaning cart* which follows a path from one center to another. There they will be ultrasonically washed. She will use this same cart which has storage compartments as a silent butler when setting the table. After dinner the used china and silver will be placed in special washing units of the cart where china will be washed and silver washed and polished.

Cubic Cluster is actually grouping of minimodule appliances in futuristic kitchen concept. Wall units, in decorative geometric pattern broken up by sunburst design, drop down for food preparation, fold away when not in use. Square in foreground contains oven with two quarter sections of counter top lifting up and out to reveal food-warming surface. This is one manufacturer's version of the kitchen of the future. However, stylists say that future design concepts will be guided by consumer demand.
Courtesy Frigidaire

No man is an island but this futuristic kitchen concept employs island concept for appliance grouping. Note two-sided access to cooking top. At far right is stacked grouping of freezer and broiler-oven units. Second island at left combines sink, dishwasher, and beverage dispenser.
Courtesy Frigidaire

The Sink of the Future—One Station Food Preparation Cleanup Center. An advance look at the exciting prospects in store for the homemaker is this sink of the future.

While it may not be an exact prototype of what's coming, many of the features included in this full-scale model will be incorporated in future sink designs already past the research stage and on the drawing boards.

Two large stainless steel bowls with push-button drain controls are the work center of the sink that was designed to handle food preparation, cooking, and cleanup at one station. Additionally there is a smaller, self-flushing center bowl, utilized for waste disposal. Dual, adjustable height spouts, and push-button temperature and volume controls complete the picture.

The opposite side of the circular work top features a bar and food preparation sink with a cutting board in front of the sink, disposer, and push-button water controls that offer instant hot or refrigerated water.

A ceramic cooktop provides infinitely adjustable linear controls.

The upper console makes it a one-stop home communications center. Recipe storage and display with controlled indexing and selection via computer makes it possible to select the dinner menu and instantly flash it on the built-in television set. Closed circuit TV keeps the homemaker in touch with all areas of the home or permits selection of a favorite television show as meal preparation progresses. A telephone is built-in and connected with the intercom system. There's even a self-contained cassette recorder for leaving messages or for automatic recording of phone conversations. The hood provides ventilation and lighting.

The basic material is easy-to-maintain stainless steel with a maple edge. Operation is simple since all controls are push-button activated in this futuristic kitchen sink concept. *Courtesy Elkay Manufacturing Co.*

This is an artist's rendition of an ultramodern kitchen concept "Kitchen in the Round." The kitchen's unique circular design saves footsteps. Some of its innovations include a computerized food storage compartment, an automatic menu selector microwave cooking, and even an environmentally controlled garden to grow such savory herbs as chives, rosemary, and thyme. *Courtesy Whirlpool*

When she is finished in the kitchen her robot floor scrubber-polisher will scurry back and forth across the kitchen floor to put it in tiptop shape. (We may not even need a polisher with all the new "no-wax" vinyls available now.) This will be much like our floor scrubber-polisher of today except that it has an electronic brain which guides it along the floor according to the path it has learned. She will also have programmed her automatic vacuum cleaner to spruce up the rest of the house before her guests arrive.

She has lots more convenience gadgets in her kitchen, too—an automatic sifting and measuring machine, a dishmaker for everyday disposable plastic dishes (recyclable and biodegradable), an automatic beverage dispenser, an ice cube dispenser, an ultrasonic blender that uses sound waves rather than chopping blades, an electronic device which will turn her appliances on or off at voice command. She will probably call the children to dinner via a tiny transistor unit connected

Two artists' concepts of the kitchen of the future indicate that it will be little more than a control center for the homemaker—computerized with push buttons and monitors. *Courtesy Hotpoint* and *General Electric*

to a button they wear. She will use her kitchen computer to adjust recipes, balance her budget, and record family appointments. And there will be other robot helpers as well. These are not really as fantastic as they seem. We have already witnessed solid state switch controls on all kinds of appliances. These integrated circuits are really mechanical brains.

And What about Laundry?

The story of laundering in the future is really a story of fabrics and appliances. Clothing, linens, and furnishings will surely all have permanent-press characteristics. Most of them have it already. Our work clothes will probably be disposable. Even now you can buy throwaway paper clothing.

Specialized appliances throughout the house will care for our no-iron clothing. In the bedroom a laundry-closet will no doubt act as a personal valet. You will hang your soiled clothing in one compartment where it will be ultrasonically washed, then automatically transferred to the storage area. Clothing that is not soiled will be hung in a freshening closet where it will be protected and kept fresh and crisp for instant wearing. Do-it-yourself dry-cleaning machines might be standard equipment in every home.

Laundry units for linens will be in the bathroom where dirty linens will collect. They will sort, wash, dry, fold, and stack the linens.

Ultrasonic waves for dishwashers and clothes washers, laser beams for garbage disintegration, and microwaves are the household tools of the future. We are developing them now and in many instances, such as electronic ovens and microwave ranges, they are on the market already.

The future doesn't just happen. It evolves and is evolving now through gradual change. Dream about the new kitchen you want and start planning it right now. Chances are the future is already happening to you.

But in the end it isn't the modern appliances or newest aids that make the kitchen such a wonderful place to be. It's the warmth and the care and the love that flourish there that make your kitchen the very heart and soul of your home.

Appendix

Where to Go for Information

Below is a list of trade associations which will give you information on where to go in your particular area for specific kitchen and laundry planning or product information. In addition to general information, they maintain lists of member companies who will also be of help to you in securing products and services locally.

For all gas products and major gas appliances:

American Gas Association
1515 Wilson Boulevard
Arlington, Virginia 22209

Gas Appliance Manufacturers' Association, Inc.
1901 North Fort Myer Drive
Arlington, Virginia 22209

For appliances (major and portable)

Association of Home Appliance Manufacturers
20 North Wacker Drive
Chicago, Illinois 60606

Edison Electric Institute
90 Park Avenue
New York, New York 10016

For lighting:

American Home Lighting Institute
230 North Michigan Avenue
Chicago, Illinois 60601

For kitchen dealers, kitchen planning:

American Institute of Kitchen Dealers
114 Main Street
Hackettstown, New Jersey 07840

For ventilating, vent hoods, and fans:

Home Ventilating Institute
230 North Michigan Avenue
Chicago, Illinois 60601

For electronics:

National Appliance and Radio TV Dealers Association
318 West Randolph Street
Chicago, Illinois 60606

For plumbing, heating, cooling, sinks, bathrooms, and laundries:

National Association of Plumbing, Heating and Cooling Contractors
1016 20th Street, N.W.
Washington, D.C. 20036

For remodeling:

National Home Improvement Council
11 East 44th Street
New York, New York 10017

National Remodelers Association
50 East 42nd Street
New York, New York 10017

For kitchen cabinets:

National Kitchen Cabinet Association
334 East Broadway
Louisville, Kentucky 40402

For home building:

National Association of Home Builders
National Housing Center
15th and M Street
Washington, D.C.

For window treatments:

Window Shade Manufacturers Association
230 Park Avenue
New York, New York 10022

INDEX

Numbers in boldface indicate illustrations.